*An Introduction
to Quantitative Methods
for Historians*

An Introduction to Quantitative Methods for Historians

RODERICK FLOUD

Methuen

First published in 1973
by Methuen & Co. Ltd
11 New Fetter Lane, London EC4P 4EE
Second edition 1979
© 1973, 1979 Roderick Floud
Printed in Great Britain by
Richard Clay (The Chaucer Press), Ltd,
Bungay, Suffolk

British Library Cataloguing in Publication Data

Floud, Roderick
   An introduction to quantitative methods for
   historians. – 2nd ed.
   1. History – Statistical methods
   I. Title
   519.5'02'497   D16

   ISBN 0-416-71660-1
   ISBN 0-416-71670-9 Pbk

In memory of my parents

Contents

Preface to the first edition

I have benefited, in writing this book, from a great deal of advice and encouragement. I am particularly grateful to R. M. Hartwell, who first suggested that I write a book on statistics for historians, to Dr Emiel van Broekhoven, who helped me in my initial work with computers, and to Professor Stanley Engerman, Professor Nathan Rosenberg, Dr Roger Schofield and Geoffrey Crossick, who read and made many helpful comments on earlier drafts. A lecture audience at Cambridge provided a very responsive audience for many of the ideas and examples which I have used. John Naylor of Methuen has been a constant source of advice and help. Above all, however, I am grateful to my wife, for her criticism, comfort and help, without which this book would truly never have been written.

Preface to the second edition

I am glad of the opportunity to bring this book up to date, and to correct errors and omissions of the first edition. I have been made conscious of these deficiencies by many students at Cambridge and London whom I have encouraged to use the book, and by numerous historians who have made helpful suggestions. In particular, I should like to thank Mrs Evelyn Caulcott, Leonore Davidoff, Stanley Engerman, Leslie Hannah, Toro Hoivik, Clive Lee, Hans Chr. Johansen and Herman Van der Wee for their long and helpful comments, although I have not been able to follow all their suggestions. Annabel Gregory has checked all the calculations and carried out computations, and Marie-Ann Bastide has typed the corrections and additions with great efficiency. My wife, who was thanked in the first edition, deserves and receives such thanks again.

Introduction

When we describe and analyse human society as it existed in the past or as it exists at present, we inevitably make use of numbers and quantities. Age, date of birth, wealth, number of wives, numbers of children – all these are quantitative characteristics of a person which we must discover if we are to give an adequate description of him. In doing this, we measure, compare him with other people, richer or poorer, older or younger, and seek by these means, as well as by a discussion of his thoughts and his work, to place him within the society in which he lived. We do this, normally, by classifying people into groups, people who behave in similar ways or have similar ideas. We use such terms as 'middle class', 'Frenchmen', 'Conservatives', to describe such groups. We must classify and group in this way, because only by such means can we reduce the diversity of human thought and behaviour to a manageable form.

Such measures as age, wealth, number of children, are explicitly quantitative. We can measure the age of a person only by calculating the *number* of years since his birth, or his wealth only by calculating the *number* or value in some *number* of monetary units of the material goods that he owns. If we use such measures in describing people who lived in the past, then we are using quantitative methods. Other measures or descriptions that we use in history are, by contrast, non-quantitative in form, and describe instead the thoughts or attitudes of individual or groups; 'Fascist', 'Renaissance man', are such descriptions. But when we are concerned with non-quantitative, or qualitative, descriptions such as these, we may often find that we can give them a full meaning, and assess their historical significance, only by measuring the *number* of people who hold such views or can be described in such terms. 'The middle class' is a description of a group in society, but for many purposes it is also a description of a *number* of people with particular incomes and attitudes in that society. If we say that 'the middle class supported the government' we mean that most, if not all, of the people whom we have described as 'middle class' supported the government, and we can conclusively establish the truth of such a statement only by counting the *number* of such people. Many qualitative judgements or descriptions used by historians thus have an implicit quantitative significance, which it is sometimes necessary to make explicit. In addition, many descriptions of the behaviour of individuals or groups have quantitative significance; such words as 'usually', 'normally', 'often', 'many', refer to quantitative concepts, and although we may often not wish to test them exactly, in principle their significance or truth can only be established by quantitative measurement.

Historians, like other social scientists, thus use quantitative concepts frequently and inevitably. This fact does not mean that all statements that they make are quantitative, or that they believe that all aspects of human behaviour can be measured and given numbers. Many facets of human beings, and of groups of human beings, and of material objects, cannot be measured or expressed in quantitative terms; although we can measure the income of a medieval peasant, we cannot measure the happiness he derived from spending it. Similarly, although we can measure the changing price of broadcloths produced in the fifteenth century, we can never know what they felt like to the touch. The historian, in contrast to other social scientists, is in fact particularly limited in his measurement; he cannot ask his subjects questions about their happiness or their attitudes, and cannot therefore hope even to produce relative measures of happiness or political attitudes, as can be done by psychologists and sociologists.

Nevertheless, the fact that some areas of human experience in the past are immeasurable is no reason not to measure those that are accessible to us. At the least, the measurable areas may help us in our interpretation of the immeasurable. Such views as that of Arthur Schlesinger jun. that 'almost all important questions are important precisely because they are not susceptible to quantitative answer'[1] ignore the fact that we may not be able to interpret the evidence on the 'important' questions without knowledge of the quantitative answers. It is much easier to explain someone's increasing happiness if we have established that his income was increasing than if we have no knowledge of his income. Thus, even if we are basically more interested in 'qualitative' than in 'quantitative' questions, the two are inextricably linked. Quantitative questions complement qualitative questions, and quantitative evidence complements qualitative evidence; neither can replace the other, and neither can pretend to comprehend the whole of historical study. A major problem of the historian, whatever his interests, is that he is always faced with inadequate evidence; we never have enough to be sure that we are right in our interpretation or description. If, in decrying the importance of quantification, the historian excludes all consideration of quantitative evidence, or relegates it to a subsidiary place, he is further reducing the already inadequate evidence that he has available. Quantitative evidence will almost certainly not provide a complete answer, but it may well provide some of the answer, and to throw it away unseen is both wasteful and irresponsible.

A more serious, but equally fallacious, criticism of quantitative history is the argument that the use of quantitative methods involves oversimplification, the loss of information about the past, the forcing of individuals into categories, and consequent dehumanization of history. Any use of methods of classification or aggregation will, of course, simplify the diversity of human historical experience, since that is its aim; no one historian can comprehend that diversity, and the mind of the historian, like the mind of anyone faced with a multiplicity of phenomena, inevitably seeks patterns and similarities, and rejects or forgets

[1] Arthur Schlesinger jun., 'The humanist looks at empirical social research', *American Sociological Review*, vol. XXVI (December 1961), p. 770.

much that cannot fit those patterns. The advantage of quantitative history, in contrast to qualitative impressionistic history, is that its systems and methods of classification, the assumptions it uses and the patterns it imposes, are stated and clear; one does not have to see into the mind of the historian, or follow his thought processes, to understand quantitative history, since the classification and the rejection of data are exposed to view. The quantitative historian, also, in searching explicitly for patterns and similarities, is forced always to recognize that he is simplifying, and to describe how he is doing so; not for him the unconscious weeding out of inconvenient items of evidence. The quantitative historian thus can never lose sight of the diversity inherent in historical evidence; his measures are designed to reduce that diversity to a comprehensible form, but also to provide a guide to the divergence of the evidence from the patterns and averages that are used.

There is some bad quantitative history, in which evidence is forced into predetermined categories, and in which the assumptions used are contrary to historical fact. It would, however, be difficult to claim that there is no bad qualitative history. What is certain is that many, though not all, statements made by historians are quantitative statements, that much historical evidence is quantitative and should be analysed by the use of quantitative techniques, and that the historian who uses quantitative methods should use them well. Just as the deciphering of medieval manuscripts, or the interpretation of the political thought of the enlightenment, needs experience, training and skill, so the handling of quantitative materials requires the knowledge of particular methods and techniques of analysis. The historian cannot simply study a table of numbers and expect to understand its significance immediately; he must learn the techniques to draw out its meaning and to relate that meaning to the other pieces of evidence which he has collected. This book is designed, therefore, to help the quantitative historian to use his materials well, and to help those who read his work to judge whether he has done so.

In the following chapters a number of quantitative techniques are discussed in relation to their application to historical problems and historical evidence. The first chapter is concerned with methods of classifying and arranging historical evidence so that it can be analysed by the methods described later in the book. In Chapter 2 methods of describing quantitative evidence in a summary form are discussed, while Chapter 3 consists of a description of some simple mathematical techniques which are useful in the analysis of evidence (no knowledge of mathematics beyond simple school arithmetic and algebra is assumed). These three chapters form, therefore, a description of the preliminary steps that the historian has to undertake before beginning his analysis.

Chapters 4 and 5 describe the first stages of analysis. In Chapter 4 a number of methods of presenting evidence in graphical and tabular form are discussed, while in Chapter 5 these methods of presenting evidence are supplemented by a discussion of measures of central tendency (averages), and measures of dispersion. In Chapter 6, all these techniques are applied to evidence which is ordered chronologically (time series), and discussed with some techniques of particular importance in time series analysis.

In Chapter 7 the methods and concepts developed earlier in the book are used in a discussion of statistical methods for establishing the existence of a relationship between two sets of evidence. Concepts of correlation are discussed, and a simple introduction is given to one of the most powerful of statistical techniques – simple linear regression.

Chapter 8 is concerned with a particular problem of historical data, which is not often considered in traditional texts on statistics – the problem of missing evidence. Building on the methods discussed in previous chapters, a number of procedures for tackling problems of missing evidence are suggested, and the concepts of sampling are introduced.

Finally, in Chapter 9 some of the tools of quantitative analysis are described: the electronic computer and the electronic calculator. The methods discussed earlier in the book do not demand the use of such equipment, but it is shown that, with these aids, quantitative analysis can be made easier and less time consuming.

This book is not a textbook of statistics, nor is it a contribution to discussions of historical method. Nor can it pretend to provide an answer to all the problems that may arise in the analysis of quantitative historical materials. In recent years there has been a very rapid growth in quantitative studies of historical problems. These studies use a variety of methods, drawn from the other social sciences, which are too numerous or, in some cases, too complex, to be described here. These studies and methods share, however, a common core of basic statistical techniques, which are explained in the chapters which follow. This book is an introduction to the skills required by the historian, whether he wishes to read books and articles which use statistical analysis, or to use quantitative evidence himself, whether for political, social, demographic, economic or even intellectual history; it is also an introduction to the many other books on statistics, computing, econometrics or mathematics, which the quantitative historian may eventually need to read or consult.

1 Classifying historical data

One of the first requirements of a systematic study of historical evidence is that the material should be classified. The historian naturally classifies his material in many ways, according to his own preconceptions and to the objects of his study. It is common, for example, for historians to classify their material into primary evidence and secondary evidence. Primary evidence is evidence produced during the period being studied, while secondary evidence has been in some way reworked, normally by other historians. Other classificatory schemes that have been employed by historians distinguish between literary and archaeological evidence, between written and printed evidence, or between quantitative and qualitative evidence. More detailed schemes of classification can be employed; one may, for example, classify primary evidence according to its source, distinguishing between diaries, legal records, court records, newspapers, election results, commercial records.

Historians have, through experience in the use of records, evolved rules that allow them to judge the value of different types of material and help them to use these different types effectively. They classify their material, therefore, partly so that these rules can easily be applied. Thus, for example, J. J. Bagley divides parish records dating from 1660 to 1760 into two groups: poll tax returns and parish registers of baptisms, marriages and burials. Having distinguished between these two groups, Bagley then argues that poll tax returns are not a reliable guide to population changes, while parish registers may sometimes be a good guide.[1]

The historian who uses quantitative materials must learn to classify his materials not only in terms of their source and their reliability but also in a way that shows how far they are suitable for different methods of analysis. The first step he must take is to examine his data, as we shall call the materials he is analysing, and to classify them in a way that will aid him in his analysis. It is possible to distinguish between three types of classification that we may be able to undertake: nominal, ordinal and interval. Whether we can classify data in any one of these ways depends upon the amount of information or evidence we possess.

(a) Nominal classification

The first and most simple form of classification is that used in normal speech, when we divide objects into generic classes by giving them names; this is often a preliminary to counting how many objects fall into each class. The compilers of Domesday Book, for example, were presenting information as nominal data when they wrote of the manor of Wye in Kent in 1086 that:

> There is land for 52 ploughs. On the demesne there are 9 ploughs, and 114 villeins with 22 borders have 17 ploughs. There is a church and 7 serfs, and 4 mills worth 23 shillings and 8 pence, and 113 acres of meadowland and woodland which yield 300 swine from pannage dues.[2]

In this example the compilers of Domesday have inspected the physical objects, men, animals and farm implements on the manor of Wye, given them names and added up the number of each type.

It is important to note several features of this description of the manor of Wye – features that apply generally to nominal

---

[1] J. J. Bagley, *Historical Interpretation, 2: Sources of English History, 1540 to the Present Day* (Harmondsworth, Penguin Books, 1971), pp. 84–154.

[2] J. J. Bagley, *Historical Interpretation, 1: Sources of English Medieval History, 1066–1540* (Harmondsworth, Penguin Books, 1965), p. 27.

classification. The first is that the names given to each characteristic of the manor of Wye are, in principle, arbitrary. It would make no difference to the description of the village if we had given the names of the characteristics in Latin, as they were given in the original manuscript, or in some new language of our own. The name given is immaterial; so long as both the compiler of Domesday and the reader of Domesday agree on the names given to particular characteristics, those names are satisfactory.

The second feature of nominal classification is that it is not implied that the order in which the characteristics are listed has any particular purpose, nor that one characteristic of the manor of Wye is more important than another. Although the characteristics are given in the order quoted in the passage it would make no difference to the accuracy of the description of the village if they were listed in a different order. In fact the compilers of Domesday Book kept to roughly the same order for each entry, which facilitates comparison between manors, but the order is immaterial within each manor.

The third important feature of nominal classification, as in the descriptions of the manor of Wye, is that the categories under which items are listed are discrete, or mutually exclusive, and that there is no relationship between them other than that they are different characteristics of the same manor. It is not possible, for example, to add swine to mills, and to conclude that the manor of Wye had 304 swine/mills, since the two categories, swine and mills, are separate and cannot be aggregated. Even in the case of ploughs, in which it might seem possible to conclude that there were in total twenty-six ploughs on the manor – nine on the demesne and seventeen off the demesne – we do not break this rule; we are not in fact adding demesne ploughs to non-demesne ploughs, two different categories, but rather creating a new category – ploughs of all types – which comprehends both of them. Such an operation, grouping categories, is always possible, but it should be realized that in grouping we are not adding two categories together, but rather creating a new category.

(b) Ordinal classification

In many cases the amount of information that we have available, or the number of assumptions about the data that we are willing to make allows us to go slightly further than merely listing the characteristics of something that interests us. It may be possible to impose some order on the categories we use, to say that one category consists of items that are larger than, older than, smaller than or richer than the items that comprise another category. If it is possible to make some such statement about the relationship between the categories we have established then the data can be regarded as being of ordinal type.

An example of ordinal classification which is frequently encountered in historical work is that of social status. In 1688, for example, Gregory King produced a listing of the social classes in the British population, together with estimates of the numbers of families in each social class. An extract from his listing, showing the upper thirteen of his twenty-six classes, the top half of the social structure, is given in Table 1.1. In such a classification by social class, the compiler of the categories is not only listing the categories, together with the number of items falling into each category, as would be the case with nominal classification, but he feels it possible to make statements about the relationship between one category and the other. Gregory King not only counted the number of families of temporal and spiritual lords, but judged that the former were superior to the latter.

Whereas with nominal classification the order in which the categories are listed is immaterial, and it would make no difference if they were jumbled up, with ordinal classification the order is, as the description 'ordinal' implies, all-important. If we were to jumble up the categories in Gregory King's table, and list them in a different order, we would have lost an important characteristic of his list.

Ordinal data, as we can for convenience call data which have been subjected to an ordinal classification, are more valuable than nominal data simply because the order of categories is an additional piece of information about the data, which can then be used in further analysis.

Table 1.1 *Numbers in social classes*, c. *1688*

Class	Number of families
Temporal lords	160
Spiritual lords	26
Baronets	800
Knights	600
Esquires	3 000
Gentlemen	12 000
Persons in greater offices and places	5 000
Persons in lesser offices and places	5 000
Eminent merchants and traders by sea	2 000
Lesser merchants and traders by sea	8 000
Persons in the law	10 000
Eminent clergymen	2 000
Lesser clergymen	8 000

Source: G. King, quoted in L. Soltow, 'Long-run changes in British income inequality', *Economic History Review*, XXI (1968), No. 1, p. 18.

(c) *Interval or ratio classification*

Just as the additional information of the order of categories distinguishes ordinal from nominal data, so further information, on the precise relationship between categories, is the distinguishing characteristic of interval or ratio classification. We are able to classify information in this way when not only the order in which the categories fall, but also the size of the intervals between the categories, is known, and this information can be used in further analysis. Most of the data used in quantitative analysis of historical materials are of the interval or ratio type, but examples that will be most familiar include income data, electoral statistics, voting figures, population statistics, yields of crops. In Table 1.2, for example, the state of the parties in Parliament after the general election of 1929 is given. With such data, not only is it possible to say that Labour had more members of Parliament than did the Conservatives but also that they had exactly 28 more members, while the Conservatives in turn had 201 more members than did the Liberals. In other words, we have a fixed unit – number of members – by which we can measure party strength. If it is possible to conceive of that unit of measurement having a zero point, as it is when we conceive of a party having no members of Parliament, then we have ratio data. Only if no zero point exists for the unit of measurement are the data theoretically interval data, the major example of such

Table 1.2 *Party strength in the House of Commons, 31 May 1929*

Party	No. of seats
Labour	288
Conservative	260
Liberal	59
Independents	8

data being measurements of temperature, where the zero point is arbitrarily assigned. This differs from a ratio scale, such as income in money, where the state of having no money has more than arbitrary significance. In practice, however, the distinction between ratio and interval data is unimportant; most historical data are of ratio type, but they are often referred to as being of interval type, and we can use the terms interchangeably for the purposes of this book.

(d) Some complications

The amount of further analysis of data which can be undertaken, after the initial classification, depends on the type of data that the historian has. Interval data are more valuable than nominal or ordinal data, because of the additional information about order and arrangement which is implicit in interval data, and we can therefore use more complicated analytical procedures with such data.

It is for this reason that it is important for the historian to be able to judge accurately whether his data are of nominal, ordinal or interval type. If he is unable to do this, he will run two risks. If he assumes that his data are nominal when they are really ordinal or interval, he will be playing safe, but will suffer the penalty that the range of analytical techniques he may use will be severely restricted. If, on the other hand, he assumes that his data are of interval type, when they are really only ordinal, then he will have made a mistaken assumption, and any statistical methods he uses which assume that the data are interval data may produce misleading results. The historian must therefore be able to judge the type to which his data best approximate, before beginning his analysis.

In most cases the type of classification which can be undertaken, or which we can assume was undertaken by the compilers of the data, will be clear, as it has been in the examples of nominal, ordinal and interval data that have been given earlier in this chapter. In other cases, it may be more difficult to decide whether the data are really of one type or another. As an example, when Gregory King made his listing of the English population by social class, as in Table 1.1, he added estimates of the yearly income of families in each class. Table 1.3 gives some of these estimates, this time for the bottom half of the social spectrum.

So far as the two left-hand columns of Table 1.3 are concerned, it is clear that together they represent ordinal data. There might be some argument about whether Gregory King has correctly specified the order, whether for instance military officers were really of a lower social class than naval officers, and both lower than shopkeepers, but it is clear that the data are of ordinal type. The difficulty comes in deciding whether the third column in the table, yearly income per family in £, is of a different type. Superficially, it is a ratio scale; £ sterling is a defined unit of measurement, with a clear zero point. The difficulty lies, however, in the sources available to King when he compiled his estimates; since he did not have full income statistics for families in 1688, his estimates must be largely guesswork, on the basis of his experience. We have to decide whether King was able to make accurate estimates from experience, or whether he simply assigned likely incomes to families on the basis of their place on the social scale. If the former, then we may treat his data as of ratio type, although regarding the exact figures with some suspicion; if the latter, then what we have are ordinal data masquerading as ratio data.

This problem, in which it is difficult to decide whether data are of one type or another, occurs quite frequently in using historical statistics, since the historian often has inadequate information about the way in which the data he is using were

Table 1.3 *Number of families and yearly income per family, classified by social class, England c. 1688*

Class	Number of families	Yearly income per family £
Freeholders of the better sort	40 000	91
Freeholders of the lesser sort	120 000	55
Farmers	150 000	$42\frac{1}{2}$
Persons in liberal arts and sciences	15 000	60
Shopkeepers and tradesmen	50 000	45
Artisans and handicrafts	60 000	38
Naval officers	5 000	80
Military officers	4 000	60
Common soldiers	35 000	14
Common seamen	50 000	20
Labouring people and outservants	364 000	15
Cottagers and paupers	400 000	$6\frac{1}{2}$
Vagrants, beggars, gipsies, thieves and prostitutes	30 000 persons	2 per head

Source: G. King.

compiled. Unfortunately, no general rules for dealing with such a problem exist; the historian has to make a judgement, and his readers have to judge his judgement. In this particular case of the King data, it might be noted, for instance, that the order of yearly incomes does not simply follow the order of social class; naval officers are said to have a yearly income over twice that of artisans and handicraftsmen, who immediately precede them, and farmers with an income of £42½ precede persons in liberal arts and sciences with £60 a year. This disparity in order might be evidence that King had some other evidence on which to base his income statistics, and was not simply assigning numbers according to his perception of social class. It might, therefore, be reasonable to regard the income data as being of ratio type.

In general it is sensible to play safe, to assume that the data are of a less informative type unless one is certain that they satisfy the rules for the more informative type of data. An alternative procedure is to use more than one type of statistical method, comparing the results. Examples of possible methods with similar objects but suitable for different types of data will be given later in the book.

(e) Reclassification and grouping

It is important to realize that the same set of information can often be classified in several different ways. In our example from Domesday Book, we learnt that there were 300 swine in the manor of Wye. Taken by itself, this is a nominal classification of information, but if we have, let us say, information on the number of swine in other Domesday manors, we can use this additional information to classify Wye and other manors, in terms of the numbers of swine they possessed. If we knew merely that Wye had more swine than another village, we would have an ordinal classification, while if we knew exactly how many more swine, we would be able to place Wye within an interval classification. This ability to classify and reclassify is very valuable, since we can exploit different features of our data in different ways, so long as we are constantly aware of the type of classification which has been undertaken.

The need to be aware of what we are doing applies to another form of classification which is often undertaken by historians. It is not an alternative to, but rather is normally combined with nominal, ordinal or interval classification. It was noted in discussion of nominal classification that two items of data – ploughs on the demesne and ploughs off the demesne – might if necessary be grouped into another category – ploughs in general. This process of grouping, or aggregation as it is sometimes called, occurs very commonly both in the evidence which the historian has to work with and in his treatment of it. In the simplest of all examples, a human being can be classified either as a single individual, or as a member of a group of children, of parents, or of grandparents. In addition, the individual will, by virtue of his job, be part of a group of occupations; by virtue of his age, of a generation, and so on. If we know enough about an individual, we can consider him or her within one or many groups. We can, in addition, subsume those groups within larger groups, as when we consider people as residents of towns which are themselves within counties. In such a case we can speak of the behaviour of an individual either as himself or herself, or as a member of a family, as a resident of a town, or as a citizen of a nation.

In other cases our knowledge may be restricted to the behaviour of a group, and we may have no knowledge of the individual behaviour of the members of a group. We then have aggregate rather than individual data, and we must be careful to note this distinction, particularly since much published evidence is aggregative. Social historians, for example, make much use of published census reports, in which are described the social and economic characteristics of groups such as the residents of particular parishes or counties. Economic historians, similarly, study demand for some commodity from a group of consumers, while political historians study election results determined by the behaviour of groups of voters. In all these cases the behaviour of the group has been determined by the behaviour of all the members of the group, but (except in the unlikely event that they all behaved in exactly the same way) we cannot deduce how any one individual has behaved. We can, in other words, work from individual data to aggregate data, but not necessarily from aggregate to individual data. This is a particular difficulty in studies which attempt to relate one aspect of individual behaviour to another, on the basis of aggregate data, and it will therefore be discussed again later in this book.

2 Arranging historical data

As well as classifying his data in the manner described in the last chapter, the historian must learn to arrange his data to suit the requirements of quantitative analysis. Different statistical methods require that data should be arranged in different ways, but there are some general principles, and a general vocabulary, which can be laid down. They are designed to secure clarity and consistency, to save time and effort, and to avoid the possibility of confusion in later stages of analysis.

(a) The data set

In the last chapter we used the word 'data' in an all-embracing sense, to describe the materials on which the historian works. We need therefore another term to describe the data to be used in a particular analysis project, and for this purpose we shall use the term 'data set' to describe a coherent selection of historical data, which a historian intends to use in a particular project. He may wish, if he is interested in more than one question, to use more than one data set in his analysis, but in that case it is still convenient to think of his material as being a series of data sets, together making up the whole body of evidence that he is considering.

The purpose of thinking of evidence as a series of data sets is to emphasize that historical data should be seen not as some vague bundle of information that has survived to us from the past, but as pieces of information relevant to particular problems which we wish to study. In any one project, we will select those pieces of information which we think are relevant to the problem we are considering, and ignore the rest. Some examples may help to clarify the concept of the data set. If we are interested in studying the pattern of English manorial society in 1086, then our data set might well be the Domesday survey; in other words, we select from the wide range of possible information about England in 1086 one set of information, which we call our data set for this particular project. Similarly, in a study of British elections, one of our data sets might well be the set of election results, like that for 1929 given in Table 1.2. A data set is thus a coherent selection of data from the whole range of historical data available to the historian, and it is selected because it relates closely to the questions that the historian wishes to consider.

(b) The case

Every data set is composed of a series of individual pieces of data, brought together to form a coherent body of evidence relevant to a particular question. Within each data set, we therefore have to arrange the data so as to facilitate the consideration of that question; the data cannot simply lie about in a jumbled fashion on pieces of paper or file cards, but must be consistently and logically arranged.

The basic unit of arrangement of any data set is the 'case', which consists of one or more pieces of information relating to a particular unit of investigation. In the Domesday survey, for example, we might regard each manor as being one case, comprising all the pieces of information describing that manor. Similarly, in a study of election results, each general election result could be considered to be one case, so that the election result of 1929 can be thought of as one case drawn from the data set of results of British general elections. Each case may, therefore, be an individual person or manor, or election result, or it may be some group or aggregate; we would not normally mix individual with aggregate data within any one data set.

(c) The variable

Each case consists of a number of pieces of information about itself. This information describes different characteristics of that case. In the Domesday survey, for example, we are told how many ploughs there are in the manor of Wye, how many serfs, how much woodland. If we take other manors, other cases, we can find information on these same characteristics of the other manors; some will have the same number of ploughs as Wye, others more and others less. The characteristic of 'number of ploughs on the manor' will vary, in other words, from case to case, and we can therefore describe it as a variable characteristic, shortened to 'variable'. We can see that each case is therefore made up of a number of different pieces of information relating to variables that are common to all cases, and we therefore say that each case is composed of a number of values, one value for each variable. The values do not have to be numerical – the name of each manor, for example, is a variable – and often it may be convenient to record each case as a mixture of numbers and words.

In our example of general election results the case is the election result, and the variables are the party strengths after each election. Thus there were four variables – Labour strength, Conservative strength, Liberal strength and Independent strength – and the values of the variables in 1929 were 288, 260, 59 and 8.

(d) The data matrix

It is convenient to arrange our data set, on the page or in our minds, so that we can see clearly what pieces of information are part of our data set, and which are cases and which are variables. One convenient method of organizing data is through the use of the 'data matrix'. An example of a data matrix, part of a data set of Domesday manors, is given in Table 2.1.

In Table 2.1 we have set out some evidence on five manors as given in Domesday Book. We have set out the information so that each case – in this table each manor – has a row to itself, while each variable (the number of ploughlands per manor, the number of acres of meadow per manor and the number of villeins per manor) is set out as a column of the table. We can think of a data matrix, therefore, as consisting of a number of rows, which will normally represent cases, and a number of columns, which will normally represent variables (in this book, in fact, we will keep strictly to this convention, but the reader should be aware that it is sometimes broken, for convenience of presentation or other reasons).

We can describe the matrix given in Table 2.1, therefore, as being a data matrix with five rows and four columns. It will often be convenient for us, in the process of analysis, to concentrate our attention either on one row or one column, or

Table 2.1 *Domesday manors*

Manor	*Ploughlands*	*Acres of meadow*	*Villeins*
Wye	52	–	114
Stiffkey	1½	2	–
Milton	15	20	14
Oundle	9	50	23
Leeds	6	–	27

A dash denotes no information.

Source: J. J. Bagley, *Historical Interpretation, 1: Sources of English Medieval History, 1066–1540* (Harmondsworth, Penguin Books, 1965), pp. 27–9.

perhaps on one piece of information, discarding the remainder of the matrix for that part of the analysis. When we do this it is often difficult to know how to refer to the particular bits of information in which we are interested; it is, for instance, rather cumbersome to say, 'the piece of information giving the number of acres of meadow in the manor of Oundle'.

To facilitate reference to individual pieces of information in a data matrix, we can use a system of matrix notation. Just as in algebra we are used to denoting numbers by letters of the alphabet, so we can denote each piece of information in a matrix (each 'matrix element') by a letter of the alphabet. Table 2.2 shows a possible method of doing this.

In this table the letter *a* stands for the figure 52, while *k* stands for 50, the corresponding entries in the data matrix given in Table 2.1. We have, by this method, facilitated reference to particular pieces of information. We can now say '*k*' instead of 'the piece of information giving the number of acres of meadow in the manor of Oundle'.

However, it is clear that this method of representing the

Table 2.2 *Domesday manors*

Manor	Ploughlands	Acres of meadow	Villeins
Wye	*a*	*b*	*c*
Stiffkey	*d*	*e*	*f*
Milton	*g*	*h*	*i*
Oundle	*j*	*k*	*l*
Leeds	*m*	*n*	*o*

elements in a matrix by letters of the alphabet is severely restricted. If we had more than twenty-six elements we should run out of letters, and many data matrices will have more than twenty-six bits of information in them. We therefore need some more general way of representing elements in a matrix, and such a generalized method is shown in Table 2.3.

Table 2.3 *Data matrix A representing five Domesday manors*

Manors	Ploughlands	Acres of meadow	Villeins
Wye	A_{11}	A_{12}	A_{13}
Stiffkey	A_{21}	A_{22}	A_{23}
Milton	A_{31}	A_{32}	A_{33}
Oundle	A_{41}	A_{42}	A_{43}
Leeds	A_{51}	A_{52}	A_{53}

In this table we have denoted each element of the matrix by the use of the letter *A*, together with a first subscript which shows the row in which the element is placed, and a second subscript which shows the column in which the element is placed. This method of notation allows us to describe a whole matrix, even a whole data set, and each element in it, by the use of one letter of the alphabet and two subscripts. We can choose different letters of the alphabet to describe different matrices or data sets.

We have so far considered matrices in which there are both more than one row and more than one column, but it is possible for a matrix to have only one row or only one column. For example, if we take the second row of Table 2.1, we have a matrix with one row, known as a row vector, as shown in Table 2.4.

Table 2.4 *Row vector of observations for Stiffkey manor*

Manor	Ploughlands	Acres of meadow	Villeins
Stiffkey	$1\frac{1}{2}$	2	–

This can be replaced, in matrix notation, by Table 2.5.

Table 2.5 *Row vector B of observations for Stiffkey manor*

Manor	Ploughlands	Acres of Meadow	Villeins
Stiffkey	B_1	B_2	B_3

Notice that we have used a different letter, to avoid confusion with the larger data matrix A, and that we have dropped one subscript. We have in fact discarded the first subscript, that giving the row; since there is only one row, the first subscript is redundant.

In a similar way, the first column of Table 2.1 could be expressed, using matrix notation, as Table 2.6, and we would say that we had a column vector C. Again we have used a different letter, and this time have dropped the column subscript; since there is only one column it is redundant.

The same pieces of data can therefore be regarded as elements of a matrix, or elements of a row vector, or elements of a column vector. Which way we choose to represent them at any one time is entirely our choice, depending on whether we are interested in the whole matrix, or simply in one case (a row vector) or one variable (a column vector).

A further useful convention is to use the letter i to represent the row subscript, and the letter j to represent the column subscript. Thus we can say that, in Table 2.3 the i subscript can have values of 1, 2, 3, 4 or 5, while the j subscript can have values 1, 2 or 3. We can in fact describe this matrix as the matrix A_{ij} where i varies from 1 to 5, and j from 1 to 3.

Table 2.6 *Column vector C of observations of number of ploughlands for five Domesday manors*

Manor	Ploughlands
Wye	C_1
Stiffkey	C_2
Milton	C_3
Oundle	C_4
Leeds	C_5

We shall use matrix notation of this kind in discussing many of the statistical methods described later in this book. Although to use such notation may seem at first sight to be introducing unnecessary complication, it will become clear that the use of such notation greatly simplifies the handling of quantitative data.

(e) Collecting data

Since data arranged in the form of a data matrix are suitable for analysis by the methods that will be described later, it follows that, unless there is some overriding consideration that prevents such an arrangement, data should be collected and set out ready for analysis in the form of a data matrix. The historian beginning a project in quantitative analysis must therefore decide firstly which unit in his evidence he will treat as his cases and secondly which variables relating to those cases he will want to study. Having decided this, he can arrange his material accordingly.

The arrangement of real data in this way is a more or less complicated procedure depending on the complexity of the underlying data. One important requirement of the arrangement of a data set into a data matrix is that of consistency; each row must consist of a case, and each column entry must contain the same kind of information as every other entry in that column. Usually, consistency of this kind is easy to attain; with the data given in Table 1.3, for example, of Gregory King's estimates of the numbers of families in each social group with their yearly incomes, there is no possibility of confusion. The data are clearly stated, with each column clearly defined. On other occasions, however, perhaps because the original data have been confusingly recorded, there is a possibility of falling into error. For example, in the Domesday survey one of the most important pieces of information collected about each manor was the area of land assessed for geld payment. Table 2.7 lists this information for four of the manors we have already considered.

Table 2.7 *Land assessed for geld in four Domesday manors*

Manor	Land assessed for geld
Wye	7 sulungs
Milton	$\frac{1}{2}$ hide
Oundle	6 hides
Leeds	10 carucates and 6 bovates

8 bovates = 1 carucate.

In this table the data refer to the same characteristic of the manors, the same variable for each case, but we would clearly be in error if, in recording our data, we simply listed them as in Table 2.8.

In Table 2.8 our column of data is not consistent, since the units in which the area of land has been recorded are not the same from case to case. In much the same way, it is possible to violate the requirement of consistency between cases. For example, if in a survey of the results of British elections we took as our cases not only the state of the parties after each general election but also the state of the parties after each by-election, we would then have an inconsistent data set. The information in each column would be correct and consistent, but the cases would differ one from the other; one case would be after a general election, when all seats are contested, another would be after a by-election, when only one seat can change hands.

Table 2.8 *Land assessed for geld in four Domesday manors*

Manor	Land assessed for geld
Wye	7
Milton	$\frac{1}{2}$
Oundle	6
Leeds	10·75

It may seem superfluous to emphasize the need for consistency when collecting data and arranging them in a data matrix, but consistency is essential when quantitative methods of analysis are used. When the historian is faced with an inconsistent data set, therefore, as in the example given in Table 2.7, he has to try to overcome the difficulty before he can proceed to analyse the data. He is faced with a choice between four courses of action. The first, and best, choice is to transform all the data into a consistent measure, transforming sulungs and carucates into hides; unfortunately, it is not always possible to do this, since the relationship between different measures may not be known. A common problem of this type in economic history is the difficulty that different types of cloth were measured using different measures, and the conversion ratios between them are not always known.

The second possibility, if it is not possible to convert the data to a common standard, is to accept the diversity, and to record the data in different columns, as if each measure of area were a separate variable, as is done in Table 2.9. The difficulty with this method is that it makes it difficult to carry out any analysis across cases; it also wastes space, which may be important if the land assessed for geld is only one of the pieces of information that need to be recorded.

Table 2.9 *Land assessed for geld in four Domesday manors*

| Manor | Land assessed | | |
	(a) Sulungs	(b) Hides	(c) Carucates
Wye	7	n.a.	n.a.
Milton	n.a.	$\frac{1}{2}$	n.a.
Oundle	n.a.	6	n.a.
Leeds	n.a.	n.a.	10·75

n.a. = not applicable.

The third possibility is to omit the atypical units; sulungs were a Kentish measure, not used in the remainder of England, and carucates were used less often than were hides. It may therefore be sensible to omit information on sulungs and carucates, and to record the information as in Table 2.10.

Table 2.10 *Land assessed for geld in four Domesday manors*

Manor	Land assessed for geld, in hides
Wye	n.a.
Milton	$\frac{1}{2}$
Oundle	6
Leeds	n.a.

n.a. = not available.

This method is less satisfactory than either of the two former methods, because information has been discarded; there is no possibility of using the data on sulungs or carucates.

The fourth method, the least satisfactory, is to omit entirely any information on the inconsistently recorded variable. In the case of our Domesday example, as in Table 2.7, this would result in losing the table altogether – an extreme measure. However, if the item causing difficulty is only one among many pieces of information to be recorded, and if it will not play a very important part in further analysis, then it may be safe to discard it altogether, rather than face the problems of lack of consistency. The chief objections to this procedure are that information is being discarded and that it is often difficult to tell, at the data recording stage, whether some piece of information will or will not prove valuable at a later stage of analysis. Therefore, unless the difficulties of doing so are impossible to overcome, it is better to keep data than to discard them.

3   Some simple mathematics

In this chapter we shall discuss the calculation of some simple, but important, statistical measures. We shall also describe some simple mathematical techniques, which simplify the calculations of these measures, and which we shall need to use later in the book. Some of these techniques will be familiar to those who can remember the mathematics they learnt at school, while others will be new to many people, and are therefore explained at some length. The concepts of statistics could, it should be said, be explained without the use of one or two of these mathematical techniques, but to do this would lead to unnecessary complications and to long-winded explanations of simple points.

(a) The frequency distribution

Each column of a data matrix consists of data values concerned with some variable characteristic of the cases in the matrix. If we are interested in one variable characteristic in particular we focus on its column in the matrix, and we see in that column a list of numbers, one for each case. In the Domesday example used in the last chapter, for example, we saw a list of areas assessed for geld, one for each manor. If we are considering only a small number of cases, as we were in the last chapter, then we can comprehend the information on assessed areas per manor without much difficulty. If, however, we are analysing data for more cases, for example for fifty manors, we shall need to comprehend or assimilate information from a much longer list, such as that shown in Table 3.1. When we are faced with such a table it is very difficult for us to distinguish at all clearly the main features of the information that the table contains; we cannot easily assimilate fifty or more numbers in our heads.

In order to assimilate large quantities of data, therefore, we need to summarize the data in some way, to bring out their main features in a memorable way. The simplest way of doing this is, as a first step, to count the number of times that each value appears in the list. In doing this, we are essentially rearranging the data; in our original data matrix, such as the column vector shown in Table 3.1, the values of the variable are arranged or listed according to the order in which the cases appeared in the matrix as it was originally collected. Now, instead, we arrange the cases according to the values they have for the variable. We distribute the cases to show the frequency with which particular values of the variable occur, and for this reason such a rearrangement of data is known as a frequency distribution.

As an example, let us consider the problems involved in analysing the data of Table 3.1. This table shows the numbers of

Table 3.1 *Woodland in Essex, c. 1086*

Place	Nos. of swine for which there was woodland, 1086
Writtle	1 200
Clavering	600
Farnham	150
,,	50
Ugley	160
Alferestuna	350
Canfield	120
Dunmow	300
Easton	150
,,	400
,,	150
Lashley	60
Thaxted	800
Yardley	30

Table 3.1—*continued*

Hersham	30
Hallingbury	100
Finchingfield	5
,,	30
Hedingham	500
,,	160
Henny	30
,,	20
Maplestead	60
,,	15 (16 in original)
Polhey	40
Saling	200
Stansted	400
Wethersfield	500
Wickham St Pauls	20
Eastwood	30
Amberden	200
Birchanger	50
,,	30
Elsenham	1 000
Saffron Walden	800
,,	30
Takeley	600
Thunderley	600
Wickham Bonhunt	80
Wimbish	60
Layer	400
,,	60
Coggeshall	30
Braxted	500
Notley	80
,,	30
,,	200
,,	100
Rivenhall	350
Unspecified (Barstable Hundred)	55
	11 915

Source: H. C. Darby, *The Domesday Geography of Eastern England* (Cambridge, Cambridge University Press, 1952), pp. 236–7.

swine for which there was woodland, in fifty Essex manors, recorded as part of the Domesday survey in 1086. In essence, the information is concerned with the amount of woodland on these manors; the compilers of Domesday did not normally give areas of woodland, but used the measure of the number of swine which could be supported on it. As Professor Darby says, 'It does not necessarily follow that these figures indicate the actual number of swine grazing in a wood: the swine were used merely as a unit of measurement.'[1] With this information, we can see that the data of Table 3.1 provide useful evidence on the extent of wood and forest in Essex in 1086. As it stands, however, the information is difficult to understand; we gain little idea, from looking at the table, of the distribution of woodland in each place, or whether there was a particular area of woodland that was commonly kept intact. To obtain this kind of information, we need to summarize the table, to reduce the information which it contains to a manageable form.

We may begin this process of summarizing the table by constructing a simple frequency distribution, such as that shown in Table 3.2. Instead of fifty numbers, one for each place, we now have forty-four numbers, of which half (those in the first column) show the values of the variable numbers of swine, and half (in the second column) show how frequently those values occurred in the data. Although there is, when one compares Table 3.2 with Table 3.1, some reduction in the amount of information that we need to assimilate, we have not simplified very much. It is still difficult to understand the contents of the table at a glance.

We can, however, construct other types of frequency distribution that will further help understanding of data such as this. For example, a first step is to group the values of the variable, and to list the frequency with which cases fall into each group; the result is known as a grouped frequency distribution, and examples are shown in Tables 3.3 and 3.4. We can choose our groupings of values very much as we please; if we wish to emphasize fine distinctions between cases, we will

[1] H. C. Darby, *The Domesday Geography of Eastern England* (Cambridge, Cambridge University Press, 1952), p. 233.

choose a large number of groups, but if we are interested only in broad distinctions, we can use a small number of groups. The groups do not necessarily have to be of the same size, but confusion can be caused when they are not; unless there is some

Table 3.2 *Frequency distribution of Essex parishes,*
c. 1086, by numbers of swine

1 Nos of swine	2 Nos of places with nos. of swine as in column 1
5	1
15	1
20	2
30	9
40	1
50	2
55	1
60	4
80	2
100	2
120	1
150	3
160	2
200	3
300	1
350	2
400	3
500	3
600	3
800	2
1000	1
1200	1

overriding difficulty, groups of the same size should be used. The one absolute requirement is that the groups should be unambiguous; there should be no possibility of disagreement as to whether a case should go into one group or another. Thus groups should always be stated, as in Table 3.3, 0–199, 200–399, etc.; if they were stated as 0–200, 200–400, etc., confusion

Table 3.3 *Grouped frequency distribution of Essex parishes, c. 1086, by numbers of swine*

Nos of swine	Nos of places
0–199	31
200–399	6
400–599	6
600–799	3
800–999	2
1000–1199	1
1200–1399	1

Table 3.4 *Grouped frequency distribution of Essex parishes, c. 1086, by numbers of swine*

Nos of swine	Nos of places
0–99	23
100–199	8
200–299	3
300–399	3
400–499	3
500–599	3
600–699	3
700–799	0
800–899	2
900–999	0
1000–1099	1
1100–1199	0
1200–1299	1

would arise as to where a case with 200 swine should be placed.

The frequency distribution is an important statistical tool, and we shall return to a more detailed consideration of its use in the next chapter. At this moment, it is necessary simply to remember that a frequency distribution represents a rearrangement of data in which the cases are listed according to the value of the variable that they possess.

(b) Summation notation

It frequently happens in the analysis of quantitative data that we wish to calculate and use the total of a set of numbers. The process of adding numbers to obtain a total, or 'sum' as it is normally called, is familiar, but it is often clumsy to have to write such instructions as 'calculate the sum of values for the variable'. It is therefore useful to have a notation that will give an instruction to sum, and can also be used to represent the sum in further calculations.

In summation notation, the Greek capital letter sigma, Σ, shows that some numbers are to be added, while other terms, placed above, below and to the side of the sigma, indicate what is to be added to what. For example, in Table 3.1, if we regard the list of numbers of swine as a column vector represented by the letter X, with values X_i running from X_1 to X_{50}, we can express the sum of that column as

$$\sum_{i=1}^{50} X_i = 11\ 915.$$

The term below the sigma, $i = 1$, indicates that i, the subscript of the X vector, first takes the value of 1, and subsequently takes consecutive positive values, 2, 3, 4, 5, etc. The term above the sigma indicates the final value of i, in this case 50, since there are fifty cases in the table, while the term next to the sigma, X_i, indicates the vector to be summed. We can vary the terms above and below the sigma, if we wish, to indicate that we are calculating the sum of only part of the list. For example, if we wished to exclude from our calculation the manors of Writtle, Clavering, Farnham and Rivenhall, and the 'Unspecified' manor in Barstable Hundred, we could express the sum of the other manors by writing

$$\sum_{i=5}^{48} X_i.$$

This would instruct us to give i the initial value of 5, and then to sum each consecutive positive value of i up to and including 48, thus excluding the first four and the last two cases on the list.

A useful general form of the instruction, for a list of any number of cases, is to call the number of cases N, and to write the summation instruction as

$$\sum_{i=1}^{N} X_i.$$

Sometimes we may wish to obtain the total not simply of a vector, but of a whole matrix. This may often be necessary when we have classified a data set in two ways, forming a data matrix such as that in Table 3.5. To obtain the total population of the British Isles in 1851 we need to sum all the elements of the matrix.

Table 3.5 *Estimated mid-year population of the British Isles, 1851 (000s)*

	Males	Females
England and Wales	8 809	9 174
Scotland	1 379	1 517
Ireland	3 181	3 333

Source: B. R. Mitchell and P. Deane, *Abstract of British Historical Statistics* (Cambridge, Cambridge University Press, 1962), p. 8.

If we express the data of Table 3.5 as a matrix, Y, we will have a matrix with elements as shown in Table 3.6.

Table 3.6 *Data matrix Y representing the estimated mid-year population of the British Isles*

	Males	Females
England and Wales	Y_{11}	Y_{12}
Scotland	Y_{21}	Y_{22}
Ireland	Y_{31}	Y_{32}

We can write the sum of all the elements of the matrix Y as

$$\sum_{i=1}^{3} \sum_{j=1}^{2} Y_{ij}$$

where the first sigma refers to the rows, and the second sigma to the columns, of the matrix Y with i rows and j columns. The complete instruction is thus to sum all the elements in the matrix. The actual procedure we would use to add up the elements would be to begin with $i = 1$ and $j = 1$, taking first the element Y_{11}, the top left-hand element if the matrix were presented as a table. We would then take, as the second element to be added, the element for which $i = 1$ and $j = 2$, the element Y_{12} before returning to the beginning of the second row and taking the element Y_{21}. In other words, the subscript of the second sigma varies within each consecutive value of the subscript of the first sigma.

The purpose of summation notation is to simplify calculation and the use of sums of numbers in statistical formulae. Instead of writing 'the total of the numbers listed in Table 3.1' we can simply write

$$\sum_{i=1}^{50} X_i$$

having defined X as the column vector shown in Table 3.1. Indeed, summation notation is often further simplified by elimination of the subscripts. When, for instance, we wish to use the sum of a vector Z, we could simply write $\sum Z$, rather than

$$\sum_{i=1}^{N} Z_i.$$

It is important, however, that no confusion should be caused by doing this, and in general the subscripts should be used.

It should be noted that when the sigma precedes a term including several symbols enclosed by brackets, it indicates that everything included in that term is to be summed, until a $+$ or $-$ sign is encountered. For example, if we want to multiply together the equivalent elements of two vectors, X and Y, and sum the results, we would write

$$\sum_{i=1}^{N} X_i \, Y_i.$$

This indicates that, for each value of i from 1 to N, we multiply the X_i by the Y_i and sum. If, however, we wanted to add to that sum some other number, for instance the number 55, we would write

$$\sum_{i=1}^{N} X_i \, Y_i + 55.$$

This would show that we wanted to add 55 to the sum of the X and Y vectors multiplied together, not that we multiplied together the X_i and Y_i and added 55 to each product, before summing; had we wanted to do this, we would have written

$$\sum_{i=1}^{N} (X_i \, Y_i + 55).$$

The $+$ sign, in fact, indicates where the summation should stop.

We can use the summation sign and its associated symbols just as we use any other algebraic quantity. Thus we can write

$$K \sum_{i=1}^{N} X_i Y_i$$

indicating that, after calculating the sum of the X_i multiplied by the Y_i, we multiply that sum by another quantity, K. Further examples of the use of summation notation which often occur in statistical work are

$$\sum_{i=1}^{N} X_i^2 = (X_1^2 + X_2^2 + X_3^2 + X_4^2 \ldots + X_{N-1}^2 + X_N^2)$$

and

$$\left(\sum_{i=1}^{N} X_i \right)^2 = (X_1 + X_2 + X_3 + X_4 \ldots + X_{N-1} + X_N)^2.$$

In these examples, the row of dots indicates that one should continue to sum all the values between that preceding the dots, in these cases X_4^2 and X_4, until reaching the end of the list with X_N^2 and X_N.

(c) Logarithms

It is often necessary for historians to calculate and analyse proportionate changes; we might wish to examine, for example, the change in British exports from one year to the next as a proportion or percentage of those in the previous year, or the proportionate change in the votes cast for a political party from one election to the next. In many problems of this kind, which are discussed in Chapter 6, it is convenient to make use of logarithms. The concept of logarithms will be familiar to most readers who have studied elementary mathematics at school although one of their main uses, that of simplifying calculations with large numbers, is less important in the age of electronic calculators. Logarithms remain important in statistics, however, and we must therefore review the main features of their use.

There are two types of logarithms which are used in statistics, logarithms to the base 10, and logarithms to the base e, but we shall be concerned only with the former, which are more commonly used. To find the logarithm to the base 10 of a number we can make use of the four-figure tables which are reproduced at the end of this book on pp. 228–30. When using these tables, we take only the first four significant (i.e. not preceded by a zero) digits of the number. With large numbers this will entail a loss of accuracy, which can be overcome by using an electronic calculator, many types of which will calculate logarithms at the touch of a button. It is sensible, however, to follow through the calculation using four-figure tables, since the underlying concept of logarithms and their use appears more clearly.

For example, to find the logarithm of 104, 869·0, we take the first four digits, rounding off the fifth, to obtain 1049. The first two digits of this number refer us to the row of the log tables, in this case to row 10. Looking along that row, the third digit, 4, refers us to the column of four-digit numbers headed 4, while the fourth digit, 9, refers us to the column of one- or two-digit numbers headed 9. The fourth column gives us the value ·0170, while adding to this the value under the column headed 9 we get ·0170 + 0037 = ·0207. Similarly, if we wished to calculate the logarithm of 1272, we would use the third row of the table, getting the result ·1045.

In finding these values, however, we have found only a part (called the mantissa) of the logarithm of these numbers. We have in addition to take account of the position of the decimal point. To do this, we have to know that (as implied by the name 'log to the base 10') the logarithm of 10 is 1·0000. The logarithm of 100 ($= 10^2$) is 2·0000, the logarithm of 1000 ($= 10^3$) is 3·0000, and so on. It follows that any number falling, for example, between 10 and 100, will have a logarithm between 1·0000 and 2·0000. The exact value between these two bounds is given by the mantissa, found as we have just shown from the log tables. The part of the logarithm giving the position of the decimal point, known as the characteristic, and the part of the logarithm independent of the decimal point, the mantissa, together make up the logarithm we use in our calculations. Table 3.7 shows the effect of altering the position of the decimal point.

Table 3.7 *The effect of the position of the decimal point upon logarithms*

log 1272·0 = 3·1045	log 0·127 20	$= \bar{1}\cdot1045$
log 127·20 = 2·1045	log 0·012 72	$= \bar{2}\cdot1045$
log 12·720 = 1·1045	log 0·001 272	$= \bar{3}\cdot1045$
log 1·2720 = 0·1045	log 0·000 127 2	$= \bar{4}\cdot1045$

The most convenient way of thinking of the location of the decimal point, and therefore of determining the characteristic of the logarithm, is to think of the number of digits past which the decimal point would need to be moved before the number had one significant figure to the left of the decimal point. For example, in Table 3.7 we would have to move the decimal point in the number 127·2 to the left past two digits before the number would be 1·272. The characteristic is therefore 2. Similarly, for numbers less than 1·000, we calculate the number of digits past which the decimal point would have to be moved to the right. In the case of 0·0001272 we would have to move the decimal point past four digits, and the characteristic is therefore $\bar{4}$.

Having discovered the logarithms of the numbers we wish to

use, we can then carry out the arithmetical operations that we wish to perform; we shall describe those shortly. The answer to an operation performed using logarithms will itself be a logarithm, and will therefore have to be transformed, through the use of tables of antilogarithms, to give us our final result (antilog tables are reproduced on pp. 229–30). Imagine that our answer is the logarithm 2·7127. We take the mantissa, and refer to the row titled ·71; we then go to the third four-figure column, finding 5152; we then refer to the seventh of the one- or two-digit columns, finding 8. Adding 5152 + 8 = 5160. We now have a four-digit number, but we shall have to decide where the decimal point shall be placed, using the information given to us by the characteristic of the logarithm, in this case 2. This tells us that we should move the decimal point two places to the right from the position of having one significant figure to the left of the decimal point (had the characteristic been $\bar{2}$, we would have moved the decimal point two places to the left). Taking our number 5160, we therefore start with the decimal point in the position 5·160, and move it two places to the right, giving 516·0. The antilog of 2·7127 is therefore 516·0.

The operations that can be carried out using logarithms can most easily be set out in tabular form, as in Table 3.8.

It should be noted that placing a bar over the characteristic of the logarithm, as in $\bar{2}$, simply shows that the logarithm is that of a number with an absolute value (without its plus or minus sign) of less than 1·0000. We ignore signs when conducting operations with logarithms, taking them into account only at the end of the operation. Thus to multiply 274·6 by −58·27 we would carry out the operations exactly as in Table 3.8, replacing the minus sign in the calculation at the end to give us the answer of −16,000·0.

The three preceding sections in this chapter have discussed all the mathematical operations that need to be known in order to understand the remainder of this book. Essentially, the historian who wishes to use quantitative methods must know how to add, subtract, multiply, divide, calculate squares and square roots, and use simple matrix and summation notation. To ease or speed up calculation he can use one of the electronic

Table 3.8 *Operations using logarithms*

Operation	Method	Example
Multiply 274·6 by 58·27	Add logarithms, take antilogarithm	$274·6 \times 58·27$ $= \log (274·6) + \log (58·27)$ $= 2·4387 + 1·7654$ $= 4·2041$ (taking antilog) $= 16\ 000·0$
Divide 274·6 by 58·27	Subtract logarithms, take antilogarithm	$274·6/58·27$ $= \log (274·6) - \log (58·27)$ $= 2·4387 - 1·7654$ $= 0·6733$ (taking antilog) $= 4·713$
Square 274·6	Multiply logarithm by 2, take antilog	$274·6^2 = \log (274·6) \times 2$ $= 2·4387 \times 2$ $= 4·8774$ (taking antilog) $= 75\ 410·0$
Take square root of 58·27	Divide logarithm by 2, take antilog	$\sqrt{58·27} = \log (58·27)/2$ $= 1·7654/2$ $= 0·8827$ (taking antilog) $= 7·633$
Take square root of 0·9854 (number less than 1·0000)	Divide logarithm by 2, take antilog	$\sqrt{0·9854} = \log (0·9854)/2$ $= \bar{1}·9936/2$ $= (\bar{2}·0000 + 1·9936)/2$ $= \bar{1}·0000 + 0·9968$ $= \bar{1}·9968$ taking antilog $= 0·9926$

calculators or computers described in Chapter 9; these remove many of the difficulties associated with hand computation, but to use them the historian must still understand the simple mathematical operations which have been described in this chapter. In general the choice of method will depend upon the type of operation that has to be carried out, and upon the accuracy that is required. If complete accuracy is required, then either hand methods or machinery with the capacity to handle large numbers must be used; if truncation to four significant figures is acceptable, then logarithms and square root tables can be employed.

4 The preliminary analysis of data, I: frequency distributions and charts

Once the data have been collected and arranged in the ways that have been described in the preceding chapters, the analysis stage of the project can begin. The first stages of quantitative analysis will vary from project to project, and from historian to historian, but it is safe to say that it is likely that at an early stage the historian will need to make use of the methods of *descriptive statistics*. Descriptive statistics are those statistical methods primarily concerned with the organization and presentation of data; they are sometimes contrasted with other methods called *analytic* statistics, but the distinction is a false one, and will not be used in this book. The descriptive statistics that we shall be considering are as much a part of the analysis of data as are more advanced statistical methods.

The function of descriptive statistics is to facilitate the understanding of quantitative material. They may help the historian to continue his analysis, or they may help the reader to understand the results of the analysis, but in both cases the aim is greater understanding. Since this is so, descriptive statistics have to be judged according to how far they succeed in increasing understanding; there are, therefore, no right or wrong ways of using descriptive statistics, although there are several ways of using them, discussed later in this chapter, which may mislead the unwary. There are, it is true, some methods of descriptive statistics that are suitable only for particular types of data; the mean, for example, cannot be calculated if the data are of ordinal or nominal type. But with these exceptions, we should choose the methods of presenting our material – that is, the descriptive statistics we use – simply with an eye to what will most clearly illuminate those features of the data in which we are most interested.

It should be stressed that the methods of descriptive statistics are useful not only in the presentation of results but at every stage of the analysis. The drawing of a graph, the work of a few minutes, may suddenly show some facet of the data that was not at all obvious when the historian was merely staring at a table of figures.

Table 4.1 shows a typical segment of a data matrix, after the collection of the data but before any rearrangement or statistical work has been carried out. The data set shown in Table 4.1 consists of information about twenty-five ships which formed part of the British merchant fleet in 1907; each ship is identified by its 'official number' (a unique identifying number somewhat like the number given to each motor vehicle and shown on its number plate). Table 4.1 contains in the order of columns given in the table an identification of each case, two nominal variables, and two interval variables. The table does not contain any ordinal data; ordinal data are rarely encountered in historical work, and it is therefore unnecessary to consider examples of them at length. Whenever a particular type of statistical method is suitable for ordinal data this fact will be mentioned; more detailed discussion of ordinal data can be found in textbooks of statistics for social scientists.

(a) The frequency distribution

In Chapter 3 we introduced the most widely used of the methods of descriptive statistics, the frequency distribution. We demonstrated that the frequency distribution essentially involved the rearrangement of the data matrix, or of individual columns of the matrix, into a form in which the information they contain is more easily intelligible. The rearrangement may simply involve ordering the cases in a new way, or it may involve grouping the cases according to the value that they have on one or other of the variable characteristics. Frequency distributions may be created from nominal, ordinal and interval data, and as

Table 4.1 *Twenty-five British merchant ships, 1907*

Official No.	Trade	Power	Tonnage	Crew size
1697	Home	Not given	44	3
2640	Home	Not given	144	6
35052	Home	Not given	150	5
62595	Home	Sail	236	8
73742	Home	Steam	739	16
86658	Home	Steam	970	15
92929	Foreign	Steam	2 371	23
93086	Home	Steam	309	5
94546	Foreign	Steam	679	13
95757	Home	Sail	26	4
96414	Foreign	Steam	1 272	19
99437	Foreign	Steam	3 246	33
99495	Home	Steam	1 904	19
107004	Home	Steam	357	10
109597	Home	Steam	1 080	16
113406	Home	Steam	1 027	22
113685	Home	Not given	45	2
113689	Home	Not given	62	3
114424	Home	Sail	68	2
114433	Foreign	Steam	2 507	22
115143	Foreign	Sail	138	2
115149	Home	Steam	502	18
115357	Home	Steam	1 501	21
118852	Foreign	Steam	2 750	24
123375	Home	Steam	192	9

Source: Crew lists held by the Registrar General of shipping and seamen.

examples we shall use the data on method of power, a nominal variable, and on crew size, an interval variable.

Method of power, the third column in our data matrix, is a nominal variable which can take one of three values, representing steam, sail and information not given. To construct a frequency distribution based on this variable, therefore, we simply count the number of times that each type of power appears in the third column of our data matrix, and enter the results into a new table, shown as Table 4.2.

Table 4.2 *Frequency distribution of data*
from column 3 of Table 4.1

Power	No. of ships
Sail	4
Steam	16
Not given	5
Total	25

Notice that we specify, in the heading of the table, the source of the data contained in the table. We also, as an aid to accuracy and to understanding, give the total number of cases in the table.

With our interval data variable, size of crew (the fifth column of Table 4.1), we have in theory a very large number of possible values, as opposed to the three possible values for our data on method of power. Some ships of this period had crews of several hundreds, but it so happens that in our sample the crew sizes range from two to thirty-three, and we can therefore limit our frequency distribution to those values. Even with this limitation, however, if we imitated the method of Table 4.2 we should have a table of 32 possible values, most of them having a zero entry in the second column. To simplify and compress the frequency distribution, therefore, we group the values together, and count the number of cases falling within each group. The result is Table 4.3.

Notice again that the groups, the first column of Table 4.3, are stated so that there can be no possibility of confusion as to whether a case should be in one group or another; had the groups been stated as 0–5, 5–10, 10–15, etc., this confusion would have occurred.

Construction of Table 4.3 immediately gives us a much clearer idea of the data than we could gain from the jumble of figures in Table 4.1. We can, if we wish, construct other types of frequency distribution, designed to illuminate particular features of the data. A popular type of frequency distribution, suitable for all types of data, is the percentage frequency

Table 4.3 *Grouped frequency distribution of data from column 5 of Table 4.1*

Crew size	No. of ships
0–4	6
5–9	5
10–14	2
15–19	6
20–24	5
25–29	0
30–34	1
Total	25

distribution. In such a table, the frequencies are expressed not as absolute numbers, the number of times each frequency appeared, but as percentages of the total number of cases. Tables 4.4 and 4.5 show such percentage frequency distributions. In each case, the total of the items in the table is 100.

Table 4.4 *Percentage frequency distribution of data from column 3 of Table 4.1*

Power	% of total no. of ships
Sail	16
Steam	64
Not given	20
Total	100*

* No. of cases: 25.

A certain amount of care is necessary in the construction of percentage frequency distributions. Percentages, which are themselves a type of descriptive statistics, can be misleading if the total number of cases is very small; if this is the case, then very small differences in frequencies can be magnified by being converted into percentages. It is for this reason that the total

number of cases should always be stated, as in Tables 4.4 and
4.5, allowing the reader to convert back to the absolute numbers
if he wishes to do so.

Table 4.5 *Percentage grouped frequency distribution*
of data from column 5 of Table 4.1

Crew size	% of total no. of ships
0–4	24
5–9	20
10–14	8
15–19	24
20–24	20
25–29	0
30–34	4
Total	100*

* No. of cases: 25.

Subtypes of frequency distributions that are sometimes useful, although appropriate only for ordinal and interval data, are
the cumulative frequency distributions and the cumulative
percentage frequency distributions. They are useful when it is
important to know how many cases are above, and how many
are below particular values. Examples are given in Tables 4.6
and 4.7.

Table 4.6 *Cumulative grouped frequency*
distribution of data from
column 5 of Table 4.1

Crew size	No. of ships
4 or less	6
9 or less	11
14 or less	13
19 or less	19
24 or less	24
29 or less	24
34 or less	25

Table 4.7 *Cumulative grouped percentage frequency distribution of data from column 5 of Table 4.1*

Crew size	% of total no. of ships
4 or less	24
9 or less	44
14 or less	52
19 or less	76
24 or less	96
29 or less	96
34 or less	100*

* No. of cases: 25.

Notice that in Tables 4.6 and 4.7 no total figure is given in the tables, since by definition the last figure in the column of frequencies must be the total number of cases, or 100 in the case of the percentage distribution.

(b) Cross-classification

We have so far discussed the use of frequency distributions in summarizing data on one or other column of our data matrix. We may also tabulate our data, by methods analogous to the construction of frequency distributions, but using data from more than one column of our data matrix. The results are known as cross-classifications.

Table 4.8 *Cross-classification of column 3 against column 4 of Table 4.1*

Power	Tonnage
Sail (4 ships)	468
Steam (16 ships)	21 406
Not given (5 ships)	445
Total (25 ships)	22 319

Table 4.8 represents the simplest type of cross-classification, in which one nominal variable, power, is classified against an interval variable, tonnage. A table such as Table 4.8 is sometimes described as a tabulation of column 3 *by* column 4.

Similar cross-classifications can be undertaken for all the variables in Table 4.1, the results appearing in different tabular forms according to the type of data involved, and the number of possible values of each variable. Table 4.9 shows what is known as a contingency table, in which the entries in the table show the number of times that cases occurred with values shown by the marginal headings. A contingency table can thus be thought of as a frequency distribution classified in two or more ways.

Table 4.9 *Contingency table, column 2 by column 3
of Table 4.1*

Power	Trade		
	Home	*Foreign*	*Total*
Sail	3	1	4
Steam	10	6	16
Not given	5	0	5
Total	18	7	25

Just as we can have percentage frequency distributions, so we can construct percentage contingency tables, such as Table 4.10. In Table 4.10 each entry in Table 4.9 has been expressed as a percentage of the total number of ships. It is also possible to construct, if we wish to do so to illuminate particular features of the data, percentage contingency tables in which the entries are calculated not as percentages of the grand total (in this instance 25), but as percentages of the total number of cases within some group. Table 4.11 is an example of such a procedure.

In Table 4.11 the entries in the table have been expressed as percentages of the column totals; no row totals are given, since they would be meaningless. One could, alternatively, calculate percentages of row totals, and in that case no column totals would be given. Notice that the process of division and rounding produces a total slightly larger than 100 in the first column.

It is possible to construct tables in which data on three

Table 4.10 *Percentage contingency table, column 2* by *column 3 of Table 4.1*

	Trade		
Power	Home	Foreign	Total
Sail	12	4	16
Steam	40	24	64
Not given	20	0	20
Total	72	28	100*

* No. of cases: 25.

or more variables are summarized, but the danger in doing so is that the table will be as obscure or difficult to interpret as the raw data. Unless there is some very specific reason for doing otherwise, therefore, tabulations should be confined to data on one or two variables.

Table 4.11 *Column percentage contingency table, column 2* by *column 3 of Table 4.1*

	Trade	
Power	Home	Foreign
Sail	16·7	14·3
Steam	55·6	85·7
Not given	27·8	0·0
Total	100·01	100·00*

* No. of cases: 25.

Tables 4.2 to 4.11 have been presented without comment on the relative advantages of one tabular method over another, or on the particular characteristics of the data that each has revealed. It should be clear, however, that each method has revealed different facets of the data; Table 4.4, for example, showed that nearly two-thirds of the ships were powered by steam, Table 4.7 that over half had crews of less than fifteen men, Table 4.9 that only one sailing ship was employed on foreign trade. All these facets of the data would be valuable to a student of shipping history, and none would have been immediately obvious simply from looking at the raw data matrix of Table 4.1. Therefore the exact choice of which tabular method to use depends on which facet of the data is to be explored (and to some extent on whether the data have been classified on a nominal or an interval scale).

(c) Charts

We have concentrated in this chapter on the use of tabular methods in presenting data. There are a number of other ways of presenting data; in particular, we may present data in some form of chart. Many people find it easier to appreciate the implications of evidence if it is charted in some way, and chart methods of descriptive statistics are therefore particularly useful in the final presentation of the results of an analysis. Moreover, the historian working with quantitative material may gain from expressing his results in chart form at preliminary stages of the analysis; expressed in such a form, the data may show patterns that he had not anticipated, and this may lead to ideas for further analysis.

One of the most common methods of presenting nominal data (and also, if desired, ordinal and interval data) is by the use of the bar chart, such as that shown in Figure 4.1. In that figure, the data from our shipping example on the method of powering ships are presented in bar chart form. The bars that give the bar chart its name are kept entirely separate from each other, to emphasize the fact that we are charting nominal data, and there is no ordinal or interval relationship between the categories. Since they are nominal data that are being charted, the order of bars along the horizontal axis is immaterial; they could be shuffled without loss of or alteration to the information that is being presented. If, on the other hand, ordinal data were being charted, it would be conventional, although not absolutely essential, to order the bars along the axis according to the order of the categories or variables. Notice also that the variable by which the cases have been classified (in Figure 4.1 the method

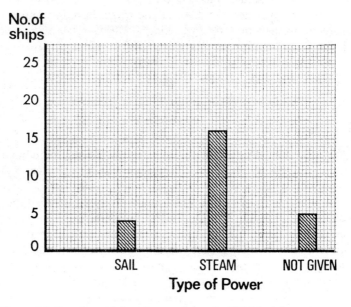

Figure 4.1 Bar chart of data from column 3 of Table 4.1.

of power) is plotted along the horizontal axis of the chart. There would be nothing wrong in presenting the bar chart so that the classificatory variable was shown along the vertical axis, with the bars horizontal, but conventionally the bars are vertical, as in Figure 4.1.

If interval data are to be charted, then we can present them in the form of a bar chart, but it would be more normal to present them as a histogram, such as Figure 4.2. Since we have interval data, the data values are not separated, as they were in Figure 4.1, but are shown next to each other along the horizontal axis. In this

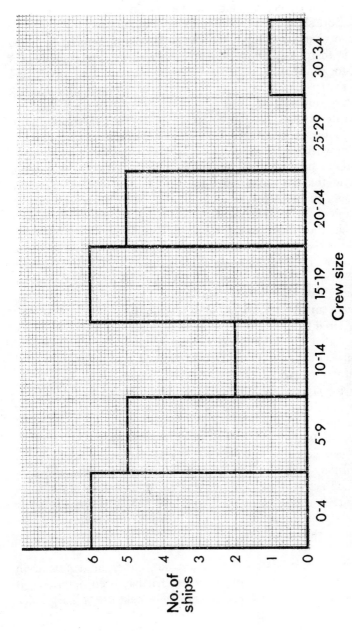

Figure 4.2 Histogram of data from column 5 of Table 4.1.

case, the different values of the classificatory variable, crew size, are shown not only by the height of the bars, as they would be in a bar chart, but by the area of the column centred on them; it is therefore important that the width of each column of a histogram should be the same, so that the areas are proportional to the frequency being presented. If they are not, a misleading impression will be given.

Interval data can also be presented in graphical form. Figure 4.3 shows, for instance, how we could graph the data on size of crew from Table 4.1. We take the groups of crew sizes, the variable by which the data are being classified, and show these along the horizontal axis; the frequencies with which these groups of crew sizes occur is shown along the vertical axis. A graph of this kind is essentially a diagrammatic form of a simple grouped or ungrouped frequency distribution.

It is also customary, when interval data are being graphed, to alter the form of the graph slightly by joining up the points on the graph, creating what is sometimes called a line graph. In theory, we should only join up the points on a graph, thus giving an impression of continuity in the variable, if we are prepared to assume that the variable is in fact continuous in the sense that it could in theory take on any value. This is an assumption that can often be made in the case of scientific data; temperature, for example, is a variable of this type, and so is distance. Most historical data, on the other hand, are not continuous but discrete; the possible values of the data proceed in steps. For example, if we measure population size, we must always measure in multiples of one person; we cannot subdivide people as we can degrees of temperature or kilometres of distance. In addition, many historical data, although theoretically continuous, are not so in practice because of inaccuracy of measurement. An example of this is ages of people; we rarely know the ages of the people we study, down to the nearest day, although theoretically if we had more information we could do so.

Since most historical data are not, either in theory or in practice, continuous, in the sense that has been described, it might seem that we should not normally make use of line graphs.

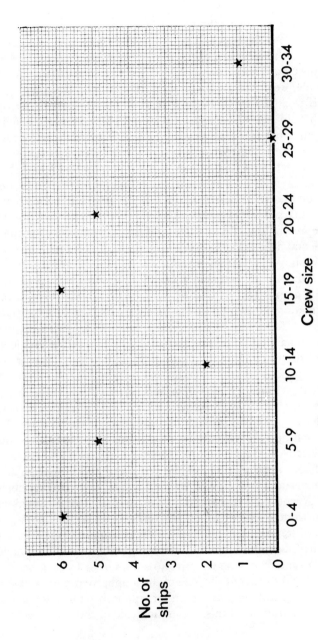

Figure 4.3 Graph of data from column 5 of Table 4.1.

In practice, however, the gain in understanding made possible by the use of line graphs is so considerable that we can feel justified in making use of them, remembering all the time that we must not treat the data as if they were continuous. As an example, we can study Figure 4.4, a line graph based on Figure 4.2. If we look first at the point marked A on the graph, we can see that this lies above the point marked 5–9 on the horizontal axis, and that it is also placed on the horizontal line from the point marked 5 on the vertical axis. Clearly, point A represents the fact that there were five ships with crew sizes of 5, 6, 7, 8 or 9 men. Point B on the graph lies on the same horizontal line as point A, but it lies on a vertical line which is between the points marked 10–14 and 15–19 on the horizontal axis. It does not represent, therefore, any group from the underlying grouped frequency distribution of crew sizes, which is being shown on the graph. We cannot say that five ships had somewhere between 10–14 and 15–19 men, and point B is therefore meaningless.

Line graphs are particularly valuable to the historian in the presentation of time series data, and we shall therefore return to them.

We can also make use of graphical methods in the presentation of the results of cross-classifications, when the data are of ordinal or interval type. We do this by constructing a diagram which is of considerable importance in statistical analysis, the scatter diagram. Figure 4.5 shows such a scatter diagram, in which a cross-classification of tonnages and crew sizes is shown. Each point on the diagram represents one ship, and the points are placed on the diagram according to the value which that ship had on the variable on the horizontal axis, tonnage, and on the vertical axis, crew size. In this case, since two variables are concerned, the question of which should be represented on the horizontal, and which on the vertical axis, is immaterial.

There are some general principles which apply to the drawing of graphs, and which, if forgotten or ignored, may lead to serious errors in interpretation. Figure 4.6 shows how, by lengthening or shortening either of the axes of the graph, we can present our data in a misleading manner, either emphasizing or minimizing fluctuations; to avoid this, a common rule of thumb is that the

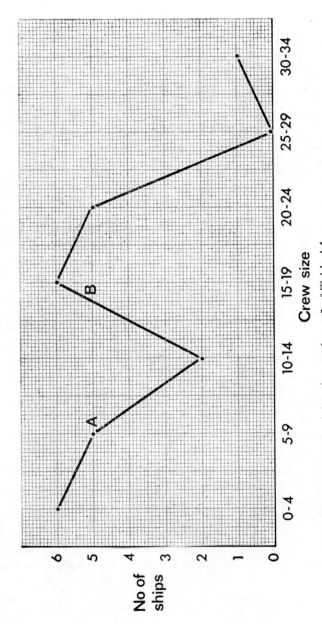

Figure 4.4 Line graph of data from column 5 of Table 4.1.

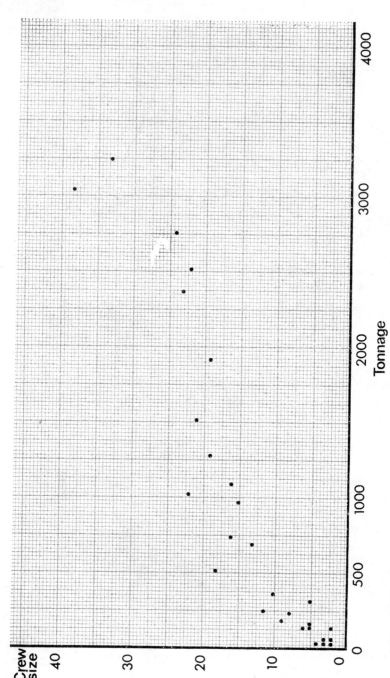

Figure 4.5 Scatter diagram. Data from columns 4 and 5 of Table 4.1.

vertical axis of a graph should be two-thirds the length of the horizontal axis. Other rules are that the zero value in a graph should always be given, and that the intervals should be clearly stated along the axes. In general, we should construct our graphs in such a way as to show clearly the characteristics of the data we wish to emphasize, but not in such a way that we mislead.

(d) Ratio scale graphs

In all the graphs that were described in the last section, the scales were constructed so that there were equal intervals between each category, both on the horizontal and on the vertical axes. If we take, as a further example, Table 4.12 and Figure 4.7, which represents imports of raw cotton into the United Kingdom between 1770 and 1800, we see that in 1772 raw cotton weighing 5,307,000 lb was imported, while in 1773 imports were 2,906,000 lb – a fall from one year to the next of 2,401,000 lb. Later in the period, between 1790 and 1791, imports fell from 31,448,000 lb to 28,707,000 lb – a fall of 2,631,000 lb. The absolute fall in both cases is similar, 2,401,000 lb and 2,631,000 lb, and therefore the falls are represented as almost equal along the vertical scale of Figure 4.7.

In historical work, however, we are often interested not so much in absolute as in relative change between two periods. This is particularly so when we are dealing with a period like that of the Industrial Revolution in Britain in which the change is rapid, and when we are dealing with the rapid growth of an industry as important as cotton processing was to Britain. We often wish to consider relative increase, proportional or percentage change, and to compare percentage change over different periods; if we take cotton imports in 1772–3 and 1790–1, for example, we find that between 1772 and 1773 the fall in imports was 45·24 per cent, while between 1790 and 1791 it was only 8·41 per cent. We cannot derive such information from a graph such as Figure 4.7, because such a graph represents absolute changes as equal, whatever the percentage

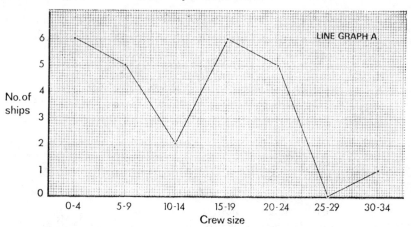

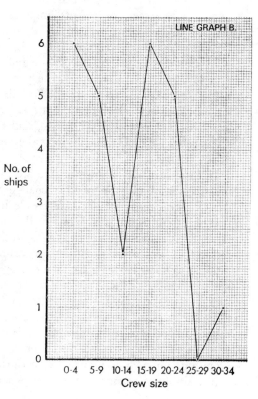

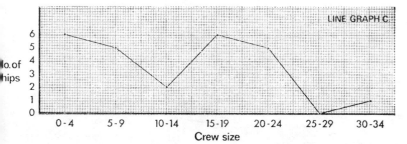

Figure 4.6 The effect of changing the length of axes and width of intervals on line graphs. Data from column 5 of Table 4.1.

changes may have been. If we are interested in representing percentage change graphically, therefore, we need to find an alternative form of graph. We need, in fact, a graph that is easily constructed, which gives us the values of the variables along

Table 4.12 *Raw cotton imports into the United Kingdom, by weight, 1770–1800*

Year	Imports ('000 lb)	Year	Imports ('000 lb)
1770	3 612	1786	19 475
1771	2 547	1787	23 250
1772	5 307	1788	20 467
1773	2 906	1789	32 576
1774	5 707	1790	31 448
1775	6 694	1791	28 707
1776	6 216	1792	34 907
1777	7 037	1793	19 041
1778	6 569	1794	24 359
1779	5 861	1795	26 401
1780	6 877	1796	32 126
1781	5 199	1797	23 354
1782	11 828	1798	31 881
1783	9 736	1799	43 379
1784	11 482	1800	56 011
1785	18 400		

Source: B. R. Mitchell and P. Deane, *Abstract of British Historical Statistics* (Cambridge, Cambridge University Press, 1962), pp. 177–8.

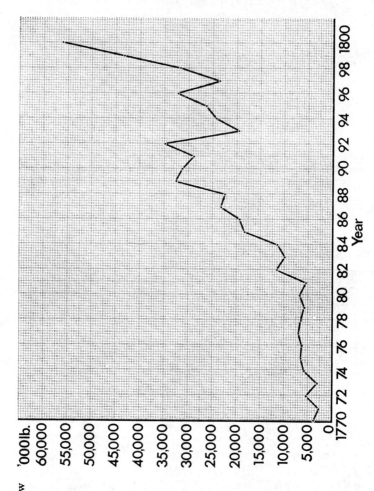

Figure 4.7 Imports of raw cotton into the U.K., 1770–1800, by weight. *Source*: see Table 4.12.

the axes (so that we can calculate the absolute changes if we wish to do so), but in which proportional or percentage change is represented by equal intervals on the scale of the graph. We can achieve this by the use of a ratio scale, normally based on logarithms.

It will be recalled from the last chapter that logarithms to the base 10 have the property that the logarithm of 10 is 1·0000, the logarithm of 100 is 2·0000, and the logarithm of 1000 is 3·0000. A rise from 10 to 100, or by ten times, is thus represented by an increase in the logarithm from 1·0000 to 2·0000, a difference of 1·0000. Similarly, the rise of ten times from 100 to 1000 is also represented by a difference of 1·0000 in the logarithm, although the absolute change from 100 to 1000 (1000−100 = 900) is much greater than the absolute change from 10 to 100 (100−10 = 90).

Logarithms thus have the property, which we wish to have in our graphical method, that equal proportional changes are represented by equal absolute changes in the logarithms. If we therefore transform each of the values in Table 4.12 into logarithmic form, and plot the result on a graph in which the vertical axis shows logarithms, we shall have achieved our main object in representing proportional changes. Figure 4.8 shows such a graph.

However, it is still a cumbersome operation to convert each of the values in Table 4.12 into logarithms, and furthermore in doing so we lose the ability to show the original values on the graph. In order to find the original values from the graph alone, we would need to use tables of antilogarithms. These difficulties can be avoided, however, by using a scale for our graph such as that in Figure 4.9, in which the values on the scale are the original values, but the distances between the points on the scale represent the differences between the logarithms of the numbers. We see, for example, that the distance on the scale between 5 million and 7·5 million, a proportional increase of 50 per cent, is the same as the distance between 10 million and 15 million, the same proportional increase.

Although it is quite easy to construct ratio scales of this type, it is much simpler to buy graph paper that has been printed

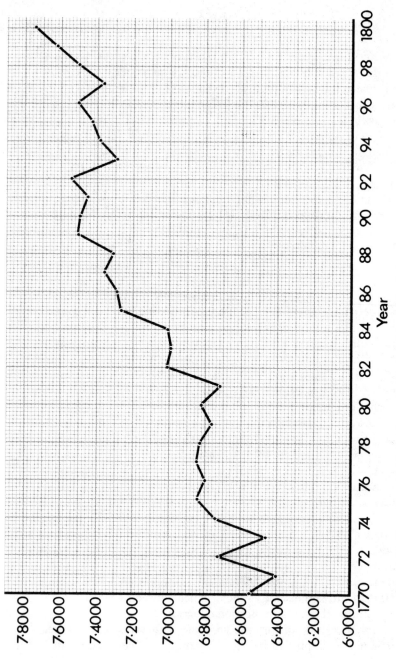

Figure 4.8 Data from Table 4.12 graphed in semi-logarithmic form.

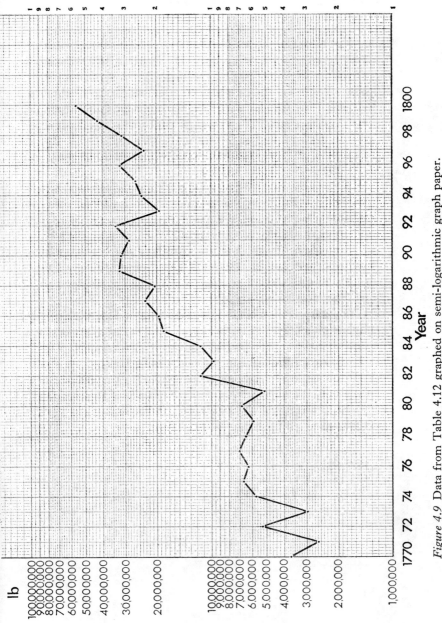

Figure 4.9 Data from Table 4.12 graphed on semi-logarithmic graph paper.

with a log scale. Before buying such paper, however, we need to know in advance the range of values that we wish to represent. Logarithms are arranged in cycles; from 1·0000 to 2·0000 is one cycle, from 2·0000 to 3·0000 a second cycle, and so on, and graph paper is set out for the representation of one, two, three or more cycles. If we wished to include on our graph, for example, data ranging from 3 to 1750, we should need to buy graph paper set out for four cycles: 1–10 (log 0·0000 to 1·0000), 10–100 (log 1·0000 to 2·0000), 100–1000 (log 2·0000 to 3·0000) and 1000–10,000 (log 3·0000 to 4·0000).

It should also be noted that Figure 4.8 is properly known as a semi-logarithmic graph, since only one axis is plotted on a logarithmic scale; it would not normally make sense to plot time changes on a logarithmic scale. When we wish to plot two variables against each other, however, and to examine proportionate changes in each, we can make use of logarithmic graphs, in which both scales are plotted logarithmically; graph paper of this type can also be bought.

The interpretation of semi-logarithmic and logarithmic scale graphs needs some care, since our eyes are normally accustomed to graphs with equal interval scales. We should remember to concentrate on the slope of the line between two points on the graph; the steeper the slope, the faster is the proportionate increase. We shall return to some further uses of logarithmic graphs and associated logarithmic transformations in the discussion of time series data in Chapter 6.

5 The preliminary analysis of data, II: summary measures

In the last chapter we considered methods by which a raw data matrix might be rearranged and presented in ways that added to our understanding of the information contained in the data. Although, in constructing grouped frequency distributions, we made some attempt to summarize the data, we did not carry this very far; we merely grouped the data into a smaller number of categories. This method cannot be carried very far, since, as the number of groups in the frequency distribution diminishes, the data lose definition. This makes it impossible to use a frequency distribution if we wish to find only one number that will adequately summarize the data; a frequency distribution with only one group would merely tell us the number of cases in the data matrix.

In this chapter, therefore, we shall consider other methods of summarizing the different types of data that we have encountered. We shall, it should be noted, reverse the order we have used so far in exposition, and begin with a method suitable for interval data, before turning to summary measures for ordinal and nominal data.

(a) The arithmetic mean

A method that will enable us to calculate one number to represent or summarize a whole set of numbers is the method of the arithmetic mean. The arithmetic mean will be more familiar as the 'average', but this is a misleading description; there are other averages, discussed below, and it is better to be precise and use the term 'arithmetic mean'. This measure can be used only with interval data.

The arithmetic mean is very easily calculated by adding up the numbers in a list, and dividing by the number of cases. For the data of Table 3.1, for example (pp. 29–30), the total number of swine given in the table is 11,915; there are fifty cases, so that the arithmetic mean is $11,915/50 = 238 \cdot 3$ swine. We can easily represent this, using summation notation and denoting the mean of a vector X by the term $\bar{X}$ (pronounced X bar), by the equation

$$\bar{X} = \frac{\sum_{i=1}^{N} X_i}{N}.$$

(It might be objected that in the data of Table 3.1 it seems that the numbers of swine are always rounded to the nearest five. In such cases, calculation of the mean may be misleading, but when the rounding is to the nearest five, rather than to some larger interval, the error is likely to be very small, and the procedure of calculating the mean acceptable.)

It is often convenient to calculate the mean of some data not from the raw data but from data rearranged into a frequency distribution. The mathematics of such a calculation are only slightly more complicated and the extra work involved is compensated for by the smaller number of cases. To calculate the mean from a frequency distribution, each value of the frequency distribution is multiplied by the frequency with which it appears, the results are summed, and the sum is divided by the number of cases in the raw data. Table 5.1 shows, as an example, the calculation of the mean of the data of Table 3.2. The result, $238 \cdot 3$, is exactly the same as the result achieved using the original data. In the general case, the mean of a frequency distribution is given by the equation

$$\bar{X} = \frac{\sum_{i=1}^{k} f_i X_i}{N}$$

where the X_i are the values of the variable, the f_i are the frequencies with which those values occur, k is the number of groups, and N the number of cases from which the frequency distribution has been compiled.

Table 5.1 *Calculation of mean from a frequency distribution*

Nos of swine X_i	Nos of places f_i	f_iX_i
5	1	5
15	1	15
20	2	40
30	9	270
40	1	40
50	2	100
55	1	55
60	4	240
80	2	160
100	2	200
120	1	120
150	3	450
160	2	320
200	3	600
300	1	300
350	2	700
400	3	1 200
500	3	1 500
600	3	1 800
800	2	1 600
1000	1	1 000
1200	1	1 200
	$N = 50$	11 915

$$\frac{\sum_{i=1}^{k} f_iX_i}{N} = \frac{11\ 915}{50} = 238\cdot3 \quad \text{(where } k \text{ is the number of groups)}$$

In Table 3.2 the data on numbers of swine per parish were presented as a frequency distribution, but no summarizing of the data took place. In Tables 3.3 and 3.4, however, the data were grouped together into groups or categories, and frequency distributions of this type are therefore known as grouped frequency distributions. When it is necessary to compute the mean or any other statistic from grouped frequency distributions of this kind, a different procedure is required, one that takes account of the fact that the true values of the data are no longer given, merely the groups into which they fall.

To calculate the mean from grouped data we hypothesize that each case falls at the midpoint of the group into which it has been placed. In order to calculate that midpoint, we have to look closely at the method of grouping we have used. In Table 3.4, for example, we have stated the groups as 0–99 swine, 100–199 swine, and so on. In doing so, we have not considered what we would do had we come across a parish with 99·7 swine; we do not need to consider such a possibility, since 0·7 swine is not a meaningful quantity. Had we been using other data, however (for instance, data on areas of land in the Domesday parishes), we might have found a parish with an acreage of 99·7 acres, and we would have had a problem in assigning such a parish to any one group. Normally, we would 'round' our figure to the nearest whole number, so that acreages of 99, 99·1, 99·2, 99·3 and 99·4 acres would be assigned to the first group, 0–99 acres, and acreages of 99·5, 99·6, 99·7, 99·8 and 99·9 acres would be assigned to the 100–199 acre group. Any acreage below 99·5 therefore would be assigned to the lower group, any acreage over 99·5 (and any acreage of exactly 99·5) would be assigned to the higher group. Thus although we have stated in Table 3.4 that our groups run from 0–99 and 100–199, in truth they run from −0·05 to 99·5, 99·5 to 199·5, and so on; for this reason, these limiting values for the groups are known as the 'true limits' (as opposed to the 'stated limits') and it is these 'true limits' that are used in calculating the midpoints of groups in grouped frequency distributions. If we return to the data in Table 3.4, we can repeat the table showing the true as well as the stated limits, and the midpoints of the groups. These are shown in Table 5.2, which demonstrates the method of calculating the mean from such a grouped frequency distribution.

Computation of the arithmetic mean from the grouped frequency distribution gives the result 262·0, as shown in Table 5.2. The result obtained from the entire vector of original data was 238·3. The difference between 238·3, the correct arithmetic mean, and 262·0, the mean calculated from grouped data, is the

Table 5.2 *Computation of the arithmetic mean from a grouped frequency distribution*

Nos of swine Stated limits	Nos of swine True limits	Group midpoints m_i	Nos of cases f_i	$m_i f_i$
0–99	−0·5–99·5	50·0	23	1 150
100–199	99·5–199·5	150·0	8	1 200
200–299	199·5–299·5	250·0	3	750
300–399	299·5–399·5	350·0	3	1 050
400–499	399·5–499·5	450·0	3	1 350
500–599	499·5–599·5	550·0	3	1 650
600–699	599·5–699·5	650·0	3	1 950
700–799	699·5–799·5	750·0	0	0
800–899	799·5–899·5	850·0	2	1 700
900–999	899·5–999·5	950·0	0	0
1000–1099	999·5–1099·5	1 050·0	1	1 050
1100–1199	1099·5–1199·5	1 150·0	0	0
1200–1299	1199·5–1299·5	1 250·0	1	1 250
			$N = 50$	13 100

$$\bar{X} = \frac{\sum_{i=1}^{k} m_i f_i}{N} = \frac{13\ 100}{50}$$

$$= 262 \cdot 0$$

price we pay in inaccuracy of the final result through using the more convenient grouped frequency distribution. The distance by which the mean obtained from the original data differs from the mean obtained from grouped data will depend on the degree to which, and the direction from which, the actual data differ from the midpoints of the groups chosen. This emphasizes the importance of choosing appropriate groups, particularly if calculations from grouped data are to be used.

The mean is easy to calculate, and it has the advantage, when compared with other summary measures that we shall discuss, that it takes account not only of the number of items in a distribution, but also of the value of each item. The compensating disadvantage of the arithmetic mean is that, because it does take account of every value, it can be affected very considerably by the existence of one extreme value.

As an example, let us take the data from column four of Table 4.1 (p. 44), which gives the tonnages of the twenty-five merchant ships. The total tonnage of the ships, $\sum X_i$, was calculated in Table 4.8 as 22,319 tons. Divided by $N = 25$, this gives an arithmetic mean tonnage of 892·76 tons. One ship, however (that with the official number 99437), had a tonnage much larger, by over 500 tons, than any other ship. If we were to exclude that one ship from the calculation of the mean, the total tonnage would be reduced to 19,073 tons, and the mean tonnage to 794·71 tons. The inclusion of that one ship, therefore, has considerably affected the mean. Similarly, the inclusion of the very small ship, No. 95757, with a tonnage of 26 tons, will have affected the mean in a downward direction.

It is partially for this reason that we need to associate with the mean some measure of the range of the data from which the mean has been calculated, and we shall therefore consider next such a measure, the standard deviation.

(b) The standard deviation

The mean is certainly the simplest and most convenient method of summarizing interval data. It is designed to focus attention on what is often called the 'central tendency' of the set of data being considered. In the simplest case, when two numbers are to be summarized, we can imagine that we have a piece of string, on which two marks have been made, representing the two numbers; the mean will then be represented by a third mark, centrally placed between the other two, as in Figure 5.1. The original numbers are shown as A and A', and the mean as $\bar{X}$.

The major difficulty with the use of the mean as a summary

measure is shown if we consider what happens if we make two further marks on the string, B and B', an equal distance from A and A' in opposite directions. Now we try to find the mean of the numbers represented by B and B'; since we have moved an equal distance from A to B, and from A' to B', it is clear that the mean of B and B' will also be at $\bar{X}$. Similarly, if we were to make two further marks, C and C', equal distances inwards from A and A', their mean would still be $\bar{X}$.

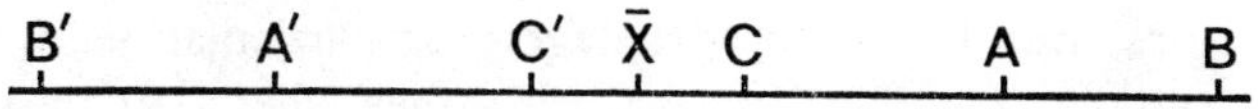

Figure 5.1 Figurative representation of the arithmetic mean.

The mean, therefore, gives no indication of how far divergent from the mean were the individual observations in the data. It is therefore desirable that, if we wish to use the arithmetic mean to summarize our data, we should also use some other method of describing the amount of dispersion or diversity of the data around the mean. It might seem that the simplest way of doing this would be to add up the amount by which each observation differed from the mean; this amount is known as the 'deviation' of each observation from the mean of the distribution of which it forms a part.

This is, however, not a correct solution to the problem of representing dispersion around the mean, since the result of this calculation will always be zero. This is because, as can be seen from observation of Figure 5.1, the individual deviations from the mean will cancel each other out. It is therefore necessary to develop another measure of dispersion which will not suffer from this disadvantage.

There are a number of such measures of dispersion, just as there are measures of central tendency other than the arithmetic mean. These other measures will be discussed later in this book, but at the moment we will concentrate on the measure that is both most convenient and most widely used, that known as the 'standard deviation'. Like the mean, the standard deviation may only be calculated when the data is of interval or ratio type.

The difficulty with the method of representing dispersion that we have just discussed is that all the observations that are greater than the mean are cancelled out by observations that are less than the mean. We could avoid this difficulty by ignoring the signs of the deviations, totalling them, and dividing by the number of observations, to give us the arithmetic mean of the 'absolute values' (values without sign) of the deviations. This result, known as the mean deviation, is sometimes used in statistics, but it has disadvantages; in particular it is very awkward to compute, particularly when there are a large number of observations, and it cannot be used in further analysis. Instead, we avoid the difficulty by getting rid of minus signs from the deviations by squaring each deviation. It will be recalled that the square of either a positive or a negative number is a positive number. We then sum all the squared deviations and, since we are interested in the average dispersion around the mean, divide by the number of items. The formula used is therefore, for a vector X,

$$\frac{\sum_{i=1}^{N} (X_i - \bar{X})^2}{N}$$

and the result is known as the 'variance'.

As an example, let us take the first ten cases from our list of numbers of swine (Table 3.1, pp. 29–30) and illustrate the process of calculation of the variance, in Table 5.3. The variance, although easy to calculate and very useful in more advanced work, has two disadvantages as a measure of dispersion. The minor disadvantage is that, particularly if the deviations from the mean are large, squaring them makes them even larger and more cumbersome to handle. The major disadvantage is that it is difficult to give the variance a substantive, as opposed to a mathematical, meaning. In the data for Table 5.3, for example, it is straightforward to say that the arithmetic mean of numbers of swine in ten places in Essex in 1086 was 348 swine; it makes very little sense to say that the average dispersion around that mean was 104,896·0 squared swine.

It is partly for this reason, and partly so that the dispersion around the mean should be expressed in the same unit as the

Table 5.3 *Calculation of the variance*

Place	Nos of swine X_i	Mean $\bar{X}$	$(X_i - \bar{X})$	$(X_i - \bar{X})^2$
Writtle	1200	348	+852	725 904
Clavering	600	348	+252	63 504
Farnham	150	348	−198	39 204
,,	50	348	−298	88 804
Ugley	160	348	−188	35 344
Alferestuna	350	348	+2	4
Canfield	120	348	−228	51 984
Dunmow	300	348	−48	2 304
Easton	150	348	−198	39 204
,,	400	348	+52	2 704

$$N = 10 \quad \sum_{i=1}^{N} X_i = 3480 \qquad \sum_{i=1}^{N} (X_i - \bar{X}) = 0 \qquad \sum_{i=1}^{N} (X_i - \bar{X})^2 = 1\ 048\ 960$$

$$\frac{\sum_{i=1}^{N} (X_i - \bar{X})^2}{N} = \frac{1\ 048\ 960}{10} = 104\ 896{\cdot}0$$

mean itself, that we use as our most convenient measure of dispersion the standard deviation, which is simply the square root of the variance. It is, for a vector X,

$$\sqrt{\left(\frac{\sum_{i=1}^{N} (X_i - \bar{X})^2}{N} \right)}$$

and it is normally represented by the letter s. In the example given in Table 5.3

$$s = \sqrt{104\ 896{\cdot}0}$$
$$= 323{\cdot}9$$

and we can therefore say that the standard deviation of the data in Table 5.3 is 323·9 swine.

It can be seen from Table 5.3 that in order to calculate the standard deviation it is first necessary to calculate the mean. We shall often need to calculate the mean, and can then use the formula for the standard deviation as given above, but we can also calculate the standard deviation directly through a number of other formulae, all of which are rearrangements of the standard formula. The most convenient of these alternatives is

$$s = \frac{1}{N}\sqrt{\left(N \sum_{i=1}^{N} X_i^2 - \left(\sum_{i=1}^{N} X_i\right)^2\right)}$$

which involves calculation only of the sum of the values of the variable and the sum of the squares of each value. Other possible formulae, and formulae for the computation of the mean from ungrouped and grouped frequency distributions, can be found in any textbook of statistics.

The calculation of the mean, and of the standard deviation, has considerable advantages when we are dealing with interval data, and the mean is in fact the best known and most used of the various 'averages' that we shall consider in this book. The major advantage of the mean and the standard deviation is that every item of data is used in their calculation, so that no information is wasted; in addition, both measures are easy to calculate, either by hand or with calculating machinery. One of the disadvantages of the mean, however, which we have already discussed, is that it is sensitive to the existence of extreme values in the distribution from which it is calculated. This can be important in historical problems, particularly in dealing with pre-industrial societies in which there were great disparities of wealth and social status within society. For example, if we were interested in calculating the mean size of household in a medieval village, we might find that the mean was biased upwards by the presence in the village of one castle, housing the lord and his servants and retainers; in this case, the mean size would give a false impression of the normal household size.

It might seem that this difficulty, which is often less obvious than in the example given, might be overcome by associating with the mean the standard deviation, as a measure of the dispersion of the data. Unfortunately, the existence of extreme values in a distribution – values, that is, that lie very far from the majority of other values – affects the value of the standard deviation also. It will be recalled that the computation of the standard deviation involves, among other things, squaring each of the deviations from the mean. Although we try to compensate for this by taking the square root, a higher weight is inevitably given to values far from the mean, as compared with values close to the mean. This is not always a disadvantage, as will be seen when we discuss more advanced statistical methods, but when the mean and the standard deviation are being considered as summary measures this difficulty should always be borne in mind. In the remainder of this chapter we shall discuss other measures of central tendency and dispersion; the use of some of these measures can help to solve this difficulty.

(c) *The geometric mean*

The geometric mean is the second type of average suitable only for interval data, but is not often used, except in problems in economics and economic history. For a vector X of N numbers, the geometric mean is calculated by the formula

$$\text{G.M.} = \sqrt[N]{[(X_1)(X_2)(X_3) \ldots (X_N)]}.$$

In other words, we multiply all the N values of X together, and take the Nth root. In practice, we would make use of logarithms, adding together the logarithms of all N values of X, dividing the result by N, and taking the antilogarithm. In some circumstances, particularly in the treatment of index numbers and when it is desired to find an average of relative changes in a variable or variables, as when one is finding an average of a number of rates of growth, the geometric mean is the most appropriate measure of central tendency. It tends, in comparison with the arithmetic mean, to give less weight to extreme values, but no measure of dispersion is directly associated with it.

(d) *The median*

The third summary measure of central tendency is the median, which can be calculated if the data are of ordinal or interval type. The median is, like the mode (see below), very simple to calculate; it is simply that value of a variable which splits an ordered list of cases into two halves, so that there are as many cases with values below the median value as there are with values larger than the median value. All that we need to do, therefore, to calculate the median is to rank the cases according to the value that they take on a particular variable; the median will then be the value half-way along the rank order. For example, if we take column 4 of Table 4.1 (p. 44), giving crew size, we can reorder the cases as in Table 5.4.

Table 5.4 *Data of column 5, Table 4.1, arranged by rank order*

Rank	1	2	3	4	5
Official No.	113685	114424	115143	1697	113689
Crew size	2	2	2	3	3
	6	7	8	9	10
	95757	35052	93086	2640	62595
	4	5	5	6	8
	11	12	13	14	15
	123375	107004	94546	86658	73742
	9	10	13	15	16
	16	17	18	19	20
	109597	115149	96414	99495	115357
	16	18	19	19	21
	21	22	23	24	25
	113406	114433	92929	118852	99437
	22	22	23	24	33

Since there are an odd number of cases (twenty-five) in Table 5.4, the median case is the thirteenth $(N + 1)/2$; the median value for this distribution is therefore, by coincidence, 13. If there had been an even number of cases, say twenty-four, in the distribution, the median would have been taken as the arithmetic mean of the twelfth $N/2$ and thirteenth $(N + 1)/2$ cases; in the example of Table 5.4 (assuming that the twenty-fifth case had been excluded), the median of the remaining twenty-four cases would have been the mean of the twelfth and thirteenth cases, i.e.:

$$\frac{10 + 13}{2} = 11 \cdot 5.$$

The median is only one of a group of measures that divide and summarize data according to the rank order of the values. In addition to the median, these measures are quartiles, deciles and percentiles. Just as the median divides the cases into two groups, the quartiles divide the data into four groups, the deciles into ten groups, and the percentiles into one hundred groups. There are, unfortunately, two conventions for the calculation of the quartiles; the most common is that the first quartile is defined as the $[(N + 1)/4]$th case, the second quartile (the median) as the $[(N + 1)/2]$nd case, and the third quartile as the $[(3N + 3)/4]$th case ('lower' and 'upper' are sometimes used instead of 'first' and 'third'). In the example of Table 5.4 this rule would give 6·5, 13 and 19·5, so after rounding we take the quartiles as being the seventh, thirteenth and twentieth cases, with values of 5, 13 and 21. Deciles and percentiles are calculated in a similar way, although their use is naturally limited to instances where the data set is composed of a sufficiently large number of cases to make it sensible to divide the data into so many groups.

Various measures of dispersion can be associated with the median, and with quartiles, deciles and percentiles; that which is most commonly used is the quartile deviation, or, more properly, the semi-interquartile range, defined as half the difference between the first and third quartiles. In the example given in Table 5.4, therefore, the semi-interquartile range is:

$$\frac{21 - 5}{2} = 8.$$

We can therefore say of this example that the median is 13 and the semi-interquartile range 8, giving us some idea of the central tendency of the distribution and of the amount of dispersion around that central tendency.

Although the median and the quartile deviation are easily

calculated and convenient measures of central tendency and of dispersion, they have several disadvantages which should normally lead us to reject their use when we have a choice, as we do when the data are of interval form; if the data are of ordinal type, we have the choice only of the mode and median. The major disadvantage of the median and the quartile deviation is that they take no account, in their calculation, of the extreme values in the distribution, other than to note that they exist – for example, let us imagine that instead of the real data given in Table 5.4 we had been presented with data such as those in Table 5.5. This distribution is clearly different in its shape

Table 5.5 *Rank order of hypothetical set of twenty-five numbers*

No. in rank order	1	2	3	4	5	6	7	8	9	10
Value (crew size)	2	2	2	2	2	2	2	4	6	7
	11	12	13	14	15	16	17	18	19	20
	7	9	10	10	10	11	12	13	16	20
	21	22	23	24	25					
	38	69	77	95	160					

from that given in Table 5.4, and only six items in the rank order have the same value in both Tables 5.4 and 5.5. Moreover, the extreme values at the top end of the rank order are much larger in Table 5.5 than in Table 5.4. Yet both the distributions have the same median, and the same quartile deviation, and this would remain true even if we altered our hypothetical distribution so that all the items from No. 20 upwards had values several times larger. It should be noted that it is in some cases an advantage to have a measure of central tendency that ignores values that are very different from most of the values in the rest of the distribution; as an example, it is useful, if we are studying the normal age at which people marry, to have a measure that ignores the spinster who gets married at 55, some 30 to 35 years after most other members of her generation. Similarly, if we are interested in the standard of living of the worker in an industrial town, the median real wage will give a better idea of the material standards of life than the mean real wage; the median will hardly be affected at all by the high real incomes of the factory-owners living in the same area. With most data, however, the insensitivity of the median to extreme values is a disadvantage. A further disadvantage of the median, which needs some emphasis, is that only a very few methods of statistical analysis make use of it. In general, if interval or ratio data are being used, it is not a very useful measure of central tendency, and its associated measure of dispersion, the quartile deviation, is similarly useful only in a few special cases.

(e) *The mode*

If we have nominal data, as in columns 2 and 3 of the data matrix shown in Table 4.1 (p. 44), the only summary measure of central tendency that we may use is the mode. The mode is simply that value which occurs most often. In the case of the variable giving the method by which the ships were powered, we know from Table 4.2 that four were driven by sail and sixteen by steam, and that the method of propulsion was not given for five ships. The modal value of the variable 'method of propulsion' is therefore 'steam'. The mode can also be used as a summary measure with ordinal or interval data; the variable 'crew size' in Table 4.1 has a mode of 2, since there are three ships with a crew of that size, and no other crew size occurred more than twice.

It is clear from these examples that the mode is of limited use in summarizing data such as those in Table 4.1; this will normally be true of the mode as applied to historical data, although there are some cases in which it is important to know the most common value in a set of data. The mode has, for example, sometimes been used by demographic historians, since changes in the age at which most people married or had their first child can affect the birth rate. The mode has the major disadvantage, however, that no measure of dispersion is associated with it, so that it is of very limited use where the data are at all dispersed.

(f) The coefficient of variation

There remains, among summary measures likely to be useful to, or used by, historians, only the coefficient of variation. This provides us, when we have interval data, with a simple means of comparing the degree to which two sets of variables differ from their respective means. It is often useful to know which of two or three variables is most dispersed around its mean; in our shipping example, for instance, it might be of interest to know whether the tonnages of ships varied more than did the crew sizes. We cannot compare the standard deviations of each variable directly, partly because they are in different units (numbers of men and numbers of tons), and partly because their means are so different. The coefficient of variation for any vector of numbers is simply the standard deviation of that vector expressed as a percentage of the mean of the vector. Thus the coefficients of variation for the data in Table 4.1 are:

$$\text{Tonnage } \bar{X} = 892 \cdot 8 \text{ tons}$$
$$s = 946 \cdot 2 \text{ tons}$$
$$\text{Coefficient of variation} = \frac{946 \cdot 2}{892 \cdot 8} \times 100 = 105 \cdot 99$$

$$\text{Crew size } \bar{X} = 12 \cdot 8$$
$$s = 8 \cdot 6$$
$$\text{Coefficient of variation} = \frac{8 \cdot 6}{12 \cdot 8} \times 100 = 67 \cdot 19$$

We can therefore say that the tonnages of the ships exhibit more variation around their mean than do the crew sizes.

(g) Which to use?

The choice of summary measure for a particular set of data can be seen to depend firstly on the type of data, secondly on the characteristics, particularly the amount of variation, of the data, and thirdly on the use to which the summary measures are to be put at a later stage of the analysis. In some cases, the choice will not be clear cut; in demographic work, for example, each of the summary measures may be best suited to illuminate some particular feature of the data – the mode will give, for example, most common age at marriage, while the median and arithmetic mean will each give 'normal' ages at marriage, the median to some extent excluding and the arithmetic mean including the most abnormal cases. In these circumstances, the different measures of central tendency are illuminating different

Table 5.6 *Age at first marriage in Colyton*

Men	*No.*	*Mean*	*Median*	*Mode*
1560–1646	258	27·2	25·8	23·0
1647–1719	109	27·7	26·4	23·8
1720–1769	90	25·7	25·1	23·9
1770–1837	219	26·5	25·8	24·4
Women				
1560–1646	371	27·0	25·9	23·7
1647–1719	136	29·6	27·5	23·3
1720–1769	104	26·8	25·7	23·5
1770–1837	275	25·1	24·0	21·8

Source: E. A. Wrigley, 'Family limitation in pre-industrial England', *Economic History Review* XIX (April 1966), No 1, p. 86. The mode is interpolated from the mean and the median not derived directly from the data.

aspects of the data, and they can usefully all be given. This has been done, for example, in Table 5.6, which is based on a study of marriages in a Devon village. Table 5.6 shows that use of one measure of central tendency, without the others, might give a misleading impression. The use of the mean alone, for example, would give an impression of very wide variation in marriage age over the centuries; the mode, on the other hand, tells us that across the centuries the most common age of marriage remained much the same. To quote either summary measure without the other would mislead; Wrigley, by quoting all three, gives us the material we need to make up our own minds.

It is important to understand and use the interrelationship between the three measures. In one simple case the interrelationship between the mean, the median and the mode is clear. If nine marriages in Colyton had occurred in the manner shown in Figure 5.2 then the mean age, the median age and the modal age would be identical; in other words, in a symmetrical distribution of data such as Figure 5.2, the three measures have the same value. In Figure 5.2 they are all 25, and we say that the

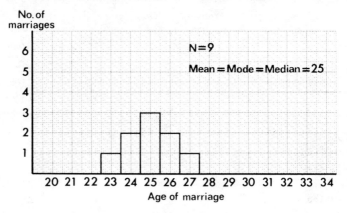

Figure 5.2 A symmetrical distribution.

'peak' of the distribution is at age 25. But we can equally imagine that each marriage took place two years earlier. If that had been so, the whole distribution would be shifted two years to the left along the horizontal axis, and the peak of the distribution and with it the mean, median and mode would now be 23; its symmetry would be maintained.

If the mean, median and mode coincide when the distribution of data is symmetrical, it is reasonable and correct to infer that when they are calculated and found not to coincide, as in Table 5.6, this is because the distribution is not symmetrical. In Figure 5.3, for example, eleven extra marriages have been added to those shown in Figure 5.2. The distribution in Figure 5.3 is clearly asymmetrical, and the measures of central tendency have different values. The mode remains at 25, but the median has

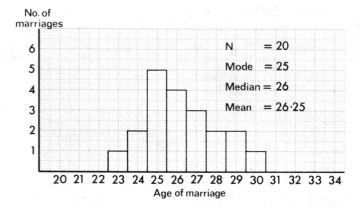

Figure 5.3 A distribution skewed to the right.

risen to 26; the mean has risen even further to 26·25. Simple experimentation will show that, if more marriages were added in the same way, at ages above the mode and particularly at ages much higher than the mode, the mean and median would diverge even further, as in Figure 5.4. To put it in other words,

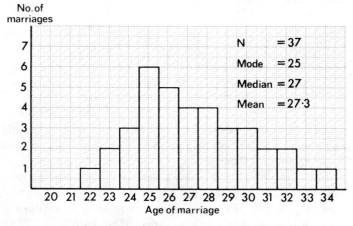

Figure 5.4 A distribution further skewed to the right.

we can call an asymmetrical distribution such as Figure 5.3 a 'skewed' distribution and say that as more marriages were added it would become more skewed. Because more marriages, in Figure 5.3, occur above (to the right) than below (to the left) of the mode, we say that the distribution is skewed to the right; if the extra marriages had occurred below the modal age then the distribution would look like that in Figure 5.5. and would be said to be skewed to the left.

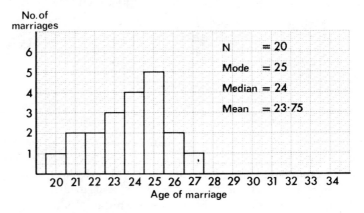

Figure 5.5 A distribution skewed to the left.

Armed with this knowledge, we can return to the measures displayed in Table 5.6. It is at once apparent that, if we look at the marriages of women, the summary measures must result not from a symmetric but from a skewed distribution. Moreover, the distribution of marriages conducted during 1647–1719 is more skewed to the right than is the distribution for 1560–1646, while in 1720–1769 the distribution is very much the same as that for the early period. The modal age remained almost exactly the same throughout all three of the periods, so we can conclude that the mean age of marriage at Colyton altered primarily because proportionately more marriages took place at ages well above the modal (or most common) age at marriage in 1647–1719 than in either 1560–1646 or in 1720–1769. (We have to say 'proportionately' more because the number of marriages altered substantially.) The mean marriage age in Colyton did not change, therefore, because the whole distribution was shifted to the right by 2·6 (29·6 — 27·0) years, but because it became more skewed to the right.

This has two implications. Firstly, it changes our view and interpretation of the historical process underlying changes in marriage in Colyton. Secondly, from the point of view of the use of statistics, it emphasises the fact that the measures of central tendency are intended to sum up and to illuminate different features of the frequency distributions from which they are calculated. They are no substitute for, but they complement, careful examination of the shape of the frequency distribution and of the nature of the historical process which may have created it.

One final point: the mode in Table 5.6 was calculated from the mean and median using the formula

$$\text{Mean} - \text{Mode} = 3 \, (\text{Mean} - \text{Median}).$$

This formula can be used only when the distribution is moderately skewed, but it is convenient if the mode is cumbersome to calculate or if, as sometimes happens, a distribution is irregular in shape and has two or more peaks.

The use of all summary measures, averages, measures of dispersion and grouped frequency distributions involves a loss of accuracy. Whether this loss of accuracy outweighs the gain in speed of computation and ease of presentation is a matter for the individual researcher to decide afresh for each project. The use of data processing machinery lessens the need for the use of grouped data and measures of central tendency as summarizing measures, but their advantages in presentation of data still remain.

6   The analysis of time series

Since this book is concerned with the quantitative analysis of historical problems, in which the dimension of time is ever present, it may seem surprising that it is only at this point that the question of 'time series' has been raised explicitly. It is important to realize, however, that the historical character of the data does not necessarily mean that they constitute, in the strict sense, a 'time series'; we give the name of 'time series' only to a set of data which is ordered chronologically. Thus neither the data on Domesday parishes nor the data on ships constitute time series. They are series of observations, the first of Domesday parishes and the second of ships, which were made sufficiently close together for us to be able to assign the same date to all the observations in each data matrix; the items are not in any way chronologically ordered.

Time series data are thus a special case of a data matrix in which the data are in chronological order rather than in any other order. The chronological ordering of the data may arise naturally, in the process of collection of the data; if we collect data on some variable at a series of points of time – daily, monthly or yearly – then our data matrix will be chronologically ordered, and each column of the matrix will be a time series. Table 6.1 shows an example of such a data matrix; many historical data are of this type: the size of the population in a series of census years, the yearly yield of the harvest, the number of unemployed at the end of each month, and many others. Alternatively, we may collect our data in some other way, so that the cases, or rows of the matrix, have no chronological ordering, but one column of the matrix consists of chronological information; for example, Table 6.2 shows, on the left hand side of the table, such a data matrix. We may construct time series data from this data matrix, either by rearranging the rows of the table into a chronological ordering, or by constructing a frequency distribution. Again, many historical data are collected in such a form; almost all data on individual people will contain chronological information, such as dates of marriage or death, which may be used to construct time series data.

Since time series data are merely one way of arranging a data matrix, the techniques that have already been discussed for summarizing and classifying data matrices may be applied to time series data wherever the problem and the nature of the data make it sensible to do this. We can, for example, calculate the mean and standard deviation of the time series shown in Table 6.1, with the aim of discovering the average

Table 6.1 *British domestic exports, 1820–1850*

	£ million		£ million
1820	36·4	1836	53·3
1821	36·7	1837	42·1
1822	37·0	1838	50·1
1823	35·4	1839	53·2
1824	38·4	1840	51·4
1825	38·9	1841	51·6
1826	31·5	1842	47·4
1827	37·2	1843	52·3
1828	36·8	1844	58·6
1829	35·8	1845	60·1
1830	38·3	1846	57·8
1831	37·2	1847	58·8
1832	36·5	1848	52·8
1833	39·7	1849	63·6
1834	41·6	1850	71·4
1835	47·4		

Source: B. R. Mitchell and P. Deane, *Abstract of British Historical Statistics* (Cambridge, Cambridge University Press, 1962), p. 282.

value of British domestic exports between 1820 and 1850, together with the dispersion around that average. We could similarly, if we wished, calculate the median and modal values of time series data, and we can also chart time series data using all the graphical methods that we have discussed. Figure 6.1 shows a line graph of the data of Table 6.1. In addition, we can use a number of methods of analysis of time series data which are not appropriate to data ordered in some other way.

(a) Objects and assumptions of the analysis of time series

Table 6.1 gives the value of exports of goods produced in Great Britain between 1820 and 1850. This was a period during which Britain was developing her manufacturing industries very rapidly, taking advantage of the new machine technology developed during the Industrial Revolution, and was exporting more and more of the products of her industry. As Table 6.1 shows, the value of her domestic exports nearly doubled between 1820 and 1850.[1] The growth was not regular, however; trade depressions, political and economic events in other countries, and the changing tastes of overseas customers, all affected the growth, so that it was faster in some years than in others. In some periods, indeed, as Figure 6.1 clearly shows, there was even a decline before the upward movement was resumed.

If we are to analyse the growth of British exports during these years, then we need to be able to think of the possible factors that might have influenced that growth, and we also need some method by which we can separate the influence of one factor from that of another. There is not much point in being able to describe various possible influences, without estimating the importance of each. Furthermore, we may be most interested not in the long-term growth of exports, but in the short, year-to-year fluctuations, and so need to be able to isolate short-term from long-term changes in the time series. We need therefore to be able to split up a time series into parts corresponding to different possible influences on the series; and time series

[1] These data are in money terms, i.e. not adjusted for changes in price levels. This problem is discussed at more length below (pp. 127–9).

methods are designed to help us to do this. The methods cannot tell us what the influences on the time series were; that is a historical question. But they can help us to distinguish between influences that operated over a long period and those that affected only individual years; once we have distinguished between such influences we can then use our historical knowledge to give names to them.

Table 6.2 *Derivation of time series from a data matrix*

Original data					Derived time series		
Name of ship	Where built	When built	Tonnage		Date of build	No. of ships	Total tonnage
Druid	Liverpool	1823	64				
Emulous	Rotherhithe	1825	129		1820	1	110
Sir Joseph Yorke	Chester	1822	62		1821	5	746
Malvina	Inverness	1824	39		1822	2	164
Enterprize	Rotherhithe	1826	318		1823	3	501
Eclipse	Greenock	1821	88		1824	3	185
William Jolliffe	Deptford	1826	235		1825	5	564
Tourist	Perth	1821	112		1826	8	1325
Ramona	Rotherhithe	1828	178		1827	0	0
Attwood	Blackwall	1825	189		1828	1	178
Harlequin	Deptford	1826	185		1829	1	34
City of London	Deptford	1824	104				
Royal Sovereign	Deptford	1822	102		The data are taken from a		
Venus	Rotherhithe	1821	112		return 'of the name and		
Soho	Blackwall	1823	292		description of all Steam		
Belfast	Belfast	1820	110		Vessels registered in the		
Dart	Rotherhithe	1825	145		ports of the United King-		
Magnet	Limehouse	1826	166		dom', *Parliamentary Papers*		
Jane	North Shields	1826	12		(1845), vol. XLVII, p. 545.		
Earl of Liverpool	Blackpool	1823	145		They are the steamships,		
Neptune	Newcastle	1824	42		registered in the Port of		
James Watt	Port Glasgow	1821	291		London in 1845, which had		
Wear	Sunderland	1825	33		been built before 1830.		
Courier	Rotherhithe	1826	103				
Majestic	Greenock	1821	143				
Ipswich	Ipswich	1825	68				
Columbine	Deptford	1826	241				
Royal Charter	Gainsborough	1826	65				
Kingston	Gainsborough	1829	34				

The methods of time series analysis assume that there may be three types of influence affecting any time series. The first influence produces long-term growth or decline in the series, and is known as the trend in the data. The second influence produces regular fluctuations around the long-term trend. One such influence is that of the seasons; bread prices in pre-industrial England were always at their lowest in the autumn, immediately

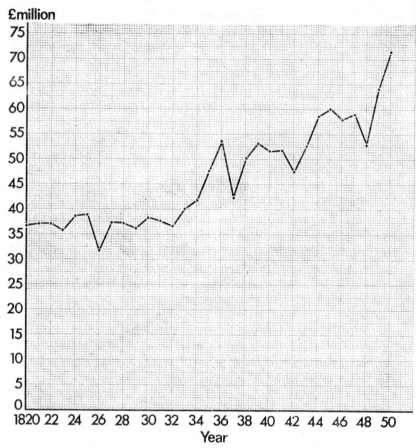

Figure 6.1 British domestic exports, 1820–50. Data from Table 6.1.

after the harvest. Another is that of changing business activity, which produced the alternation of boom and slump, the so-called 'business cycle', in the economies of many countries. The third influence is irregular, and produces short-term, un-repeated, fluctuations in the series. War or plague or a change in government policy may all produce such fluctuations. The statistical analysis of time series therefore consists in splitting a time series into parts that correspond to these different possible influences, some long term, some short term, some regular and some irregular. By using the methods of time series analysis we can isolate each, or all, of these influences.

The assumption of time series analysis is that a time series is composed of the effects of these three types of influence, and in carrying out an analysis by these methods we are accepting that assumption. We must therefore be very careful that this assumption does not conflict with what we, as historians, know about a particular set of data. If we do not believe, as historians, that a particular series has a regular cyclical influence on it, then we should not use a method of analysis that assumes that such an influence exists. We shall take up this point again later in this chapter, but first we shall discuss the analysis of the time series of Figure 6.1.

(b) The rate of growth

It is apparent from Figure 6.1 that British domestic exports rose between 1820 and 1850. If we wish to analyse that growth in detail, however, we need also to know how fast that growth was, both over the whole period and over parts of it. It will be of interest for us to discover, for example, whether the growth was faster at the beginning of the period than at the end. In addition, if we wished, for example, to compare the growth in exports with the growth in imports, we would need some measure of growth by which to compare the two series.

From Table 6.1 we can see that exports nearly doubled between 1820 and 1850. This is clearly a substantial rise, but expressed in the form 'nearly doubled over thirty-one years' it is difficult to compare with changes in other periods, either shorter or longer. It would facilitate such comparisons if we could express the growth as an average growth per year. It might seem that we could calculate such an average growth per year very simply by dividing the difference between exports in 1820 and 1850 by the number of years between them; we would then have

$$\frac{71 \cdot 4 - 36 \cdot 4}{30} = 1 \cdot 167$$

and we could say that the mean increase per year in British exports was £1·167 million. This would be true, but it would not help us very much in making comparisons with other series, since we would not know the base from which the growth began. An increase of £1·167 million per year from a starting point of £1 million would be much more spectacular than from a starting point of £100 million, but our average increase would not distinguish between these two. It would also be useful to have a measure of change independent of the original unit, in this case £ sterling, in case we wanted to compare our series for export values with, for example, a series of imports of tea in cwt.

These two requirements – the need to take account of the base, and the need to have a measure independent of the original units – suggests that a measure based on percentages would be appropriate. A further requirement is that the measure should be cumulative, expressing each year's growth as a percentage of the value for the previous year; it should be calculated, in fact, as a compound interest rate, rather than a simple interest rate. The growth rate that satisfies all these requirements is the percentage growth rate calculated from the formula

$$r = \left(\sqrt[m]{\left(\frac{X_N}{X_T} \right)} - 1 \right) 100$$

where r is the desired growth rate, X_N is the value for the last period, X_T is the value for the first period, and m is the difference in years between the first and last period.

Calculation of the growth rate is greatly simplified by the use of logarithms. For the data of Table 6.1 for example, to calculate the growth rate between 1820 and 1850 we find the logarithms of X_N (log 71·4 = 1·8537) and X_T (log 36·4 = 1·5611). Subtracting, log X_N — log X_T = 0·2926. Dividing by m = 30 to take the thirtieth root we get 0·0098. The antilog of 0·0098 is 1·023, and, subtracting 1 and multiplying by 100, we find that the average percentage growth rate was 2·3 per cent per annum.

(Growth rates may also be found, without the trouble of calculation, by the use of published tables. It should also be noted that, although in our example we have calculated the growth rate per year, the same method can be used for growth rates over any time period.)

Growth rates are a very valuable and much used means of describing time series data, but they need to be used with caution, particularly when there are marked fluctuations in the series. In these circumstances, the choice of terminal years, between which the growth rates are calculated, is of great importance. We can calculate some other growth rates from the data of Table 6.1 to illustrate this; Table 6.3 shows such growth

Table 6.3 *Growth rates of the data of Table 6.1*

Terminal years	Length of period	% growth rate per annum
1820–1850	30 years	2·3
1820–1848	28 years	1·4
1826–1850	24 years	3·5
1823–1847	24 years	2·1

rates, while Figure 6.2 shows them plotted on a semi-logarithmic scale graph. A semi-logarithmic graph is appropriate because a growth rate is a measure of constant proportionate (or percentage) rate of increase, for example of 2·3 per cent each year. As was shown in Chapter 4, the use of a logarithmic vertical scale gives a graph which represents a constant proportionate change as a straight (but not horizontal) line, and the faster the change the steeper the line; thus in Figure 6.2 the differ-

Figure 6.2 British domestic exports, 1820–50. Growth rates. Data from Table 6.3. Semi-logarithmic scale.

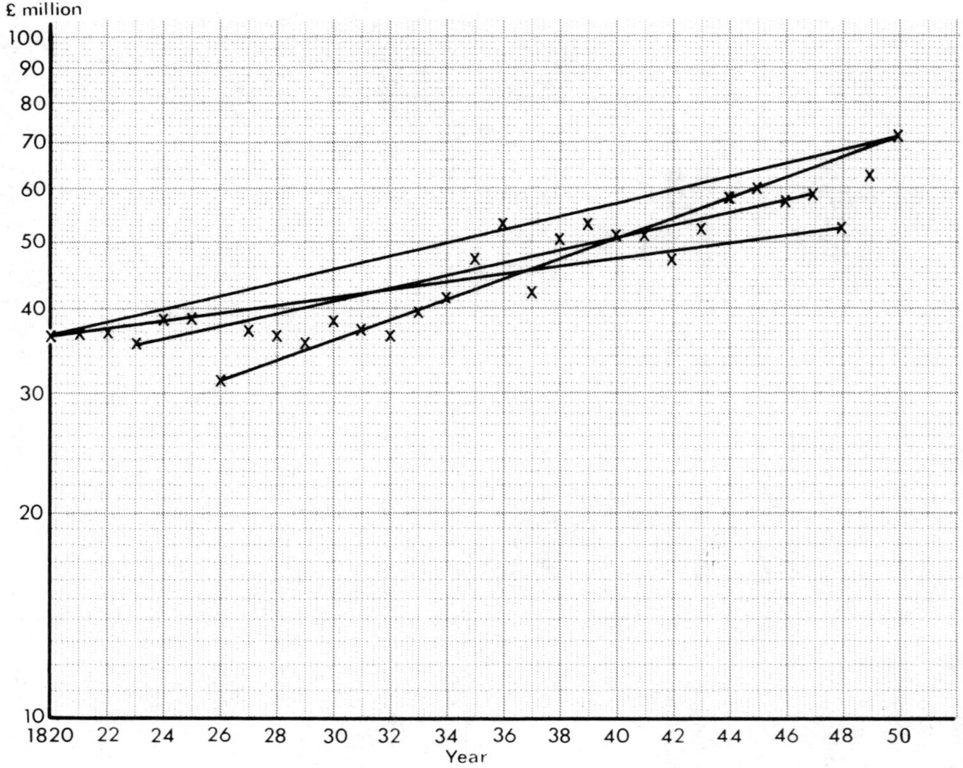

ence in slope between the line linking 1820–50 and that linking 1826–50 shows that growth was faster over the latter period. On a graph with a linear scale (such as Figure 6.1) constant proportionate growth is shown by a curve, which is more difficult to draw and makes comparison between lines less easy.

All the growth rates in Table 6.3 are correct; all give the annual percentage growth rate between the terminal years. Yet, individually, they suffer from severe deficiencies as a measure of the whole time series; the impression we gain of the growth of British exports between 1820 and 1848 is very different from the impression we gain of the growth between 1826 and 1850, although the time period over which we are measuring is not very different.

The reason for the differences that occur in Table 6.3 between growth rates is clear if we study Figure 6.2, in which the terminal years used in Table 6.3 have been linked together by bold lines. We see that in choosing 1820 and 1848 as terminal years, we have measured from a high point in 1820 to a low point in 1848, while between 1826 and 1850 we have done the reverse. Even when we take the terminal years 1820 and 1850, we see that the line connecting these two years passes above almost every other data point. Only when we take 1823 and 1847 do we seem to have chosen reasonably typical years on which to base our calculation of the growth rate.

This is not simply a statistical problem. In order to choose terminal years for such calculations we need to be extremely careful that we do not choose atypical years, since to do so may distort our results. For example, much of a lengthy historical debate over the changes in the standard of living of the British workers during the Industrial Revolution was concerned with the choice of appropriate terminal years. If some were chosen, then it appeared that the cost of living rose; if others, it appeared to fall.

(c) The trend

If we look again at Figure 6.2, it appears that part of the difficulty over the choice of appropriate terminal years may be connected with the fact that we have to choose two, and only two, terminal years with which to describe the growth of the whole series. The data for other years do not, therefore, enter into the calculation. It would clearly be more sensible, if we want to find a measure of the growth of the whole series, to find a measure that allows us to use the whole series. We want, in fact, to describe the long-term trend in the data, the first influence which is assumed, in time series analysis, to affect a time series.

We shall begin by assuming that British exports grew by a constant absolute amount each year, and use all the data in the series to make an estimate of that absolute amount. A series which changes by a constant absolute amount can be represented by a straight line on a graph with a natural scale, and we shall therefore use the data as they are shown in Figure 6.1. Later in the chapter we shall consider a method which is appropriate when we think that a series grew not by a constant absolute amount but by a constant proportion each year; such a series and the long-term trend in such a series can be represented as a curved line on a graph with a natural scale or (as in Figure 6.2) as a straight line on a semi-logarithmic graph. It is sometimes difficult to decide whether the long-term trend in a data series is best represented by a straight line ('linear') form, or by a curved ('curvilinear'), and we must therefore know the methods appropriate to each case.

We calculated in the last section that the average absolute growth of exports between 1820 and 1850 was £1·167 million per year. In making that calculation, we used data for the value of exports only in 1820 and 1850, ignoring the intervening years. As we can see from Figure 6.3, that calculation was equivalent to drawing a line to connect the data points for 1820 and 1850 on a natural scale graph, and measuring the distance along the vertical axis by which that line rises for each movement of one year along the horizontal axis. As we saw in the last section, however, it may be misleading to use data only for 1820 and 1850, since those years may be atypical. Ideally, in order to take full account of the data for every year, we need to find a line which passes through all the data points. From inspection

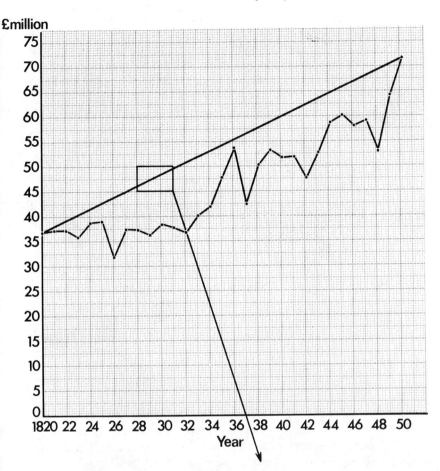

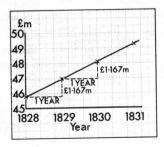

Figure 6.3 British domestic exports, 1820–50. Average annual growth, 1820–50. Data from Figure 6.1.

of Figure 6.3, however, it is clear that we cannot find such a straight line that will connect all the data points on the graph. As a second best, therefore, we will try to find a straight line that passes as close as possible to all the data points, a line that is, in a sense, an average of all the possible lines through the points of the graph. Some of the points will lie on the line, others below or above it. We could of course try to draw in such a line on the graph, on the basis of our judgement as to where it should lie, but our judgement is likely to be fallible, and to be disputed by other people. We need, therefore, to calculate a line on the basis of some theory, which is agreed to give the best possible fit to all the points on the graph.

It can be shown that the line of best possible fit is that calculated by the 'least-squares method'. Figure 6.4 illustrates the logic of this method. We try to choose the line (line B on the graph) passing through the points on the graph such that, if we draw vertical lines from each data point to the line (as we have done for the years 1835–45), measure the distances, square each of them and add them together, the result (the sum of squares of the deviations from the line) is smaller for the line we have chosen than it would be for any other line drawn on the graph. The line found by this method will give the best possible fit to all the points on the graph, and will therefore be the most appropriate line to use to represent the long-term trend in the data.

We could try to discover this best fitting line by trial and error, drawing lines on the graph, measuring deviations and calculating sums of squares, but this would clearly be a cumbersome procedure. Instead, we make use of two formulae, which together allow us to describe the line that satisfies the condition that the sum of squared deviations should be as small as possible. In order to understand this, we must consider how we might describe a line, such as line B on Figure 6.4. Line B, or indeed any other straight line, such as line A, drawn on a graph, has two important characteristics. The first is that, if it is extended as far as the vertical axis of the graph, it will cut that axis at a particular point. The second characteristic is that the line is sloped in relation to the horizontal axis of the graph.

million

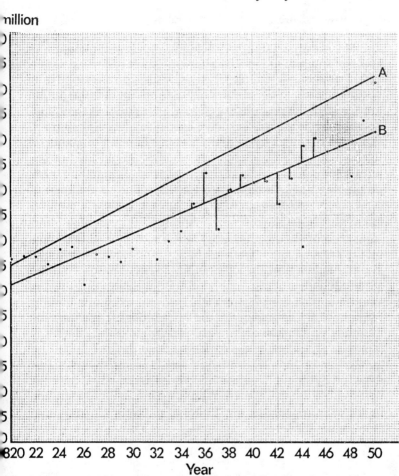

Figure 6.4 British domestic exports, 1820–50. Trends. Data from Table 6.1.

In order to draw a particular straight line on a graph we therefore need to know two things about it: firstly the point at which it crosses the vertical axis, and secondly how far it is sloped in relation to the horizontal axis. The first of these, known as the intercept, will simply be a number in the units of the vertical axis. Line A on Figure 6.4, for example, cuts the vertical axis at the point representing £35 million. The second piece of information is slightly more complicated. In order to draw the line stemming from the intercept we need to know how far up or down the line should go, as we move along the horizontal axis. If we look again at line A, we see that in 1820 it represents the value £35 million, in 1822 it represents £37·5 million, in 1824 £40 million, and so on. In other words, for every year out along the horizontal axis, we add another £1·25 million on the vertical axis. After ten years, we should have added £12·5 million, after twenty years £25 million, and we can see that line A in fact is a line that traces these values.

Therefore, in order to be able to draw line B, the line that best fits our data, we need to know two things, the intercept and the slope, and it is these two pieces of information that the two formulae based on the least squares method give us. The two formulae are

for the intercept:

$$a = \frac{\sum Y - b\sum X}{N}$$

and for the slope:

$$b = \frac{N\sum XY - (\sum X)(\sum Y)}{N\sum X^2 - (\sum X)^2}.$$

In these formulae, N is, as usual, the number of values. When we are calculating the trend in a time series, X is the vector of number of years since the beginning of the time series, and Y is the vector of data values. The two vectors for the data of Table 6.1, X and Y, are shown as the second and third columns of Table 6.4, which also shows the method of calculation of the other quantities needed to solve the formulae for a and b.

Having calculated these sums, and sums of squares, we can calculate first b, and then a, as shown in Table 6.4. We find that

Table 6.4 *Calculation of linear trend, from data of Table 6.1, by long method*

Year	Data (Y)	Time Units around 1820 (X)	X^2	XY
1820	36·4	0	0	0
1	36·7	1	1	36·7
2	37·0	2	4	74·0
3	35·4	3	9	106·2
4	38·4	4	16	153·6
5	38·9	5	25	194·5
6	31·5	6	36	189·0
7	37·2	7	49	260·4
8	36·8	8	64	294·4
9	35·8	9	81	322·2
30	38·3	10	100	383·0
1	37·2	11	121	409·2
2	36·5	12	144	438·0
3	39·7	13	169	516·1
4	41·6	14	196	582·4
5	47·4	15	225	711·0
6	53·3	16	256	852·8
7	42·1	17	289	715·7
8	50·1	18	324	901·8
9	53·2	19	361	1 010·8
40	51·4	20	400	1 028·0
1	51·6	21	441	1 083·6
2	47·4	22	484	1 042·8
3	52·3	23	529	1 202·9
4	58·6	24	576	1 406·4
5	60·1	25	625	1 502·5
6	57·8	26	676	1 502·8
7	58·8	27	729	1 587·6
8	52·8	28	784	1 478·4
9	63·6	29	841	1 844·4
50	71·4	30	900	2 142·0

$\sum Y = 1429·3$ $\quad \sum X = 465$ $\quad \sum X^2 = 9455$ $\quad \sum XY = 23\ 973·2$

(continued)

Table 6.4—*continued*

$$b = \frac{743\ 169 \cdot 2 - 664\ 624 \cdot 5}{293\ 105 - 216\ 225}$$

$$= \frac{78\ 544 \cdot 7}{76\ 880 \cdot 0}$$

$$= 1 \cdot 02.$$

$$a = \frac{1\ 429 \cdot 3 - 1 \cdot 02(465)}{31}$$

$$= \frac{1\ 429 \cdot 3 - 474 \cdot 3}{31}$$

$$= 30 \cdot 81.$$

$$\therefore\ Y_T = 30 \cdot 81 + 1 \cdot 02 X_T.$$

for these data the intercept of the line is 30·81, and the slope is 1·02. This means that our line cuts the vertical axis at the value of £30·81 million, and that for each year along the horizontal axis it rises by £1·02 million. Knowing this, we know that for 1820 the line passes through the point representing the value £30·81 million, that for 1821 it passes through the point representing £31·83 million, that for 1830 it passes through the point £30·81 + 10(1·02) = £41·01 million, and so on. Line B is that line, and we say that it is fitted by least squares methods to the data of Table 6.1; it represents the 'linear trend' in the time series.

We can calculate the values through which line B will pass by using a simple formula

$$Y = a + bX$$

where a, b, X and Y are defined as in the least squares formulae for a and b. This formula is known as the general formula for a straight line, the values of a and b altering to describe any particular line. For example, we could describe the line A on Figure 6.4 by the equation

$$Y = 35 + 1 \cdot 25 X$$

and line B is described by

$$Y = 30 \cdot 81 + 1 \cdot 02 X.$$

Similarly, if we remember that we calculated that the absolute growth each year between 1820 and 1850 was on average

£1·167 million, we can say that the line connecting those two dates on Figure 6.3 could be described by the equation

$$Y = 36·4 + 1·167X.$$

It is only line B on Figure 6.4, however, which has the desired property of having the best fit to all the data points.

The considerable labour of calculating the linear trend can be eased by a computing device shown in Table 6.5. Instead of measuring X as time units from the beginning of the time series, as we did in Table 6.4, we measure from the middle of the time series, so that $\sum X = 0$. If this is done, the two least squares equations reduce to the much simpler form of

$$a = \frac{\sum Y}{N}$$

and

$$b = \frac{\sum XY}{\sum X^2}$$

and we compute the linear trend as in Table 6.4.

To calculate growth rates on the basis of the linear trend, we simply take the values of the two points on the linear trend line which correspond to the dates between which we wish to measure growth. From our formula for line B, $Y = 30·81 + 1·02X$, we know, for example, that the value for 1820 is 30·81, while the value for 1850 is 61·41; calculating a growth rate between these terminal years, we get a rate of 2·3 per cent per annum. (In Table 6.5 we calculate that $a = 46·11$; this is because we have taken the time units as centred around 1835, so that when we calculate the trend value for 1835, $X_{1835} = 0$, so $Y_{1835} = 46·11$.) We can calculate growth between any two other points on the trend line in the same way.

In this particular case, the growth rate of the linear trend between 1820 and 1850 is the same as the growth rate calculated from the terminal dates of the data; that they should be exactly the same is entirely coincidental and the two methods of calculating the growth rate must be considered as theoretically completely separate, even if in this particular example the result is the same. In general, it is greatly preferable to calculate the growth rate from the linear trend, since that trend takes account of all the individual values in the time series.

Table 6.5 *Calculation of linear trend, from data of Table 6.1, by short method*

Year	Data value (Y)	Time units around 1820	Time units (X)	X^2	XY	Trend values
1820	36·4	0	−15	225	−546·0	30·81
21	36·7	1	−14	196	−513·8	31·83
22	37·0	2	−13	169	−481·0	32·85
23	35·4	3	−12	144	−424·8	33·87
24	38·4	4	−11	121	−422·4	34·89
25	38·9	5	−10	100	−389·0	35·91
26	31·5	6	−9	81	−283·5	36·93
27	37·2	7	−8	64	−297·6	37·95
28	36·8	8	−7	49	−257·6	38·97
29	35·8	9	−6	36	−214·8	39·99
30	38·3	10	−5	25	−191·5	41·01
1831	37·2	11	−4	16	−148·8	42·03
32	36·5	12	−3	9	−109·5	43·05
33	39·7	13	−2	4	−79·4	44·07
34	41·6	14	−1	1	−41·6	45·09
35	47·4	15	0	0	0	46·11
36	53·3	16	+1	1	+53·3	47·13
37	42·1	17	+2	4	+84·2	48·15
38	50·1	18	+3	9	+150·3	49·17
39	53·2	19	+4	16	+212·8	50·19
40	51·4	20	+5	25	+257·0	51·21
1841	51·6	21	+6	36	+309·6	52·23
42	47·4	22	+7	49	+331·8	53·25
43	52·3	23	+8	64	+418·4	54·27
44	58·6	24	+9	81	+527·4	55·29
45	60·1	25	+10	100	+601·0	56·31
46	57·8	26	+11	121	+635·8	57·33
47	58·8	27	+12	144	+705·6	58·35
48	52·8	28	+13	169	+686·4	59·37
49	63·6	29	+14	196	+890·4	60·39
1850	71·4	30	+15	225	+1071·0	61·41
	1429·3			2480	+2533·7	

Table 6.5—*continued*

$$a = \frac{\sum Y}{N} = \frac{1429 \cdot 3}{31} = 46 \cdot 11$$

$$b = \frac{\sum XY}{\sum X^2} = \frac{2533 \cdot 7}{2480} = 1 \cdot 02$$

$$\therefore Y_T = 30 \cdot 81 + 1 \cdot 02 X_T.$$

Once we have estimated the linear trend in the data, we can then subtract the trend values from the original data values, as in the second and third columns of Table 6.9 (see p. 120). The result is a time series composed of the fluctuations in the original series, and we can therefore proceed to analyse those fluctuations, free from the complications caused when the data include a long-term trend. The time series of deviations from trend is shown plotted as Figure 6.5.

We have concentrated so far on the advantages of the linear trend as a method of summarizing a time series, and of concentrating on fluctuations around the trend. The method has the disadvantage, however, that it is designed to fit a straight line to the data, while many historical time series do not seem to be very straight. If we compare Figure 6.1, for example, with Figure 4.7, which shows the growth of raw cotton imports into the United Kingdom between 1770 and 1800, we can see the difference between a series which has a reasonably linear form and one which has a curvilinear form. Where the series is non-linear, it would clearly be inappropriate to fit a straight line to the data by the method which we have just described, since such a straight line would give a misleading impression of the trend; it would be more appropriate to fit a curved line to represent the trend. Although it is often possible to do this, the mathematics involved are much more complicated than the mathematics involved in calculating a linear trend. An alternative solution which is often adopted, therefore, is to transform the series into logarithmic form; this is particularly sensible, as we saw in looking at rates of growth in the last section, when we can assume that the series changed by an equal proportionate amount each year. When the data for raw cotton imports are plotted on a semi-logarithmic graph, as they were in Figure 4.9,

£million

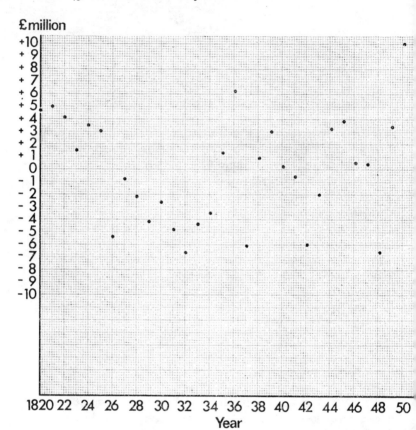

Figure 6.5. British domestic exports, 1820–50. Deviations from trend. Data from Table 6.1.

it can be seen that the values take on much more closely a straight line form, and it is therefore appropriate to calculate the linear trend, using the logarithms of the original data values. Once this has been done, as in Table 6.6, the trend values can be plotted on the semi-log graph, as in Figure 6.6, giving a straight line, or on the original graph, after conversion by the use of antilogarithms, giving a curved line, as in Figure 6.7. This method has the further advantage that the rate of growth is immediately apparent from the calculated trend equation. The equation is $Y = ab^x$, where b is equal to 1 plus the annual average rate of growth. The rate of growth of cotton imports is therefore immediately seen as 9·3 per cent per annum. The advantage of this is so considerable, in fact, that calculation of the linear trend in the logarithms is often preferred to calculation of the linear trend in the original data, even when the original data fall approximately on a straight line.

(d) Regular fluctuations in time series

In the last section we concentrated on the advantages of using the linear trend for the calculation of growth rates. In addition, as we saw, the linear trend represents the influence of long-run factors in the time series. In the case of the data of Table 6.1, for example, we might argue that this represented the long-run growth in the strength of British manufacturing and the growth in demand for British products in foreign countries. In addition to this long-term trend for exports to grow, Figure 6.5 clearly indicates that there were marked fluctuations around the trend, and we can now proceed to discuss how we can analyse those fluctuations.

The methods of time series analysis assume that there are three possible types of fluctuation, two regular and one irregular. The first type of regular fluctuation is that known as seasonal fluctuation, which includes fluctuations as the result of the weather, patterns of work and leisure within a week or within the year, and other regular weekly, monthly, quarterly or annual occurrences. In pre-industrial societies, such fluctuations, and in particular those caused by the weather, exerted a considerable influence on working patterns and on many other aspects of life: travel was difficult in winter, mills lacked water to drive them in the summer, food prices rose in the winter and before the harvest. Even in modern societies, particular annual holidays

Table 6.6 *Calculation of the linear trend in the logarithms of data on imports of raw cotton into the U.K., 1770–1800*

Year	Data (Y)	log Y	X	X²	X log Y	log trend values	Trend values
1770	3 612	3·5577	−15	225	−53·3655	3·5369	3 443
1	2 547	3·4060	−14	196	−47·6840	3·5758	3 765
2	5 307	3·7249	−13	169	−48·4237	3·6147	4 118
3	2 906	3·4633	−12	144	−41·5596	3·6536	4 504
4	5 707	3·7564	−11	121	−41·3204	3·6925	4 926
5	6 694	3·8257	−10	100	−38·2570	3·7314	5 388
6	6 216	3·7935	−9	81	−34·1415	3·7703	5 892
7	7 037	3·8474	−8	64	−30·7792	3·8092	6 445
8	6 569	3·8175	−7	49	−26·7225	3·8481	7 049
9	5 861	3·7680	−6	36	−22·6080	3·8870	7 709
1780	6 877	3·8374	−5	25	−19·1870	3·9259	8 431
1	5 199	3·7160	−4	16	−14·8640	3·9648	9 221
2	11 828	4·0730	−3	9	−12·2190	4·0037	10 090
3	9 736	3·9884	−2	4	−7·9768	4·0426	11 040
4	11 482	4·0599	−1	1	−4·0599	4·0815	12 060
5	18 400	4·2648	0	0	0	4·1204	13 190
6	19 475	4·2896	1	1	4·2896	4·1593	14 430
7	23 250	4·3664	2	4	8·7328	4·1982	15 790
8	20 467	4·3111	3	9	12·9333	4·2371	17 260
9	32 576	4·5130	4	16	18·0520	4·2760	18 880
1790	31 448	4·4976	5	25	22·4880	4·3149	20 650
1	28 707	4·4581	6	36	26·7486	4·3538	22 580
2	34 907	4·5429	7	49	31·8003	4·3929	24 710
3	19 041	4·2797	8	64	34·2376	4·4316	27 020
4	24 359	4·3867	9	81	39·4803	4·4705	29 540
5	26 401	4·4216	10	100	44·2160	4·5094	32 310
6	32 126	4·5069	11	121	49·5759	4·5483	35 340
7	23 354	4·3683	12	144	52·4196	4·5872	38 660
8	31 881	4·5035	13	169	58·5455	4·6261	42 280
9	43 379	4·6373	14	196	64·9222	4·6650	46 240
1800	56 011	4·7483	15	225	71·2245	4·7039	50 580
		127·7309		2480	96·4981		

$$\log a = \frac{\Sigma \log Y}{N} = \frac{127 \cdot 7309}{31} = 4 \cdot 1204$$

$$\log b = \frac{\Sigma X \log Y}{\Sigma X^2} = \frac{96 \cdot 4981}{2480} = 0 \cdot 0389$$

$$\log Y = 4 \cdot 1204 + 0 \cdot 0389 X$$

taking antilogs $Y = (13\ 190)(1 \cdot 093)^X$

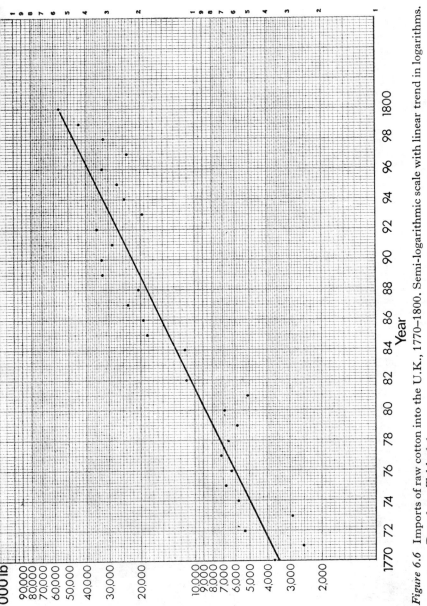

Figure 6.6 Imports of raw cotton into the U.K., 1770–1800. Semi-logarithmic scale with linear trend in logarithms. Data from Table 6.6.

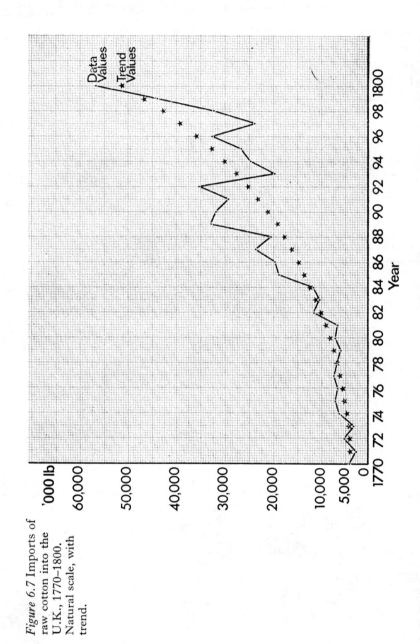

Figure 6.7 Imports of raw cotton into the U.K., 1770–1800. Natural scale, with trend.

such as Christmas or Easter affect working patterns, and food prices still alter through the seasons. Any time series, therefore, which consists of data collected at intervals of less than a year, may be affected by seasonal fluctuation; a time series such as that of Table 6.1 cannot of course be affected by seasonal changes, since the data are collected only at yearly intervals.

To illustrate the method of isolating the seasonal fluctuations in a time series, we shall therefore use another set of data, consisting of prices paid for wheat by Winchester College from 1713 to 1718. These prices were collected by Lord Beveridge as part of his great study of prices and wages in England, and they are important evidence for the study of living standards. We need to remove the seasonal influences from the series, principally to allow us to study short-term fluctuations which might have produced famine or glut in particular years, but also to allow us to study the long-term trends in the prices, unaffected by regular movements within each year.

To isolate the seasonal component we have first to estimate the trend values, since, as can be seen from Table 6.7 and Figure 6.8, the series has a downward trend; if we did not remove the influence of this trend, it would affect our estimates of seasonal variation. We therefore estimate the linear trend, and calculate the deviations of the series from the trend values, giving the series shown in column 3 of Table 6.7. In order to calculate the regular seasonal component, we now take all the values for the first quarter of each year, and calculate their arithmetic mean, repeating this operation for the second, third and fourth quarters, giving the values shown in column 4 of Table 6.7. These values represent the average rise or fall in the series for each quarter, which is what we mean by the seasonal component. Subtracting these seasonal values from the deviations from trend gives us the residual (column 5) representing the influence of factors other than the long-term trend or the seasonal component. We may also (as in column 6) subtract the seasonal component from the original series, giving us a further series including both the long-term trend and the residual fluctuations, but excluding the seasonal effect.

If we had data collected on a weekly or monthly basis, we

Table 6.7 *Calculation of seasonal fluctuation in wheat prices for Winchester College, 1713–18*

Time period		Wheat price (s. per qtr of wheat)	Trend value[1]	Deviation from trend	Seasonal component[2]	Detrended, deseasonalized series	Deseasonalized series
1713	1st qtr	42·67	46·71	−4·04	−0·09	−3·95	42·76
	2nd qtr	56·88	45·86	11·02	1·55	9·47	47·41
	3rd qtr	49·78	45·01	4·77	0·73	4·04	49·05
	4th qtr	46·21	44·16	2·05	−2·19	4·24	48·40
1714	1st qtr	32·00	43·31	−11·31	−0·09	−11·22	32·09
	2nd qtr	32·00	42·46	−10·46	1·55	−12·01	30·45
	3rd qtr	32·00	41·61	−9·61	0·73	−10·34	31·27
	4th qtr	28·44	40·76	−12·32	−2·19	−10·13	30·63
1715	1st qtr	46·21	39·91	6·30	−0·09	6·39	46·30
	2nd qtr	49·78	39·06	10·72	1·55	9·17	48·23
	3rd qtr	42·67	38·21	4·46	0·73	3·73	41·94
	4th qtr	35·56	37·36	−1·80	−2·19	0·39	37·75
1716	1st qtr	39·10	36·51	2·59	−0·09	2·68	39·19
	2nd qtr	39·10	35·66	3·44	1·55	1·89	37·55
	3rd qtr	40·29	34·81	5·48	0·73	4·75	39·56
	4th qtr	33·77	33·96	−0·19	−2·19	2·00	35·96
1717	1st qtr	43·84	33·11	10·73	−0·09	10·82	43·93
	2nd qtr	32·00	32·26	−0·26	1·55	−1·81	30·45
	3rd qtr	32·00	31·41	0·59	0·73	−0·14	31·27
	4th qtr	32·00	30·56	1·44	−2·19	3·63	34·19
1718	1st qtr	24·89	29·71	−4·82	−0·09	−4·73	24·98
	2nd qtr	23·70	28·86	−5·16	1·55	−6·71	22·15
	3rd qtr	26·67	28·01	−1·34	0·73	−2·07	25·94
	4th qtr	24·89	27·16	−2·27	−2·19	−0·08	27·08

[1] The trend values were calculated from the estimated linear trend equation, calculated by the short-cut method, of Price = 36·93 − 0·85 Time.

[2] The seasonal component was calculated by taking the mean of the deviations from trend for the first quarter of the year, then the mean of deviations for the second quarter, etc. This gave values of −0·08, 1·56, 0·74, −2·17; summing these values gave 0·05, but by definition the seasonal variation should have a neutral or zero effect over the whole year. We therefore adjusted the seasonal means by approximately −(0·05/4) in each case, taking them as −0·09, 1·55, 0·73 and −2·19, which sum to zero, and used these values as the estimates of seasonal variation.

Source: Beveridge, *Prices and Wages in England*, vol. I, p. 82.

would follow exactly the same procedure, finding the mean of deviations for corresponding weeks or months during the year. There are, it should be noted, a number of other methods of isolating seasonal variation, which can be found described in detail in the books on statistics listed in the bibliography.

Once any seasonal fluctuations have been eliminated from the

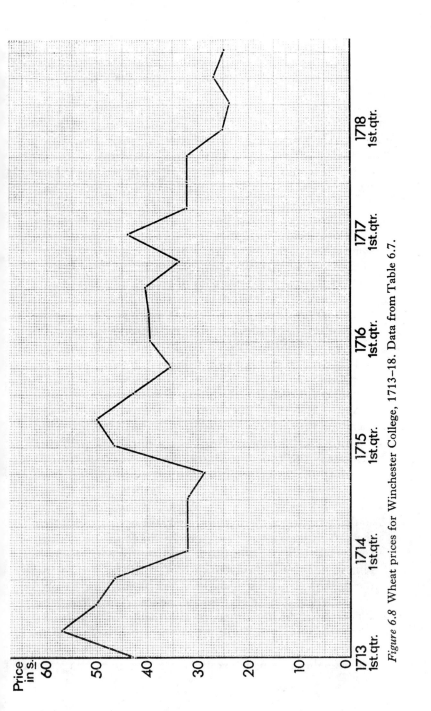

Figure 6.8 Wheat prices for Winchester College, 1713–18. Data from Table 6.7.

data, we are left with two other types of fluctuation, one regular and one irregular. The first, the regular fluctuation, is normally known as cyclical fluctuation, and is distinguished from seasonal fluctuation in that cyclical fluctuations are normally said to occur at intervals longer than one year. The most common type of such fluctuations are those known as business or trade cycles, which are used by economic historians to describe the regular or semi-regular alternations in economic activity which occurred most obviously in the nineteenth century; business cycles have a regular alternation from slump to boom and back to slump, over a period usually of seven to ten years, although some economic historians have tried to distinguish 'long waves' in economic activity lasting over centuries.

As we have said, the methods of time series analysis assume that there may be cyclical fluctuations in a time series, and therefore provide means of isolating the effects of those fluctuations. Whether a historian should use these means of isolating cyclical fluctuations depends entirely, however, on whether he feels that there are such cycles in his historical series. It is a historical, not a statistical question. The historian may feel, for example, that there is no reason to believe that any regular cyclical factor affected his data, and that his time series was therefore affected only by a long-term trend and by irregular fluctuations. If he believes this, then he should not use methods that attempt to remove a non-existent cyclical component and he can ignore the next few paragraphs.

If, however, we have some grounds for believing that there is a cyclical component in a time series, then we need to isolate it so that we can study it, and also study the irregular fluctuations that will be left when we have removed both trend and cyclical component from the time series. The most common method of removing the cyclical component from a series is that known as the method of moving averages. The procedure and results of the method of moving averages can be seen from Table 6.8 and Figure 6.9, which show a set of hypothetical data with an absolutely regular cyclical fluctuation, with a peak every four years, and a trough every four years. If, as shown in Table 6.8, we take the arithmetic mean of the first four values, then the mean of the second to fifth values, then the mean of the third to sixth values, etc., we get a series that is absolutely regular and linear – that is, with no fluctuations in it. We have therefore removed the effect of the cyclical component by taking moving averages.

This method has, however, a number of difficulties which are normally insufficiently appreciated by historians. With the data of Table 6.8 we have removed the cyclical component by taking moving averages over a four-year period; we have done this, rather than taking the average over, for example, three years, because our hypothetical series has an absolutely regular periodicity (distance from peak to peak or from trough to

Table 6.8 *Method of calculating moving averages: hypothetical data*

Time period	Data value	Total of four years	Average of four years	Total of five years	Average of five years
0	6				
1	5	20	5		
2	4	20	5	26	5·2
3	5	20	5	25	5·0
4	6	20	5	24	4·8
5	5	20	5	25	5·0
6	4	20	5	26	5·2
7	5	20	5	25	5·0
8	6	20	5	24	4·8
9	5	20	5	25	5·0
10	4	20	5	26	5·2
11	5	20	5	25	5·0
12	6	20	5	24	4·8
13	5	20	5	25	5·0
14	4	20	5	26	5·2
15	5				
16	6				

Note: The totals of *n* years, and the moving average values, are by convention placed in the table opposite the midpoints of the time periods from which they are calculated.

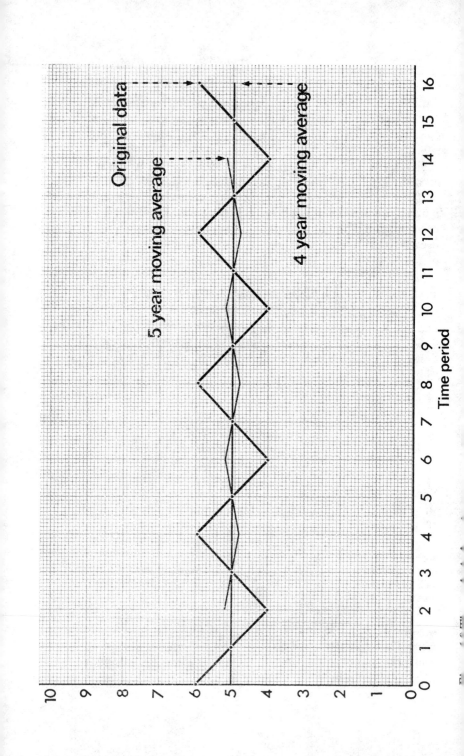

Original data

5 year moving average

4 year moving average

Time period

trough) of four years. The method works, therefore, when we know what the periodicity of the cycle is; we can then choose our moving average to suit that periodicity.

In most historical examples, however, it is difficult to decide exactly what the periodicity of the cycle is. Business cycles in the nineteenth century varied in length, for example, from five to ten years. It might seem that we could simply fix on some average length of cycle, say nine years, and use that as the basis for a moving averages calculation. Unfortunately, the success of the moving averages method is highly dependent on the choice of the period over which it is taken, and a wrong choice can produce extremely misleading results. This can be seen from Table 6.8; if we had, for some reason, taken a five-year moving average of our data, we would not have produced a smooth series. Moreover, the peaks in our five-year moving average series would correspond with the troughs in the original series, and the troughs with the peaks; the series based on moving averages would be a totally inaccurate reflection of the original series.

In the example of Figure 6.9 it is obvious that a misleading impression has been created. In real historical examples, however, it may be very much less obvious, and the historian who wishes to use the moving average method should always be alert to the possibility that, in removing the cyclical component, he is distorting the time series that remains.

(A further difficulty with the method of moving averages is that it has been shown that it can introduce regular fluctuations into a series in which no regular fluctuations existed. Further investigation of the effects of this possibility on historical time series is needed; in the meantime historians should be wary of using moving average methods with long time series.)

If the historian is satisfied that there is a regular cycle in a time series, and if he can clearly identify the periodicity of that cycle, then the method of moving averages is appropriate. Table 6.9 (columns III, IV and V) shows a five-year moving average applied to the data of Table 6.1, on the historical assumption that there is a five-year cycle of economic activity affecting British domestic exports between 1820 and 1850. Column V of that table gives the cyclical component of the

Table 6.9 *Method of splitting time series of Table 6.1 into three influences*

Year	I Data value (I)	II Trend value (II)	III Deviation (I–II)	IV Sum of five deviations	V Moving average of III: cyclical fluctuation	VI Non-cyclical fluctuation
1820	36·4	30·8	+5·6			
1821	36·7	31·8	+4·9			
1822	37·0	32·9	+4·1	+19·6	+3·9	0·2
1823	35·4	33·9	+1·5	+17·0	+3·4	−1·9
1824	38·4	34·9	+3·5	+6·7	+1·4	+2·1
1825	38·9	35·9	+3·0	+1·8	+0·4	+2·6
1826	31·5	36·9	−5·4	−1·9	−0·4	−5·0
1827	37·2	38·0	−0·8	−9·6	−1·9	+1·1
1828	36·8	39·0	−2·2	−15·3	−3·1	+0·9
1829	35·8	40·0	−4·2	−14·7	−2·9	−1·3
1830	38·3	41·0	−2·7	−20·5	−4·1	+1·4
1831	37·2	42·0	−4·8	−22·7	−4·5	−0·3
1832	36·5	43·1	−6·6	−22·0	−4·4	−2·2
1833	39·7	44·1	−4·4	−18·0	−3·6	−0·8
1834	41·6	45·1	−3·5	−7·0	−1·4	−2·1
1835	47·4	46·1	+1·3	−6·5	−1·3	+2·6
1836	53·3	47·1	+6·2	−1·2	−0·2	+6·4
1837	42·1	48·2	−6·1	+5·3	+1·1	−7·2
1838	50·1	49·2	+0·9	+4·2	+0·8	+0·1
1839	53·2	50·2	+3·0	−2·6	−0·5	+3·5
1840	51·4	51·2	+0·2	−2·4	−0·5	−0·7
1841	51·6	52·2	−0·6	−3·5	−0·7	+0·1
1842	47·4	53·3	−5·9	−3·2	−0·6	−5·3
1843	52·3	54·3	−2·0	+0·4	+0·1	−2·1
1844	58·6	55·3	+3·3	+1·5	+0·3	+3·0
1845	60·1	56·3	+3·8	+7·8	+1·6	+2·2
1846	57·8	57·3	+0·5	+3·2	+0·6	−0·1
1847	58·8	58·4	+0·4	+3·1	+0·6	−0·2
1848	52·8	59·4	−6·6	+9·3	+1·9	−8·5
1849	63·6	60·4	+3·2			
1850	71·4	61·4	+10·0			

Note: Addition of column II (Trend), column V (Cyclical fluctuation) and column VI (Non-cyclical fluctuation) gives column I (Original data).

series, which is subtracted from the detrended series (column III) to leave a residual series (column VI).

Before discussing this residual series, we should note that the method of moving averages has one further disadvantage; it gives no values for several years at the beginning and end of the time series. This is particularly serious when a long-period moving average is used; the thirty-one-year moving average used by Beveridge for some of his agricultural price series involves the loss of information on fifteen years at the beginning and fifteen years at the end of each series. Whether or not the disadvantage is sufficient to preclude the use of the method of moving averages will depend on the characteristics of the time series being studied, and on the importance of the values at the beginning and end of the series.

Once we have removed the cyclical component from the series, we are left with a residual time series, shown in column VI of Table 6.9. This represents the irregular fluctuations in the series, since we have removed from the series both the trend and the regular fluctuations. If we had considered that it was not possible to discern a cyclical fluctuation in the series, then we should have regarded column III of Table 6.9 as being composed of irregular fluctuations. No further simple manipulation of the series can be carried out, and the historian must use other skills and historical knowledge to explain why these irregular fluctuations occurred when they did. The substantial upward fluctuation in 1836, and the downward fluctuation in 1837, for example, can be closely related to the boom and then collapse of the American economy; British exports to the United States were cut by two-thirds between 1836 and 1837.

We must conclude this section on the analysis of fluctuations in time series by emphasizing once again that the historian must ensure that the assumptions of time series analysis are matched by historical assumptions which he can make about the specific time series with which he is concerned. This necessity is most apparent when the method of moving averages is being used; for this reason one common use of moving averages – to give an impression of the trend in the series – is of very doubtful validity, unless a regular cycle of known periodicity can be assumed to exist in the time series. If the assumptions of time series analysis can be met, however, then the methods are very useful in allowing the historian to study the different components in a time series, and to explain them without possibility of confusion between long- and short-term, regular or irregular movements.

(e) The use of ratios and index numbers

It is often useful, when analysing a time series, to express each value in the series as a proportion of the value in one year, often the value of the first year in the series. By doing this, we can easily see what proportionate changes are taking place in the series. In examining the data on British exports, for example, it would be useful to know by what proportion exports in 1830, 1840 and 1850 exceeded those in 1820, thus giving an impression of the growth in the value of exports. We can calculate these proportions simply, by dividing each of the values for 1830, 1840 and 1850 by the value for 1820, with the result shown in Table 6.10.

Table 6.10 *British domestic exports, as proportion of 1820 value*

Year	Original value (£ million)	Original value divided by 1820 value
1820	36·4	1·0000
1830	38·3	1·0522
1840	51·4	1·4121
1850	71·4	1·9615

We could, if we wished, express each value in the time series as a proportion of the 1820 value, thus creating a new time series with values starting at 1·0000 in 1820, and ending with 1·9615 in 1850. We can also, and it would be more normal to do this, express the values not as proportions but as percentages of the 1820 value. Thus 1820 would have the value 100·0, 1830 would be 105·2, 1840 would be 141·2, and 1850 would be 196·2.

We call this process 'transforming the series into ratio form, with a base year 1820 = 100'. To express a series in this form has several advantages, principally that it is easier to appreciate proportional changes when we are shown ratios than if we have to do mental arithmetic to express 51·4 as a proportion of 36·4. This can be particularly valuable when the units of the time series are awkward to handle; wage rates, for example, are often given in shillings and pence, and changes in them can be much more easily appreciated when they are given in the form of a ratio series. A further advantage of ratios is that it is easier to compare one series with another. For example, if we wish to compare the growth in exports from 1820 to 1840 with the growth of imports over the same period, it is easier to compare a rise from 100 to 141·2 in exports, and from 100 to 168·3 in imports, that a rise from £36·4 million to £51·4 million in exports with a rise from £54·2 million to £91·2 million in imports.

Table 6.11 *British domestic exports as ratio series, with different base years*

Year	Original value (£ million)	1820 = 100	1830 = 100	1840 = 100	1850 = 100
1820	36·4	100·00	95·04	70·82	50·98
1830	38·3	105·22	100·00	74·51	53·64
1840	51·4	141·21	134·20	100·00	71·99
1850	71·4	196·15	186·42	138·91	100·00

The value of the ratio is clearly dependent on the value in the base year. Series of ratios derived from the same original series' will vary according to the base year that is chosen. Table 6.11 shows the effect of choosing different base years on the series of export values given in Table 6.10.

It is apparent from Table 6.11 that not only do the values of the ratios change with changes in the choice of base years, but so also, as a natural consequence of the method, do the intervals between the values. Thus it is as true to say that the interval between the value of exports is 2·66 (base 1850 = 100) as it is to say that the interval is 5·22, or 4·96, or 3·69. The higher the value for the base year, the smaller will be the intervals in the ratio series between years with lower values.

It is important that we should be conscious of this fact when we choose the base year on which to calculate our series. In a series, such as that of British domestic exports, which has a rising trend, choosing an early year as a base will give an impression that the series is growing rapidly (e.g. from 100 to 196·15), while choosing a later year will seem to reduce the growth (e.g. from 50·98 to 100). There is in fact no difference in the proportional change, but a different impression is created, at least on the casual reader. Equally, in a series that shows considerable fluctuations, the series of ratios will give a different impression depending on whether the base year chosen is a year of considerable upward or downward fluctuation from the trend.

The choice of base year is thus crucial to the use of ratio series. It is rarely possible to say that there is a correct answer to the problem of choice, although in general we should choose a year with a value close to the trend line. It may also be sensible to choose a year close to the centre of the series, but these two requirements may unfortunately conflict. Moreover, the problem is often complicated by the need to use the ratios to compare two or more series. In such a case, we must choose a base year for all the series which will least distort any one of them, a task that is often very difficult and for which no rules can be laid down.

These drawbacks of ratios have to be set against the very real benefits in clarity that the use of ratios makes possible. The drawbacks can be mitigated by stating the original values together with the index numbers, so that the reader can see how far presentation in index number form is altering his impression of the data.

So far in this section we have considered the case in which one or more time series are transformed individually into ratio form. Another, possibly more important, use of ratios is to produce a composite index, linking together a number of different time series. The most familiar example of such an index is the index of retail prices, and others that have been used in historical work are indices of wage rates and indices of the cost of living. Such indices are extremely important in the consideration of such problems as that of whether living standards have improved or fallen, as for instance during the Industrial Revolution. In order to answer such questions, it is necessary to compare costs of living with income or wages; if this is to be done then indices of living costs and wages need to be prepared.

As an example of the methods by which such indices are prepared, and of the difficulties, both statistical and historical, that are involved, we shall consider the preparation of an index of living costs between 1890 and 1900. The term 'living costs' includes expenditure on food, rent, clothing, fuel and miscellaneous goods, and we must therefore take account of movements in the costs of each of these items. Any one of these items, in addition, is itself made up of a number of different costs; we must take account of the fact that the price of bread may alter in a different way from the costs of meat or fish or other foods. Let us assume for the sake of clarity, however, that we have compiled indices of the main components in living costs; these are given in Table 6.12.

Our problem is to merge these indices of different living costs into one index. One method might be simply to take the arithmetic means of the different index numbers for each year. For 1890, for example, this would give us

$$\frac{101 + 93 + 102 + 80 + 89}{5} = \frac{465}{5} = 93.$$

The difficulty with this procedure is that we are trying to compile an index that will give us an impression of changing living costs for real people between 1890 and 1900. Now it is extremely unlikely that anyone spent equal parts of their family income on each of the five component living costs. Most people spend more on food than on other requirements, and there is certainly no reason why expenditure on clothing should have been the same as expenditure on fuel. Therefore, in order that we should be able to apply our cost of living index to the problem of changing living standards between 1890 and 1900, we have to take account of the differing importance in the family budget of different expenditures. Simply taking an arithmetic mean of the five items is therefore unsatisfactory; we need instead to give more weight, for example, to changes in food prices than to changes in fuel prices, since changes in food prices will have a greater effect.

We do this by assigning 'weights' to each of our five items. These weights are given in Table 6.12. Essentially, we judge that for the average family in this period, expenditure on food was five times as great as expenditure on clothing so that changes in food prices should be regarded as five times more important than changes in the price of clothing. To calculate our composite

Table 6.12 *Components of an index of living costs, 1890–1900*
        (base: 1900 = 100)

Year (weights)	Food (60)	Rent (16)	Clothing (12)	Fuel (8)	Sundries (4)	Composite index
1890	101	93	102	80	89	97·68
1891	103	94	102	78	85	98·72
1892	104	95	101	78	81	99·20
1893	99	96	100	85	81	96·80
1894	95	96	99	73	75	93·08
1895	92	97	98	71	75	91·16
1896	92	98	99	72	75	91·52
1897	95	98	98	73	75	93·28
1898	99	99	97	73	74	95·68
1899	95	99	96	79	76	93·72
1900	100	100	100	100	100	100·00

Source: A. L. Bowley, *Wages and Income in the United Kingdom since 1860* (Cambridge, Cambridge University Press, 1937), pp. 120–1.

index for each year, therefore, we multiply the index number for each item by its weight, and divide by the sum of the weights (in this case $60 + 16 + 12 + 8 + 4 = 100$, but the weights need not sum to 100) to give us our composite index number, shown in the last column of Table 6.12. For example, for 1890 we have $(101 \times 60) + (93 \times 16) + (102 \times 12) + (80 \times 8) + (89 \times 4) = 9768$, and dividing by 100 (the sum of the weights) we get 97·68 as our composite weighted index number of living costs.

The calculation of a weighted index is thus a comparatively simple arithmetical exercise. The difficulty of the construction of composite index numbers of this kind lies not in the statistical procedures, but in the historical assumptions and decisions about evidence that have to be made. For example, in calculating the index in Table 6.12, and calling it our index of U.K. living costs, we have assumed that the weights we have used are those of an average family budget in the 1890s, and apply to upper class or working class families, Scottish or Devonshire families, with or without children. In calculating the food price index, we have had to make similar assumptions about the weights to be given to each type of food. We have assumed, further, that family budgets in 1890 were divided up in the same way as in 1900, so that we can use the same weights; while this may be sensible over a ten-year period, it is much more difficult to make a similar assumption for 1870 or even 1914. In addition, we have made a choice of 1900 as a base year; the difficulties of such a choice have already been discussed.

All these assumptions and decisions have to be made if we are to derive a composite index. The point of emphasizing the difficulties of constructing such indices is not to suggest that the task should not be attempted; composite indices are too valuable to the social and economic historian. They must be constructed, however, in full knowledge of these difficulties, since the accuracy and usefulness of the final index depends, to a greater or lesser extent, on the validity of each of the assumptions made.

The major use to which an index of living costs, such as that which we have just produced, might be put is in the interpretation of other data on prices and incomes. It is often very important for an economic or social historian to know whether price or income changes that he observes were the result of 'real' changes – in, for example, the quality of the goods whose price he is studying, or the skill of the worker whose wage he has discovered – or whether the changes were the result of general inflationary or deflationary pressures. In the sixteenth century, for example, the general 'price revolution' raised prices considerably over the century, and it is important for the historian studying the price of one commodity to isolate the effect of the general price movement from the particular price movements affecting that one commodity; he would need to calculate the 'real' price of the commodity. Similarly, the historian who wishes to study changes in the standard of living of the working class needs to be able to discover the 'real' wage, that is the wage adjusted for the changes in the prices of goods that the worker has to buy; wages have to be expressed, in other words, in terms of their purchasing power.

In both these cases, a set of 'money' values, either of prices or of wages, has to be deflated by a price index, to produce a set of 'real' values. As an example, we can use the index of living costs, calculated in Table 6.12, to deflate a series of wages. The wage series is shown in the first column of Table 6.13; it was produced in much the same way as the composite index of living costs, by taking a weighted average of a number of wage series for different occupations. The index was originally calculated with a base of 100 in 1914, and has been recalculated and displayed in the second column of the table with a base of

Table 6.13 *Construction of an index of real wages, 1890–1900*

Year	Money wages (1914=100)	Money wages (1900=100)	Cost of living (1900=100)	Real wages (1900=100)
1890	83	88·3	97·7	90·4
1891	83	88·3	98·7	89·5
1892	83	88·3	99·2	89·0
1893	83	88·3	96·8	91·2
1894	83	88·3	93·1	94·8
1895	83	88·3	91·2	96·8
1896	83	88·3	91·5	96·5
1897	84	89·4	93·3	95·8
1898	87	92·6	95·7	96·8
1899	89	94·7	93·7	101·1
1900	94	100·0	100·0	100·0

Sources: Money wage index from E. C. Ramsbottom, reprinted in B. R. Mitchell and P. Deane, *Abstract of British Historical Statistics*, p. 345. Cost of living index from Table 6.12.

1900 = 100; this is done simply by dividing each value by 94 (the value for 1900) and multiplying by 100. The third column of Table 6.12 shows the composite cost of living index. We divide each value of the cost of living index into the corresponding value of the money wage index, multiply the result by 100 and give the final figure in the fourth column of the table.

It can easily be seen from Table 6.13 that the 'real' wage index that we have just calculated differs significantly from the money wage index. The money wage index is stable from 1890 to 1896 and then rises to 1900, while the real wage index falls to 1892, then rises to 1895–6, and then falls slightly before rising to 1900. The historian studying such matters as trade union history in this period would need to be aware of this divergence; knowledge of the money wage rates alone would probably not be a good guide to the labour history of the period.

It has only been possible, in this section, to discuss the most simple of several different methods of constructing indices, together with the most common of the uses to which they can be put. Methods of construction differ not so much in the underlying logic, which has been presented in this section, but in the ways of assigning weights, choosing base years, and similar matters. Historians faced with problems involving indices should therefore consult one of the books listed in the bibliography, in the light of the logical concepts that have been presented.

7 Relationships between variables

We have discussed, in earlier chapters, the bulk of quantitative techniques that have been used by historians; until recently few books or articles on historical topics made use of more complicated methods than those, such as frequency distributions, measures of central tendency and of dispersion, and methods of time series analysis, that we have described. The use of these statistical methods has produced a very large amount of important historical work. Yet a historian who is willing to use quantitative techniques should not stop at this stage, but should be willing to use other, more complicated methods which will help him in the analysis of historical materials. It is impossible in this book to discuss all such methods, and we shall therefore concentrate in this chapter on techniques that explore a central problem in the writing of history – that of the relationship between two sets of historical events. The methods that will be discussed fall under the general heading of 'correlation and regression techniques'.

Many problems discussed by historians can be summed up as problems of whether a 'relationship' exists. We want to know, for example, whether there is a relationship between crew size and type of power in our study of the shipping industry in 1907, or between income and social status in 1688, or between number of swine and size of parish in 1086, or between the result of one vote in the House of Commons and the result of another vote, or between exports from and imports into Great Britain in the nineteenth century. In asking whether a relationship exists we simply wish to know whether two or more events are entirely independent of each other, or whether there is some connection, however tenuous, between them. Having decided whether a relationship exists, we can go on to ask how strong it is, and what form it has. We ask, for example, whether it is so strong that when A happens, B is bound to follow, or weaker such that B will follow A on most, but not all, occasions. We ask whether the relationship has the form that when A increases, B increases, or whether the relationship is inverse, such that B decreases when A increases.

A large body of statistical techniques exists to help us to answer questions such as these. It is important to recognize, however, that these techniques can help us only if we have used our historical knowledge to ask sensible, historical questions. Thus it would be perfectly possible to use these statistical techniques to test for the existence of a relationship between votes in the House of Commons and phases of the Moon and it might well happen that, by coincidence, a statistical connection could be shown to exist between them. This connection would, however, have no historical meaning, and would be a worthless result to a historian. It would be a stupid question to ask whether such a connection existed, and we would naturally get a stupid result. In other words, before we use correlation and regression methods we must be able to specify how we think two variables might be related, and then see whether our theory is supported by the statistical evidence; we must be able to describe the likely relationship in historical as well as in statistical terms.

There are, in essence, three questions that we may try to answer about the relationship between two or more historical events. They are:

1 Is there a relationship?
2 What is the strength of the relationship?
3 What is the form of the relationship?

We shall now discuss the statistical techniques that will help us to answer such questions.

(a) Is there a relationship?

Let us imagine that, as the result of a historical study, we believe that one series of events is related to another series of events. In other words, we have a hypothesis that has the form 'I think that variable 1 is related to variable 2'. In some cases, the hypothesis may be trivial, and the proof self-evident; the statement 'The beheading of traitors in Tudor England was related to their deaths' is such a hypothesis. Most interesting hypotheses about relationships will not be of this form; they will not be testable by reference to some law of physiology that people cannot live without their heads, but will require more complicated proof.

We can most easily approach the problem of how we can prove the truth of a hypothesis such as 'Variable 1 is related to variable 2' by contrasting that hypothesis with an alternative hypothesis, 'Variable 1 is not related to variable 2'. This alternative hypothesis is equivalent to the hypothesis that 'Variable 1 is independent of variable 2', by which we mean that we expect to find no relationship between a value of variable 1 and a value of variable 2 (other than the trivial relationship that they both relate to the same case). A further equivalent hypothesis is that 'A value of variable 1 gives us no help at all in predicting the value of variable 2 for the same case'. As an example, we can contrast the hypothesis that 'Crew size is related to size of ship' with the alternatives, 'Crew size is not related to size of ship', or 'Crew size is independent of size of ship', or 'Knowing crew size does not help us at all to predict size of ship'.

The value of restating our initial hypothesis in terms of these alternative hypotheses is that we can then proceed, in investigating the relationship between the two variables, to ask 'What might the data set look like if the two variables really were independent of each other?' We construct, in fact, an alternative data set, based on the hypothesis that the variables are independent, and contrast this with the actual data set on which we have based our first hypothesis that the two variables are related. If the two data sets, one real and one hypothetical, look much the same, then we shall probably conclude that it is safest to assume that the two variables are not related. If the two data sets differ considerably from each other, then we shall be safe in assuming that there is probably some relationship between the variables. We will still not know what form the relationship is, merely that the data do not support the hypothesis of no relationship. With our shipping example, for instance, we construct an alternative data set, based on the hypothesis of independence, and contrast it with our actual data set; if we find that the two are very dissimilar, we conclude that there is a relationship between crew size and size of ship. We then continue, partly through further statistical work and partly on the basis of historical knowledge, to investigate what the relationship might be caused by.

In order to be able to carry out this process of contrasting the real with the hypothetical data set, we need to do two things. We need to construct the alternative hypothetical data set, and we need to judge whether that hypothetical data set really differs from our real data set. We shall discuss two methods of doing this. The first, the calculation of the contingency coefficient C, is suitable whether the data are of nominal, ordinal or interval type; the second, the calculation of the correlation coefficient R, is suitable only when the data are of interval type. We shall not discuss several other methods that are suitable when the data are of ordinal type; ordinal data are uncommon in historical work, and these methods are therefore unlikely to be used frequently.

It should be noted, however, that it is sometimes sensible to make use of methods suitable for ordinal data, when the data are apparently of interval type, but when one has some doubts about them. An example is that of the Gregory King data on incomes and social classes, quoted in Chapter 1. In such cases, ordinal methods can be used as a safety measure, the results being compared with those from methods suitable for interval data. Information on tests suitable for use with ordinal data may most conveniently be found in an invaluable book: S. Siegel, *Nonparametric Statistics for the Behavioural Sciences*.

We shall first consider the calculation and interpretation of the contingency coefficient C; as its name implies, its most frequent use is in deciding whether a relationship exists between variables that have been tabulated in the form of a contingency table. We can illustrate its use most clearly through the use of a simple example, drawn from the political history of

Britain. The Parliament elected in 1841 was one in which the allegiance of members of Parliament to their respective parties, Liberal and Conservative, was quite strong, but in which, on some issues, other loyalties transcended party ties. On the question of the abolition of the Corn Laws in 1845–6, for example, a large number of Conservatives voted against the Conservative leader and Prime Minister, Sir Robert Peel. It is therefore of interest to discover whether voting followed party lines on other issues in that Parliament. For example, we may investigate whether party ties determined voting behaviour in the division at the end of the debate in 1844 on whether the daily labour of children in cotton factories should be limited to ten hours. In that division, 94 Liberals and 100 Conservatives voted in favour of limitation, while 56 Liberals and 135 Conservatives voted against. This vote is set out in the form of a contingency table on the left-hand side of Table 7.1.

We are interested in whether party ties were related to the votes of M.P.s on this issue. Our initial hypothesis is therefore that party ties and votes were related, while our alternative hypothesis is that party ties and votes were independent of each other. In order to choose between these hypotheses we need to construct an alternative pattern of voting, on the assumption that party ties and votes were independent; having done this, we can contrast the real voting pattern with the hypothetical voting pattern.

If the proportion of, for example, Liberal members voting for the bill was much greater than the proportion of all members voting for the bill, we would naturally suspect that allegiance to the Liberal party would be likely to produce a vote for the bill. By contrast, if party ties did not affect votes on this issue at all, then we would expect to find that the proportion of Liberals who voted for the bill would be roughly the same as the proportion of all members voting for the bill. This contrast, based on commonsense, suggests how we might begin to build up our hypothetical voting pattern, imagining that there was no connection between party tie and vote.

A total of 385 members voted in the division, of whom 194, or 50·4 per cent, voted in favour, and 191, or 49·6 per cent, voted against. Of the 385 who voted, 150 were Liberals, and the remaining 235 Conservatives. Taking the Liberals first, if there had been no connection between Liberal ties and voting on the bill, then we would expect that roughly 50·4 per cent of them would have voted for the bill, and 49·6 per cent against.

Table 7.1 *Actual and hypothetical votes on the Ten Hours Bill, 1844*

| | Observed voting figures | | | Expected voting figures | | |
	For	Against	Total	For	Against	Total
Lib.	94	56	150	75·6	74·4	150·0
Con.	100	135	235	118·4	116·6	235·0
Total	194	191	385	194·0	191·0	385·0

Source: W. O. Aydelotte, 'Voting patterns in the British House of Commons in the 1840s', *Comparative Studies in Society and History*, vol. V (1963), pp. 134–63, Table 3.

Calculating that 50·4 per cent of 150 is 75·6, we argue that, on the assumption of independence, or no connection, we should have expected 75·6 Liberals to vote for the bill, instead of the 94 who actually did so. This figure of 75·6 is known as the 'expected value' (expected under the assumption of independence) of Liberals voting for the bill; the figure of 94 is known as the 'observed value'.

We can then calculate expected values for the other possible combinations of party tie and vote, and, arranging the results in a contingency table, can contrast the 'expected' with the 'observed' voting pattern, as in Table 7.1. Note that we have calculated, and given on both sides of the table, the row, column and grand totals. This serves two purposes: firstly it enables us to check our calculation of expected values, by ensuring that the row and column totals are the same as in the original data, and secondly it provides us with a convenient method of calculating the expected values. This is because the expected value for each cell of the table can be found by multiplying the total of the row in which it falls by the total of the column in which it falls, and dividing the result by the grand total. Thus, for the Liberals voting for the bill, the expected value is given by

$$\frac{150 \times 194}{385} = 75 \cdot 6$$

which is the same result as we achieved earlier.

We have now carried out the first part of our task, that of constructing an alternative, hypothetical, data set under the assumption of no relationship between voting behaviour and party tie. We have secondly to compare the observed with the expected voting figures, to determine which of our hypotheses (that the variables are related or that they are not related) appears to be most acceptable. We do this by subtracting each cell of the table of expected votes from the equivalent cell of the table of observed votes, squaring to remove the minus signs, and dividing by the expected value for the cell to express the result in a relative form. We then sum the result for all, giving us a quantity that is known as χ^2, pronounced as 'ky square' and written 'chi-square'. For Table 7.1 the calculations are therefore

$$\chi^2 = \frac{(94 - 75 \cdot 6)^2}{75 \cdot 6} + \frac{(56 - 74 \cdot 4)^2}{74 \cdot 4} +$$

$$\frac{(100 - 118 \cdot 4)^2}{118 \cdot 4} + \frac{(135 - 116 \cdot 6)^2}{116 \cdot 6}$$

$\chi^2 = 14 \cdot 8$.

The general form of the formula for χ^2 is, therefore

$$\chi^2 = \sum_{i=1}^{R} \sum_{j=1}^{C} \frac{(O_{ij} - E_{ij})^2}{E_{ij}}$$

where R is the number of rows, C is the number of columns, i is the row subscript, j the column subscript and the O_{ij} and E_{ij} are respectively the observed and the expected values for each cell.

In the particular case of a contingency table with two rows and two columns, such as Table 7.1, the general formula will produce an inflated result for chi-square. We must therefore use an alternative formula, which is both simpler to use and more accurate. If we label the cells of a 2×2 contingency table, as in Table 7.2, chi-square is given by the formula

$$\chi^2 = \frac{N\left(|AD - BC| - \dfrac{N}{2}\right)^2}{(A + B)(C + D)(B + D)(A + C)}.$$

(In this formula, $|AD - BC|$ indicates the 'absolute value' of $AD - BC$; that is, we ignore the sign, and treat the term as positive even if BC is greater than AD.)

For the data of Table 7.1, chi-square computed by this formula is

$$\chi^2 = \frac{385(|(94 \times 135) - (56 \times 100)| - 385/2)^2}{(150 \times 235 \times 194 \times 191)}$$

$$= 14 \cdot 02.$$

This alternative formula must be used for a 2×2 contingency table when N is larger than 40. If this latter condition is not satisfied, Siegel[1] should be consulted for alternative procedures.

Table 7.2 *Labelling the cells of a 2×2*
contingency table

A	B	$A + B$
C	D	$C + D$
$A + C$	$B + D$	N

Since we have a 2×2 contingency table, with $N = 385$, we will use a value for chi-square of $14 \cdot 02$ in taking the next step in our calculation, the computation of the contingency coefficient C. This is related to chi-square by the simple formula

$$C = \sqrt{\frac{\chi^2}{N + \chi^2}}$$

so that, for our data

$$C = \sqrt{\frac{14 \cdot 02}{385 + 14 \cdot 02}} = 0 \cdot 1875.$$

[1] S. Siegel, *Nonparametric Statistics for the Behavioural Sciences* (New York, McGraw-Hill, 1956), p. 110.

We must now interpret this result in terms of our desire to discover whether a relationship existed between party tie and voting behaviour for this vote on the Ten Hours Bill. If we go back to the first formula for chi-square, we can see that, if our actual data had been identical to our hypothetical data, so that observed values were equal to expected values, χ^2 would have had a value of zero. If we now look at the formula for C, we can see that, if chi-square were zero, then C would also be zero.

We have in fact found a non-zero value for C, indicating that the actual voting pattern and the hypothetical voting pattern differed from each other. The voting pattern thus does not support the alternative hypothesis, that party tie and voting behaviour were unrelated, and we can conclude that there was some connection between voting behaviour and party tie in the vote on the Ten Hours Bill. We should note, however, that we have not yet considered either how strong the connection was, nor what form it took, nor what other factors might also have been connected with voting behaviour; we shall return to these questions later in the chapter, but at the moment our concern is simply with whether a relationship exists.

The contingency coefficient thus provides a means by which we may contrast an actual data set with a data set constructed on the basis of a hypothesis of no relationship between the variables. It is a measure that can be widely applied, to data of different types. When we have data of interval type, however, we may as an alternative make use of a different method – that of the correlation coefficient. This measure makes use of the additional information that interval data give us, and it is also of considerable use in more advanced statistical work; for both these reasons, R should be preferred to C when we have interval data.

We shall consider the computation of R (or, to give it its full name, 'Pearson's product-moment coefficient of correlation') through the example of the shipping data which we used in Chapter 4 (see p. 44). Among the variable characteristics of the ships, we listed the tonnages of the ships, and the size of the crews. A student of the history of shipping at this period, around 1907, will be aware that there was a tendency for the average size of ships to increase. It is possible that this increased the demand for seamen, in that bigger ships needed more men to man them; on the other hand, it is also possible that much of the increasing size was cargo space, which did not increase the demand for seamen so much as the demand for shore-based cargo handlers. It is therefore of interest to investigate whether there is, for the data of Table 4.1, a relationship between the tonnage of ships and the size of their crews.

The initial hypothesis is that there is such a relationship. The alternative hypothesis is that tonnage and crew size are independent. Let us consider, initially, how we would expect our data to appear, under each of these hypotheses. If crew size and tonnage are related, then we would expect that knowledge of one of these variables, for a particular ship, would give us some information, however rough, about the probable size of the other variable for that ship. For example, we would probably expect that a large ship would have a large crew, and a small ship a small crew. We might even expect that, comparing one ship with another, a ship with twice the tonnage of another might be expected to have roughly twice the crew size of the other.

By contrast, if crew size and tonnage were entirely independent, we would not expect that high values of one variable would be associated with high values of another. Indeed, we would expect that, for each value of tonnage, there would be a scatter of values of crew sizes, some higher, some lower, some in the middle. Knowledge of the tonnage would not help us in any way even as an aid to guessing what the size of crew might be.

In distinguishing between these two hypotheses, we have described a possible case where the two variables are related as being one in which, if the tonnage is high, so is the crew size; for the alternative hypothesis, if the tonnage is high, then crew size might be high or low. The questions that immediately arise are: 'What does one mean by high or low?' 'How do we measure these relative concepts?' It will be recalled that one method of judging whether a particular value of a variable is high or low is to discover whether it is above or below the mean of that variable, and how far it is from the mean. We can therefore re-phrase our two hypotheses, and say that, firstly, if the two variables are related to each other, we would expect that a ton-nage above the mean tonnage would be related to a crew size above the mean crew size. If, secondly, the two variables are independent, then a tonnage above the mean tonnage would be just as likely to be accompanied by a crew size below the mean crew size as by one above the mean crew size. Under the assumption of independence, part of the data set might look like the situation represented in Table 7.3.

Table 7.3 *Hypothetical shipping data, under assumption of independence between variables*

Ship	A: Relationship to mean tonnage	B: Relationship to mean crew size	$A \times B$
1	Above mean (+)	Below mean (−)	A negative no.
2	On mean (0)	On mean (0)	Zero
3	Above mean (+)	Above mean (+)	A positive no.
4	Below mean (−)	Below mean (−)	A positive no.
5	Below mean (−)	Above mean (+)	A negative no.

If, for each ship, we multiply its deviation from mean ton-nage, A, by its deviation from mean crew size, B, we shall sometimes get a positive, sometimes a negative quantity, depend-ing on which of the situations represented in Table 7.3 suits the particular ship. Over the long run, these positive and negative quantities will tend to cancel each other out, so that the sum of the positive and negative quantities, the products of the devia-tions from the means, will be close to zero.

Alternatively, if the two variables are related, then we might have a situation which is like that represented in Table 7.4.

Over the long run, again, a situation such as that represented in Table 7.4 will produce, summing all the products of deviations, a large positive number.

This suggests that one way of deciding whether the two variables are related is to examine the result of taking, for each case, the product of its deviation from the mean of each variable, and summing over cases. If the result is close to zero, then it will be likely that the two variables are not related, but if the result is some way from zero, it will be reasonable to suppose that a relationship exists.

Table 7.4 *Hypothetical shipping data, under assumption of relationship between variables*

Ship	A: Relationship to mean tonnage	B: Relationship to mean crew size	A × B
1	Above mean (+)	Above mean (+)	A positive no.
2	Above mean (+)	Above mean (+)	A positive no.
3	On mean (0)	On mean (0)	Zero
4	Below mean (−)	Below mean (−)	A positive no.
5	Above mean (+)	Above mean (+)	A positive no.

In order to discover whether two variables are related, therefore, we may begin by looking at the deviations from the mean of each variable for each case. We will, in terms of a formula, calculate

$$\sum(X - \bar{X})(Y - \bar{Y}).$$

If the result of this calculation is zero, we shall be safe in assuming that the two variables are unrelated. If, however, the result differs from zero, there will appear the difficulty that the result is likely to be larger the more cases there are; it will also be larger if the variables are expressed in, for example, millions rather than hundreds, although the proportional deviations may be no different. In order to facilitate comparisons between different sets of data, therefore, we can divide our result firstly by the number of cases, and secondly by the product of the standard deviations of each variable. This removes the effect of having differing numbers of cases, and of some sets of data having a larger spread of values around the mean than others.

The resulting formula,

$$\frac{\sum(X - \bar{X})(Y - \bar{Y})}{Ns_X s_Y}$$

where s_X is the standard deviation of one variable, and s_Y the standard deviation of the other variable, is the formula for R, the product-moment correlation coefficient. It will have the value of zero if the two variables are unrelated, and a value either larger or smaller than zero if the two variables are related.

If we remember that the standard deviation of X is given by

$$s = \sqrt{\left(\frac{\sum(X - \bar{X})^2}{N}\right)}$$

we can rewrite the formula for R as

$$R = \frac{\sum(X - \bar{X})(Y - \bar{Y})}{N\left[\sqrt{\left(\frac{\sum(X - \bar{X})^2}{N}\right)}\right]\left[\sqrt{\left(\frac{\sum(Y - \bar{Y})^2}{N}\right)}\right]}.$$

This formula can be rewritten in a more convenient form, removing the need to calculate deviations from the mean, as

$$R = \frac{N\sum XY - \sum X \sum Y}{\sqrt{([N\sum X^2 - (\sum X)^2][N\sum Y^2 - (\sum Y)^2])}}$$

and Table 7.5 shows the procedure for calculating R from the shipping data of Table 4.1.

As Table 7.5 shows, the value of R for the shipping data is non-zero, and we can therefore conclude that the real shipping data differ from the hypothetical data which we might have constructed under the assumption of independence between the variables. In calculating R we do not actually construct an alternative data set, as we did with the contingency coefficient C, but the principle remains the same – of contrasting a real data set with a hypothetical data set. In essence, with both measures we ask the question: 'Is the data set we have different from the data set we would have expected if the variables were independent?' If either C or R are non-zero, then this question is answered by 'Yes' and we reject the hypothesis of independence in favour of the hypothesis that the variables are related.

(b) *How strong is the relationship?*

We have, in the previous section, discussed how one may determine whether two variables are related to each other. As we pointed out, this does not exhaust the questions one may ask

Table 7.5 *Calculation of correlation coefficient R, for data of Table 4.1*

Official no.	Crew size Y	Tonnage X	Y^2	X^2	XY
1697	3	44	9	1 936	132
2640	6	144	36	20 736	864
35052	5	150	25	22 500	750
62595	8	236	64	55 696	1 888
73742	16	739	256	546 121	11 824
86658	15	970	225	940 900	14 550
92929	23	2 371	529	5 621 641	54 533
93086	5	309	25	95 481	1 545
94546	13	679	169	461 041	8 827
95757	4	26	16	676	104
96414	19	1 272	361	1 617 984	24 168
99437	33	3 246	1 089	10 536 516	107 118
99495	19	1 904	361	3 625 216	36 176
107004	10	357	100	127 449	3 570
109597	16	1 080	256	1 166 400	17 280
113406	22	1 027	484	1 054 729	22 594
113685	2	45	4	2 025	90
113689	3	62	9	3 844	186
114424	2	68	4	4 624	136
114433	22	2 507	484	6 285 049	55 154
115143	2	138	4	19 044	276
115149	18	502	324	252 004	9 036
115357	21	1 501	441	2 253 001	31 521
118852	24	2 750	576	7 562 500	66 000
123375	9	192	81	36 864	1 728

$\Sigma Y = 320$ $\Sigma X = 22\,319$ $\Sigma Y^2 = 5932$ $\Sigma X^2 = 42\,313\,977$ $\Sigma XY = 470\,050$

$$R = \frac{N\Sigma XY - \Sigma X \Sigma Y}{\sqrt{([N\Sigma X^2 - (\Sigma X)^2][N\Sigma Y^2 - (\Sigma Y)^2])}}$$
$$= \frac{25(470\,050) - (320)(22\,319)}{\sqrt{[(25(42\,313\,977) - 22\,319^2)(25(5932) - 320^2)]}}$$
$$= 0.9093.$$

about relationships between variables. A second question in which we are likely to be interested is: 'How strong is the relationship?'

A simple, but over-simple, answer to this question would be that the more either C or R differs from zero, the stronger is the relationship between the two variables. While this is true, it is not a complete answer to the question since one would also like to know what the value of C or R is if two variables are perfectly related; by 'perfectly related' we mean that there is some fixed relationship between the two variables, such that knowledge of a value of one variable for a particular case enables one to know exactly what the value of the other variable will be for that case. Having defined the range of values that C and R might attain, from independence to total dependence, one could then judge the strength of the relationship in any particular set of data, and also compare one set of data with another in terms of the strength of relationship between variables that each displays.

If we consider the contingency coefficient C, we find that, as we know, the case of independence will produce a value of zero. Unfortunately, the maximum value of C is dependent on the size of the contingency table. For a 2×2 table, perfect relationship between the variables will give $C = 0.707$; for a 3×3 table the maximum value of C is 0.816. Knowing this allows us to say that, in our example, the association between party tie and vote of the Ten Hours Bill, with $C = 0.1875$, is rather weak, well down in the possible range of values of C for a 2×2 table. We cannot, however, compare a value of C from a 2×2 table with a value of C from a 3×3 table, and, in addition, we do not know the maximum values for C for contingency tables where the number of rows is not equal to the number of columns. These are serious drawbacks of the use of the contingency coefficient, and of other measures based on χ^2 which are used to study the degree of relationship between variables. The contingency coefficient has been described in this text, therefore, not because it is an ideal measure, but because it is perhaps the most frequently used measure, and because the logic used in its calculation underlies many other tests. The historian wishing to make use of tests of this type would therefore be well advised to consider other tests, described in books mentioned in the bibliography.

If we have interval data, however, we are more fortunate, in that the possible range of values of the correlation coefficient R is clearly defined; R will be zero if the variables are unrelated, will have a value of $+1$ if the variables are perfectly and positively related, and will have a value of -1 if the variables are perfectly and inversely related. By positively related we mean that, if one variable has a high value, it is likely that the other variable will also have a high value; in an inverse relationship, one variable will have a high value when the other has a low value and vice versa. Since the possible range of values of R is so clear, we can say that the closer the value that we get from our data is to $+1$ or -1, the closer is the relationship between the variables. Since also the range of values is not dependent on the number of cases, we can compare directly the R value from one set of data with the R value from another set of data.

Our data on tonnage and crew sizes of merchant ships have produced an R of $+0.9093$. This indicates that there is quite a strong positive relationship between these two variables in the data we have used. If these data are representative of all ships in 1907, then we might be able to say that a strong relationship existed between tonnage and crew size for all British merchant ships in 1907; this, however, is a separate question which will be considered in the next chapter. For the moment, it must be emphasized that the existence of a particular R for one set of data does not imply that a similar R, or a similar relationship, exists for all data of the same kind.

Since values of R from different sets of data can be directly compared, we might continue our investigations of merchant shipping by calculating the correlation coefficients between tonnage and crew size for other years, to see whether the relationship between tonnage and crew size was strengthened or weakened as time passed. Before doing this, however, we should be quite clear about the exact interpretation of R, and of differing values of R, which are further discussed in the next section.

(c) *The form of relationships*

In some historical problems it is sufficient simply to try to establish that two variables are related, and to make an estimate of the strength of the relationship. Provided that the relationship is reasonably strong, and the historian is satisfied that it is more than coincidental (a question to which we return in the next chapter), he can then bring his historical knowledge to bear, and explain the historical meaning of the relationship. In many cases, however, attention will be focused not on the existence of a relationship, which can be assumed to exist or which is self-evident, but rather on the exact form of the relationship.

For example, a student of economic history can normally

assume that there is some relationship between the volume of a particular article being manufactured and the price at which the article can be sold. He will therefore not be particularly interested in establishing that the relationship exists, but will wish instead to investigate exactly how price varies with the quantity offered for sale. By contrast, a student of political history in the nineteenth century may consider that a demonstration that M.P.s voted according to party ties is an important contribution to knowledge by itself. As can be seen from these examples, one of the important factors determining which feature of a relationship is of interest is the state of theoretical or empirical knowledge about the relationship. It can, however, be assumed that the goal in all studies, from whatever theoretical or empirical base they began, is to discover as much as possible, and we shall proceed on this basis during the rest of this section.

Let us first take the question of what we mean by the form of the relationship between two variables. We mean the way in which the two variables are related, which we shall discover by answering such questions as: 'Is the relationship positive or inverse?' 'By how much does variable X have to alter to produce a change in variable Y?' 'Do changes in variable X explain all changes in variable Y, or are other factors involved?'

If our data are of nominal type, have been classified in contingency tables and analysed by the use of the contingency coefficient or a similar measure, these questions are either inapplicable or cannot be answered by any specific method of statistical analysis. The contingency coefficient, unlike the correlation coefficient, always has a positive value, so that its calculation does not tell us whether the relationship between two variables is positive or inverse. But in fact we do not need a test to tell us this; if we ask, was being a Liberal positively related to voting for the Ten Hours Bill, we can answer by looking directly at the vote. It makes little sense, however, to ask whether party tie in general was positively or negatively related to vote on the Ten Hours Bill; the two variables were either related or not related, and we use the statistical tests we have described to find out.

Statistical analysis can, however, help considerably with a question which is important in deciding the form of a relationship between two nominal scale variables. We have considered the vote on the Ten Hours Bill in terms of the question: 'Were party ties important in determining votes on the bill?' In deciding that they were, however, we have not considered the question of whether other factors acting on M.P.s were of equal, or even greater, importance. We might in fact expect that party tie would be one factor that an M.P. would take into account, but that he would also have definite 'ideological' views which would sometimes lead him to oppose his party. One such group of views, which led many Conservatives to oppose Peel in 1846, was that concerned with the importance of protecting British agriculture. If this hypothesis, that M.P.s, individually or in groups, had common 'ideologies' in addition to their party allegiances, then it should be possible to identify such ideologies through a study of the votes of M.P.s on a number of issues. Methods that aid in the solution of historical problems of this type are those known as Guttmann scaling techniques, which test contingency data for the existence of a spectrum of issues, and, ideally, allow individuals to be placed along the spectrum, according to their votes on each of the issues. M.P.s who vote in favour on all issues will be at one end of the scale, those who vote against on all issues will be at the other end, and those in favour on some issues and against on others will occupy intermediate positions. If a scale of this type can be identified in the data, as it has been by Professor Aydelotte in his study of the British Parliament of the 1840s,[1] then it can give valuable information about the voting behaviour of M.P.s, and, to return to the subject of this section, on the relationship between votes on one issue and votes on another issue.

With the exception of techniques such as those of the Guttmann scale, however, the identification of the form of relationships with nominal data depends very greatly on the nature of the data and of the historical questions being considered. A number of studies are listed in the bibliography to show the different approaches that can be made to this question.

When the data are of interval type, on the other hand, the

---

[1] W. O. Aydelotte, 'Voting patterns in the British House of Commons in the 1840s', *Comparative Studies in Society and History*, vol. V (1963), pp. 134–63.

range of statistical techniques available is considerably greater, and we may attempt with some chance of success to answer the questions about the form of the relationship between two variables which we posed earlier in this section. With interval data, the use of the correlation coefficient enables us to establish whether a relationship exists between two variables, while the sign of the correlation coefficient tells us whether the relationship is positive or inverse. Calculation of R for the data on ships' tonnages and size of crew, for example, showed that a relationship existed between those two variables, that it was a reasonably strong relationship ($R = +0.9093$) and that it was positive: as tonnage increased, so did crew size.

Neither the correlation coefficient nor its sign, however, tells us very much about the exact form of the relationship between the variables. They do not, for example, tell us by how many tons the size of a ship had to increase before an extra seaman was needed to help to man the ship. Yet such information is valuable; if we are interested in the impact of an increasing size of ship on employment in the shipping industry, we need this information. Similarly, one of the major controversies about British industry between 1870 and 1914 is concerned with whether output per man was increasing or decreasing; information on the number of men required to deal with ships of particular sizes would be relevant to this, particularly if comparisons could be made with earlier periods than that to which our data relates.

What we need to know is the relationship between a rise in tonnage and a rise in crew size. We need to be able to answer a question such as: 'How big a rise in tonnage was needed to produce a demand for one additional seaman?' Figure 7.1 shows the shipping data as a scatter diagram with tonnage on the horizontal axis and crew size on the vertical axis. If we look at this graph, we can see that the question we have just asked ('On average how much must tonnage rise to produce a demand for one extra seaman?') is equivalent to asking: 'How far along the horizontal axis must we go to produce a rise of one unit on the vertical axis?' It will be recalled that this is very much like the question we considered when calculating the linear trend in

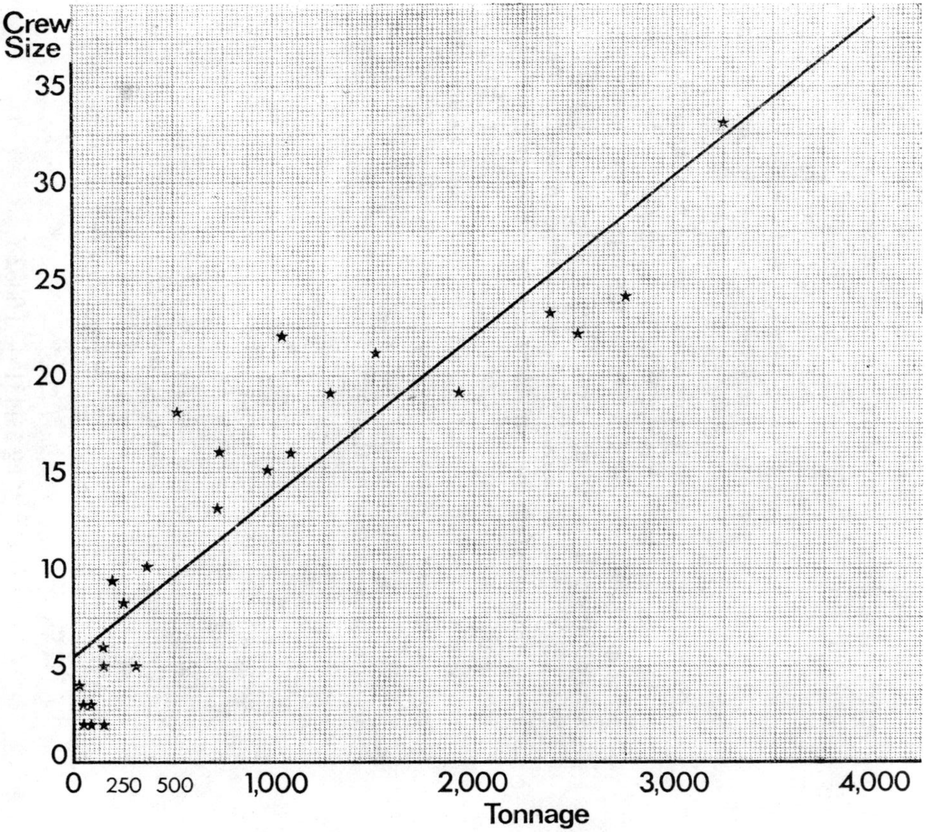

Figure 7.1 Scatter diagram showing crew size plotted against tonnage. Data from Table 4.1.

time series data: 'How far along the horizontal axis, representing time, must we go to produce a rise on the vertical axis?' This similarity suggests that we can use the same method, of fitting a line as close as possible to a set of data points, to answer our question about the relationship between tonnage and crew size.

It will be recalled that we fitted a line to our time series data by the use of the least-squares method (see pp. 97–109). The same methods are equally appropriate to the present problem; *a*, the intercept term, has the same meaning exactly, being the point at which the fitted line crosses the vertical axis above the zero point on the horizontal axis. The slope, *b*, represents in this case the number of times by which a change in tonnage must be multiplied to find the equivalent change in crew size – just as, in the time series example, it represented the number of times by which a change in years had to be multiplied to find the equivalent rise in exports. Again, just as with the time series example, application of the least squares formula will allow us to write an equation of the form

$$Y = a + bX$$

where *a* is the intercept term, *b* the slope, *Y* the crew size and *X* the tonnage.

Table 7.6 shows the calculations involved in applying the least squares formula to the shipping data, with the result that we can fill in the values for *a* and *b* in our equation, and state that the relationship between tonnage and crew size is described by the equation

$$Y = 5{\cdot}4481 + 0{\cdot}0082X.$$

The line which has been fitted to the data, and which is described by this equation, is shown as the line drawn on Figure 7.1.

This process of fitting a line to a set of data points is known as 'fitting the linear regression line of *Y* on *X*'; or, alternatively, as 'regressing *Y* on *X*'. In this particular example we have regressed crew size on tonnage. We could, simply by calling crew size the *X* variable, and tonnage the *Y* variable, have carried out the alternative procedure of regressing tonnage on crew size; this would, however, make little historical sense. It

Table 7.6 *Calculation of regression line, data of Tables 4.1 and 7.5*

$$\sum Y = 320 \qquad\qquad \sum Y^2 = 5932$$
$$\sum X = 22\,319 \qquad\qquad \sum X^2 = 42\,313\,977$$
$$\sum XY = 470\,050$$

$$b = \frac{N\sum XY - \sum X \sum Y}{N\sum X^2 - (\sum X)^2} = \frac{11\,751\,250 - 7\,142\,080}{25(42\,313\,977) - 498\,137\,761}$$
$$= 0{\cdot}008\,235.$$

$$a = \frac{\sum Y - b\sum X}{N} \qquad \frac{320 - 183{\cdot}797\,0}{25}$$
$$= 5{\cdot}4481$$

Regression line $Y = 5{\cdot}4481 + 0{\cdot}0082X$

seems most likely that shipowners in 1907 built ships of a tonnage that they wanted to have and then found the crew to man them; it seems very unlikely that they found a crew and then built a ship of the correct size to employ them. In other words, historically it seems likely that crew size was dependent on tonnage rather than vice versa, and we therefore try to fit the regression line so as to answer the question: 'Exactly how was crew size dependent on tonnage?' For this reason, the Y variable, in this case crew size, is known as the 'dependent variable', and the X variable, on which the Y variable depends, is known as the 'independent variable'. We choose which variable should be regarded as dependent, and which as independent, on the basis of our historical knowledge.

The regression equation, $Y = 5{\cdot}4481 + 0{\cdot}0082X$, which we have just derived by fitting the regression line of Y on X, tells us the relationship, on the average, between the two variables, tonnage and crew size. The line is, in fact, an estimate of the relationship; it is the best estimate that we can make on the basis of the data that we have been given, but we do have to recognize that it is only an estimate, since the line does not pass exactly through all the data points, but merely as close as possible to them. We therefore need to know how close the line is to the data points, which is equivalent to knowing how good the estimate is of the relationship between the variables.

If the 'fit' to the data points is very close, and the estimate therefore good, we shall have confidence in our statement, 'On average, an increase of tonnage of one ton produced an increased demand for seamen of 0·0082 seamen' (or, more easily: 'On average, an increase in tonnage of 1000 tons produced an increased demand for seamen of 8·2 seamen'); if the fit is not very good, then we shall not be so fully confident, and shall be less certain in describing the effects of changing size of ships on the labour force.

One measure of the goodness of fit of the regression line to the data is the correlation coefficient. If the data points fall in a straight line, so that the higher the tonnage the higher the crew, then the correlation coefficient will be 1. As the data points diverge from the line, the correlation coefficient will tend towards zero. The correlation coefficient, in this case $R = + 0·9093$, therefore tells us that, as we have already seen, the relationship between the variables is quite strong, and the fit of the regression line to the data points is quite good.

An alternative method of considering the goodness of fit is to consider how far the calculation of the regression line of X on Y helps us to explain the variation in Y. If we recall our time series example, we remember that we calculated the linear trend in the time series and obtained the trend values. We then agreed that these trend values could be regarded as representing that part of the time series determined by, or explained by, the influence of the passing of time, and we therefore subtracted the trend values from the time series; the result of this subtraction we regarded as being that part of the time series determined by other factors, such as cyclical fluctuations. By 'the passing of time' we meant of course a whole complex of changing conditions, represented in the time series by the passing of years.

In a similar way, we can try to separate changes in Y (crew size) into two parts, the first explained by the changing tonnage, and the second regarded as being due to other factors. The part explained by tonnage will be represented by the regression line (as the part explained by time was represented by the least squares trend), while the part explained by other factors will be represented by the deviations of the data points from that line. We consider the changes in, or variation in, crew size, as being a variation around the mean crew size, as we have done before to express them in a relative form. Essentially, we are arguing that crew size varied (around its mean) for a number of reasons, one of which was changing tonnage; we want to find how much of the variation was the result of changing tonnages, and how much was due to other factors.

Figure 7.2 demonstrates how we can do this. For each data point, such as that shown as A on the graph, the distance from the mean is divided into two parts, the first from the mean to the regression line, and the second from the regression line to the data point. (An alternative method of looking at this process is to consider how far knowledge of the regression line allows us to improve a guess of the value of crew size for a particular value of tonnage. If we know nothing about the relationship between crew size and tonnage, the best guess of the crew size, for any tonnage, will be the mean crew size. Knowledge of the regression line allows us to improve on this, by the distance between the mean crew size and the crew size estimated from the regression line. The measure of how far our guess is improved is the closeness of the regression estimate to the actual data point.)

If, on this basis, we regard the variation between the mean and the regression line as being that part of the variation in crew size explained by the influence of tonnage, we can see that a measure of the goodness of fit of the regression line (and thus of the accuracy of our estimate of the relationship between tonnage and crew size) is the proportion that this 'explained variation' is of the total variation of crew size about its mean.

In Figure 7.2 we have shown the relationship between total, 'explained' and 'unexplained' variation about the mean crew size for just one data point. To calculate the variation explained by the regression equation about the mean, for all data points, we square all the variations (to remove the effect of positive and negative variations cancelling each other out) and sum over all

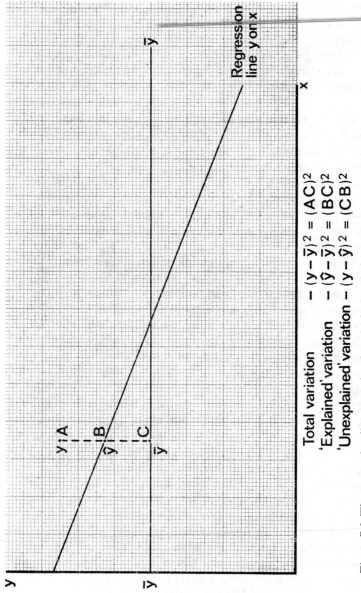

Total variation $-(y - \bar{y})^2 = (AC)^2$
'Explained' variation $-(\hat{y} - \bar{y})^2 = (BC)^2$
'Unexplained' variation $-(y - \hat{y})^2 = (CB)^2$

Figure 7.2 The regression line as an 'explanation' of variation.

the data points. The result, known as the coefficient of determination is then

$$\frac{\sum(\hat{Y} - \bar{Y})^2 \text{ (distances between mean and regression estimates)}}{\sum(Y - \bar{Y})^2 \text{ (distances between mean and data values)}}.$$

The calculation of this coefficient of determination is somewhat laborious, although arithmetically simple once the regression line has been calculated. For this example, it is 0·8268, and we therefore argue that the regression line fits so well to the data points that it explains 0·8268, or 82·68 per cent of the variation in Y. In other words, 82·68 per cent of the variation in crew size is explained by variations in tonnage.

In practice we do not need to calculate the coefficient of determination directly, since it can be shown that it is equal to the square of the correlation coefficient R. For this reason the coefficient of determination is normally written as R^2. The best measure of the goodness of fit of the regression equation is hence the square of the correlation coefficient, since it tells us exactly what proportion of the variation in Y we have explained by the regression equation of Y on X, as being due to the influence of X. This fact also helps us to judge the strength of the relationship between two interval scale variables, which we discussed in the last section. If we calculate that the correlation between two variables is, for example, 0·9, then 81 per cent of the variation in the dependent variable is being explained by the influence of the independent variable; if the correlation coefficient is, in another case, only 0·6, then only 36 per cent of the variation is being explained. One should, for this reason, not claim too much for relationships for which R is less than 0·7, since less than half of the variation can be attributed to the influence of the relationship, more than half being due to other factors.

In conclusion, four important points about correlation and regression analysis must be emphasized. The first is that, throughout this chapter, we have been concerned only with linear correlation and regression – that is, with a situation in which the data points can be represented by a straight line. It is perfectly possible for a very strong non-linear relationship to exist between two variables; if this is so, calculation of the linear correlation coefficient R will give a very low correlation, and a linear regression line will give a very poor fit to the data. For this reason, it is sensible always to plot data on a scatter diagram such as Figure 7.1, before calculating R and the regression line. They should be calculated only if a straight-line relationship appears to exist; if a curved line would seem likely to give a better fit, then textbooks of advanced statistics discuss appropriate methods.

Secondly, we have considered an example in which only one independent variable is considered to affect the dependent variable. The methods described can be extended to examples in which there are more than two or more independent variables. If this is so, the techniques are those of multiple regression analysis, rather than the simple regression analysis discussed here; again, advanced statistics textbooks should be consulted for detailed advice.

Thirdly, correlation and regression techniques are often used in historical work to make general statements about the relationship between two variables on the basis of limited evidence. We might wish, for example, to make a general statement about the relationship of crew size to tonnage, on the basis of our evidence, which is limited to data on twenty-five merchant ships in 1907. The problems that arise from such an attempt are considered in the next chapter; in this chapter we have been solely concerned with relationships in the data we have in front of us, not with generalization from those data.

Fourthly, we must emphasize again that the methods of correlation and regression analysis, and similar methods for nominal and ordinal data, make sense and should be used only when the historian has a clear theory which connects the variables whose relationship he is trying to describe. Well-fitting regression lines, and hence high R^2s, can appear for totally fortuitous reasons, and no credence should be attached to them unless the relationship they purport to describe can be understood and explained in a way entirely divorced from the statistical method.

(d) Correlation and regression with time series data

A historian will often wish to explore the relationship between two variables, each of them a time series. Indeed, this is a much more likely project in historical research than the type of example that has been used in the last section, often called a 'cross-sectional' study, in which there was no element of time. The reason for using that example, however, was that the element of time introduces complications into correlation and regression analysis, which can only be discussed after the principles of that analysis have been considered. It will not be possible to consider more than one of these complications, and any historian actually contemplating carrying out regression analysis on time series data should consult more advanced textbooks for further information.

The major complication in the application of regression methods to time series data is that the correlation of two linear trends will always be perfect – perfectly positive if both trends are moving in the same direction, perfectly negative if they are not. This can easily be seen from Figure 7.3, in which two linear trends are plotted separately against time, and then together in a scatter diagram, where all the points on the scatter diagram fall in a straight line, indicating a perfect correlation. It follows from this that, if we calculate the correlation coefficient between two time series, each of which has a linear trend, the value of R will be affected by the presence of the trend. If, for example, we are interested in the relationship between British imports and exports in the early nineteenth century, the fact that both had rising time trends will tend to make the correlation coefficient quite high, and positive. If what we are interested in showing is that both imports and exports were rising, then this will not matter. It is more likely, however, that what we are interested in is the relationship between fluctuations in imports and exports; we want to know whether a rise in imports results in a rise in exports – and if so, by how much. If we are interested in the relationship between fluctuations, then clearly we do not want the correlation and regression estimates to be influenced by the linear trends.

It is therefore important for the historian to know if time trends are affecting his results. Sometimes the effects of time acting in this way are apparent from an inspection of a graph or scatter diagram, but sometimes such evidence can be ambigu·

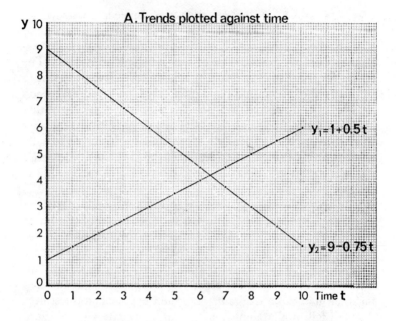

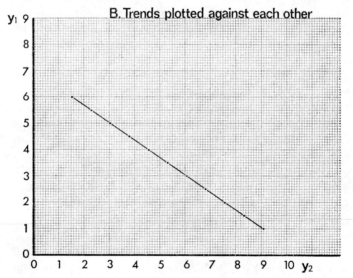

Figure 7.3 Correlation of two linear trends.

ous. It is sensible, therefore, to make use of some measure of the possible disturbing effects of time, and it is for this reason that many historians use a test known as the Durbin–Watson test, which leads to the calculation of a value called $d*$. To understand this test, which is also known as a test for autocorrelation, we must return to the method described in the last section, and graphed in Figure 7.2, by which the variation in the dependent variable was seen as being made up of two parts – one 'explained' by the variation of the independent variable, and the other an 'unexplained' variation. For each data point, the difference of the value of the dependent variable from the mean of all values was similarly partitioned, into the difference of the regression line from the mean (BC in Figure 7.2) and the remainder (AB in Figure 7.2); this remainder is often known as 'the residual', and the set of such remainders for all data points as 'the residuals from the regression equation'. It is an important assumption of regression analysis that successive residuals are 'independent' of each other; statistical independence is a concept which is explained more fully in Chapter 8, Section (b), but broadly it means that the value of one residual should have no effect on the value of the next. If this is not so, then this underlying assumption of regression is violated, autocorrelation is said to exist, and the values of the regression coefficients a and b in the equation

$$Y = a + bX$$

and of the coefficient of determination R^2 may be affected so as to make them an unreliable representation of the true relationship between Y and X.

The effects of time on two time series make it very likely that successive residuals will not be independent when the series are regressed one on the other. Data points from contiguous time periods, for example successive years, are likely to be close together, and their residuals from the regression line are thus likely to be correlated. Autocorrelation produced by the effects of time is a common problem for the historian, who should therefore conduct the Durbin–Watson test whenever two time series are regressed. The calculation of $d*$ is quite simple, for if the e_t (where t is the time period) are the residuals then

$$d^* = \frac{\sum\limits_{t=2}^{n}(e_t - e_{t-1})^2}{\sum\limits_{t=1}^{n} e_t^2}.$$

The interpretation of the value of d^* normally requires reference to a set of tables. As a rough guide, a value of d^* of approximately 2 will indicate that there is no autocorrelation, while values close to 0 or to 4 will indicate that there is positive or negative autocorrelation. The historian who uses the test should report both the value of d^* and its interpretation. Dr N. von Tunzelmann, for example, studied the relationship between British imports and exports in the early nineteenth

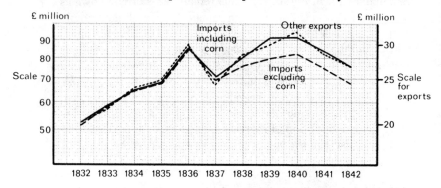

Figure 7.4 Imports including and excluding corn, and Other Exports. *Source:* N. von Tunzelmann, in 'On a Thesis by Matthews', *Economic History Review*, vol. XX (1967).

century, with exports to countries other than Europe ('Other Exports' – X_0) as the dependent variable.[1] Imports including corn was the independent or explanatory variable in one regression analysis, and imports excluding corn in another; in both analyses, logarithms of both independent and dependent variables

[1] N. von Tunzelmann, in 'On a Thesis by Matthews', *Economic History Review*, vol. XX (1967), pp. 548–54. I am grateful to Dr von Tunzelmann and to the Editors of the *Economic History Review* for allowing me to reprint graphs 7.4–7.6 from this article.

were used since the interest lay in the relationship between the growth of the series. The series are graphed in Figure 7.4. In the first analysis, there was a very strong relationship between the two series, suggested in the graph and demonstrated by an R^2 of 0·991. However, the Durbin–Watson statistic d^* is 3·55; this is close to 4, which indicates negative autocorrelation, and this is demonstrated graphically by the 'saw-tooth' pattern which is found when the actual values of X are compared with the estimated values, as in Figure 7.5. In the second analysis,

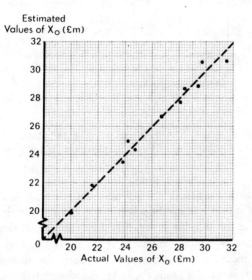

Figure 7.5 Actual values of Other Exports and of estimated values from a regression of Other Exports on Imports including corn. *Source:* N. von Tunzelmann.

R^2 was 0·965, and d^* was 0·85. This indicates positive auto-correlation, and the pattern of residuals was that in Figure 7.6; most of the early values lie above, and the later values below, the regression line, showing the effects of time on the estimated relationship. This could also be demonstrated by graphing the residuals from the regression equation against time.

The effects of time do not make analysis impossible, however, since various methods exist by which the data can be transformed

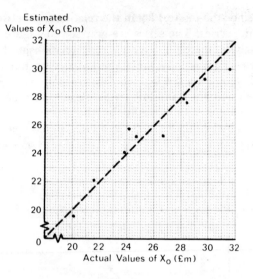

Figure 7.6 Actual values of Other Exports and of estimated values from a regression of Other Exports on Imports excluding corn. *Source:* N. von Tunzelmann.

to remove a disturbing time trend. One way to do this, described in Chapter 6, is to calculate the linear trend in each variable and to subtract the trend value from each data value; this creates a 'detrended' series which can then be used in the regression analysis. Similarly, a new series can be created by removing a strong cyclical influence from the data. An alternative method, which is particularly appropriate when we are interested in the relationship between year-by-year changes in two time series – such as the changes from year to year in Figure 7.4 – is to create a new series for each by subtracting each yearly value from its predecessor. Such a series is known as a series of first differences. Dr von Tunzelmann used a slightly more complex method and found that the regression of exports on the import series including corn then gave an $R^2 = 0.993$ and $d^* = 2.04$; for imports excluding corn $R^2 = 0.882$ and $d^* = 1.80$. In both cases, therefore, the transformation of the data series eliminated any serious autocorrelation, but did not seriously affect the strength of the relationship between the series as measured by R^2. The existence of autocorrelation does not, therefore, present an insuperable obstacle to regression analysis of time series, but the historian should be aware of its possible effects and of the use and meaning of the Durbin–Watson statistic.

8   The problem of imperfect data

Every historian, as he approaches a historical problem, forms in his mind a picture of the evidence that he would like to have to enable him to solve his problem. We can consider this ideal as a set of data, the possession of all of which would provide a complete answer to whatever question the historian wishes to ask. Each historical problem will have, in this schematic sense, its own ideal data set, although clearly one data set will overlap with another, just as one historical problem overlaps with another. We can consider each ideal data set as consisting of a set of cases; each case is composed of a set of variable characteristics which distinguish one case from another, and the whole makes up an ideal data matrix.

In some historical problems, it is easy to specify what such an ideal data matrix would contain. Suppose that we are interested in the demographic history of one parish in the eighteenth century; our ideal data matrix would then contain, as the minimum necessary to establish the chronology of population change, dates of the birth, marriage and death of each inhabitant of the parish during the century. If we are interested in exploring the causes of population change we may wish to add such variables as occupation and income to our data set. In other historical problems, the ideal data set may be less easy to define, but can easily be imagined to exist.

In the ideal data matrix, there will be information available on all cases and on all variables for each case. We shall have enough, and just enough, information to enable us to answer the question we wish to ask. In the process of collecting our evidence, discussed earlier in Chapter 2, we will try to fill up the data matrix to provide evidence on each case, and on each variable of each case, so that, at the end of the process of collecting data, we shall have a real data matrix, of the same size as our ideal matrix, on which to begin the analysis of the data.

Unfortunately, so far as the majority of historical problems are concerned, the real data that we are able to collect will not fit our ideal matrix so exactly or completely. The most common complaint of historians is phrased, 'If only we knew more about such and such', while this complaint is closely followed by: 'I've got so many data I don't know what to do with them!' The real data matrix will, in other words, almost certainly differ in some way from the ideal data matrix which the historian has, either consciously or unconsciously, set up for himself as he begins to consider his problem.

The real data matrix may differ from the ideal in many ways, but it is possible to reduce the divergences from the ideal into four stereotypes, recognizing that any real data matrix may exhibit one, more than one, or all of these divergences from the ideal. The four are:

(*a*) That there is too much information.
(*b*) That information is missing on one or more complete cases.
(*c*) That information is entirely missing on one or more variables.
(*d*) That information is missing on some variable characteristics of some cases, but no case or variable is entirely missing.

The first of these possible divergences from the ideal is peculiar in that no data are missing; rather, the problem is that there are too many data for the historian to be able to use them effectively. It is considered here because such a situation represents a divergence of the real from the ideal data set and because the methods by which this imperfection may be overcome are relevant to the discussion of missing data situations.

(*a*) *Too much information: the selection of variables*

While the use of computers and electronic calculators has made it possible for historians to analyse material of great bulk and complexity, there are still some situations in which the historian has too much material. Lack of access to electronic aids is still common, and some historical data sets are so large that even with computers the task of processing the data effectively is too great. In such situations, if the historian wishes to continue to study the problem, he has to make a selection from the available evidence, and must base his conclusions on that selection. In other words, he selects cases and variables from his real data set until he has filled up his ideal data set. The problem that he faces is to establish the principles on which the selection should be made.

We shall consider first the problem of making a selection of variables, and take as an example a method of historical inquiry which is increasingly used, that of 'collective biography'; by this term is meant the accumulation of biographical information about as many as possible of those men and women who took part in some political or economic activity. This method may be contrasted with the more traditional approach of considering only a few men or women who played a leading role. Professor Aydelotte, for example, has collected information about all the members of the Parliament of 1841, and has studied the actions of that Parliament through this information, rather than by the traditional approach of studying the actions of the party leaders, Peel, Graham, Russell, Bentinck, Disraeli and a few others.[1] Instead of studying merely the major figures in the great English overseas trading companies in the seventeenth century, Professor Rabb has collected information on all those who invested in the companies.[2] Other studies have been carried out of Frenchmen at the time of the Revolution of 1789,[3] Nazi supporters in Germany in the 1930s[4] and British industrial-

---

[1] W. O. Aydelotte, 'Voting patterns in the British House of Commons in the 1840s', *Comparative Studies in Society and History*, vol. V (1963), pp. 134–63.

[2] T. K. Rabb, *Enterprise and Empire* (Cambridge, Mass., Harvard University Press, 1967).

[3] C. Tilly, *The Vendée* (Cambridge, Mass., Harvard University Press, 1964).

[4] W. S. Allen, *The Nazi Seizure of Power* (Chicago, 1965).

ists,[1] and the term 'collective biography' has also been applied to the collection of comparative information about a number of parishes, towns and even countries.

In all these studies, the historians concerned have had to decide what information should be collected about the subjects of the study, and hence what information should not be collected. Often a decision of this type is forced upon the historian by the nature of the available evidence; Professor Rabb, for example, limited his study to the consideration of three variables for each investor: his social status, his membership of a Parliament and the companies in which he invested. Other information, such as dates of birth and death, office held, etc., was collected and used as an aid to identifying particular investors, but was not used in the analysis of data because it could be collected only for some of the 8683 investors whom Rabb identified. Professor Aydelotte was forced, for similar reasons, to omit information on the wealth and religion of his members of Parliament.[2]

A decision not to collect information about a particular variable may secondly be taken because it is believed that the variable is not relevant to the questions that are to be asked of the material. For example, Professor Rabb did not collect information on investment in three 'very important new enterprises of the period: . . . fen draining, shipbuilding and fisheries', because 'they would have taken me too far afield'.[3] In saying this, Professor Rabb is admitting that information on such investment would be very interesting, but is arguing that it is not relevant to the limited questions he wishes to answer about English investment overseas. Decisions about whether a particular set of information is, or is not, relevant to the subject being investigated must be taken in the light of historical knowledge of that subject. What the historian must do, on the basis of his knowledge, is to construct a theory which links

[1] C. Erickson, *British Industrialists: Steel and Hosiery* (Cambridge, Cambridge University Press, 1959).

[2] W. O. Aydelotte, *Quantification in History* (Reading, Mass., Addison-Wesley, 1971), p. 146.

[3] T. K. Rabb, p. 164.

together the questions he wants to ask with the evidence he will try to collect. Professor Rabb, for example, had in mind a theory of the determinants of English overseas investment which regarded social status, membership of a Parliament or investment in other ventures as important, and investment in other new projects (such as the three he mentioned) as relatively unimportant. Since these other investments are relatively unimportant, information concerning them does not need to be collected.

Such a theory, linking questions with evidence, is often given the name of a 'model'. In constructing a model, the historian draws on his historical knowledge, and on his knowledge of, for example, economic theory, to construct a picture of the determinants of a historical event or process. On this basis, he can then collect the relevant evidence and attempt to answer the questions that interest him. Such models can be simple, connecting only a small number of variables. Professor Rabb, for example, has three. Models can also be very complex, particularly in economic history; a model constructed by Professors Fogel and Engerman, for example, used twelve variables to describe the growth of the American iron industry in the nineteenth century.[1] However complex the model, its value is that it specifies precisely the theory that the historian has about his evidence and about the logical relationships between different variables. The model may of course be modified during the course of the study; that is indeed often the aim of the study, to produce a better theory to explain some historical process. But only if we have a clear idea of what our model or theory is, do we have a firm basis on which to decide whether a particular variable should be included in, or excluded from, our study.

We have so far considered the choice of variables as it is determined by the availability of evidence and by the model or theory developed by the historian. A third type of choice may be based on excluding variables that do not add any additional

[1] R. W. Fogel and S. L. Engerman, 'A model for the explanation of industrial expansion during the nineteenth century: with an application to the American iron industry', *Journal of Political Economy*, vol. 77 (1969), pp. 306–28.

information of any value to the information gained from other variables. In the most simple case, information may appear in two different forms; we may, for example, know from one source that a man was married, and from another source that he was 26 when he married. There is no point in using both these pieces of information, since the latter implies the former. In more complicated cases, the historian may feel that one variable is adequately represented by another; in his study of the impact of British railways, for example, Dr Hawke considered the importance of the railways for the carriage of wheat, but not their importance for the carriage of other grains. Since wheat was the most important grain transported, it was unlikely that the conclusions from his study would have been altered by the inclusion of other grains, and they were therefore excluded.[1] Just as with choices based on a model, such a choice to ignore a variable must of course be justified by the historian; but it is often acceptable, on the general principle that there is no point in duplicating information.

In general, variables should only be omitted as a result of conscious decision by the historian. Even when a variable has to be omitted because the evidence is not available, the historian should always be aware that something is thereby missing from his analysis. As Professor Aydelotte has written, 'The scholar must be guided by his knowledge of what is left out . . . as well as what is included, . . . and must take care not to draw inferences which, though consistent with the figures which he cites, do violence to the evidence which he has had to omit.'[2]

(b) Too much information: the selection of cases

While few general principles, other than those of care and honesty, can be laid down for the omission of variables, the theory of the selection of cases is well developed. It forms, as 'the theory of sampling', the basis for most textbooks of statistics. Since this is so, we shall not consider sampling methods in

[1] G. R. Hawke, *Railways and Economic Growth in England and Wales, 1840–1870* (Oxford, Clarendon Press, 1970), p. 192.
[2] W. O. Aydelotte, p. 147.

very great detail, but merely indicate the main principles that underlie them. This will serve the dual purpose of making it easier for historians to understand textbooks on sampling, should they ever wish to sample, and of providing a background for the discussion of missing data problems later in this chapter.[1]

In sampling, we make a selection of cases from our data. We want to reduce the amount of data with which we have to deal, without greatly reducing the accuracy of the results that we derive from the data. Our object therefore is that any conclusion we reach on the basis of our study of a selection of cases should be the same as the conclusion we would have reached if we had been able to study all the cases. In other words, we want the sample to provide us with a good estimate of the true result. If, for example, we are interested in discovering the mean tonnage of merchant ships in 1907, we will try to select a sample of ships whose mean tonnage will be the same as the mean tonnage of all ships. We might, similarly, be interested in more complicated characteristics of merchant ships – perhaps the proportion powered by steam, or the mean and standard deviation of crew size. Our aim is always the same: to find a sample that will allow us to make a good estimate of the characteristics in which we are interested.

Any method of selecting or sampling cases from the total data set will provide one with some sample data on which to form such an estimate. We could, for example, simply choose the first ten cases, or pick with a pin, or choose every ship we have heard of or those that have interesting names. Having made our selection, we could then calculate, for example, the mean tonnage of the ships in our sample, and we would have an estimate of the mean tonnage of all ships. Unfortunately, we would have no means of judging how accurate that estimate was; it might be very accurate, or wildly inaccurate, and we have no means of knowing whether it is one or the other. The purpose of sampling theory is therefore firstly to provide us with a means of

---

[1] An excellent discussion of sampling is that by R. S. Schofield, 'Sampling in historical research' in E. A. Wrigley (ed.), *Nineteenth-Century Society* (Cambridge, Cambridge University Press, 1972).

selecting cases that will give us an accurate estimate, and secondly to enable us to estimate how accurate the estimate is likely to be.

The theory and methods of sampling are based upon two concepts – that of the normal distributions, and that of independent random sampling – and upon theorems derived from these two concepts. We shall consider the normal distribution and independent random sampling separately, and then demonstrate how they help us in determining sampling methods.

The normal distributions are a particular form of frequency distributions. They have the particular property that a constant proportion of cases in the distribution lie between the mean of the distribution and any given distance from the mean, when distances from the mean are expressed in multiples of the standard deviation of the distribution. For example, 68·26 per cent of the cases in the distribution fall between one standard deviation above and one standard deviation below the mean; 95·46 per cent of the cases fall between two standard deviations above and two below the mean. Thus, if we have a set of data that is normally distributed (i.e. with a shape approximating to that of a normal distribution) with a mean of 175 and a standard deviation of 25, we know that 68·26 per cent of the cases in this distribution have a value between 150 and 200, and that 95·46 per cent of the cases have a value between 125 and 225. There are an infinite number of normal distributions, one for each set of mean and standard deviation, but all of them possess this property. Furthermore, each of these normal distributions can be converted into what is known as the standard form of the normal distribution; this is a normal distribution with a mean of zero, and a standard deviation of one. The values of any other normal distribution can be converted into values of this standard form by the formula

$$Z = \frac{X - \bar{X}}{s}$$

where X is each value of the original normal distribution, $\bar{X}$ and s its mean and standard deviation, and Z is each value of the standard form normal distribution.

Figure 8.1 shows the standard form of the normal distribution, together with the number of cases falling within particular distances from the mean of the distribution.

The second basis of sampling theory is independent random sampling. By a random sample we mean a sample of cases taken so that each case has an equal chance of being chosen as part of

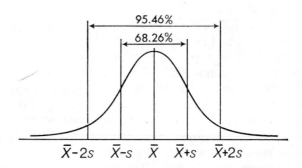

Figure 8.1 Standard form of the normal distribution.

the sample, and that each combination of cases has an equal chance of being chosen. By 'independent' we mean that the choice of one case to appear in the sample should not affect the chances of any other case appearing in the sample. It should be emphasized that a sample is random only if these conditions are fulfilled; a random sample is not one that happens to have survived through historical accident, or one that consists of cases that happen to take our fancy. In practice we select a random sample and ensure that these conditions are fulfilled by making use of tables of random numbers. These are tables so constructed that the chances of any one number appearing at any point in the tables, or of any combination of numbers so appearing, are equal. The numbers listed in tables of random numbers thus fulfil the conditions of random sampling. A small part of such a table of random numbers is shown as Table 8.1; the full tables are either published in book form or incorporated in books of statistical tables. In addition, many electronic calculators will generate random numbers.

Let us imagine that we wish to use the table of random numbers to choose a random sample of the Essex manors listed in Domesday Book, and listed in Table 3.1 (pp. 30–1). There are fifty manors listed in Table 3.1, and we will take a random sample of ten from the list.

Table 8.1 *Extract from a table of random numbers*

75	56	97	88	00	88	83	55	44	86
23	79	34	87	63	90	82	29	70	22
94	68	81	61	27	56	19	68	00	91
18	28	82	74	37	49	63	22	40	41
13	19	27	22	94	07	47	74	46	06

We first number the fifty manors from the first Writtle manor, which we call 1, to the unspecified manor, which we call 50. These fifty are known as the 'population' from which we are sampling. We then start at any point in the table of random numbers; let us, for example, start at the top of the third column with the number 97. This is larger than 50, so we cannot use it. We therefore take the number immediately below, 34 (we could equally well have moved horizontally to 88). 34 is less than 50, and we therefore select the thirty-fourth manor, Elsenham, as the first manor in our sample. Continuing down the column we next have 81 and 82, which we discard, and then 27; Wethersfield, the twenty-seventh manor in our list, is thus the second manor in our sample. We can now move either to another column, or another row, of the table. Let us assume that we simply move to the top of the fourth column, and continue, finding 22, therefore taking the twenty-second manor. Continuing with the fifth column, we find 27. Now we have already selected the twenty-seventh manor for our list; if we selected it again, then we would have a sample in which one manor appeared twice, which would be wasteful, since we would be duplicating information in our sample. We may therefore ignore that number (although there is no need to do so) and move on, taking 37, 47, 7, 19, 29 (ignoring 22), 44, 40 (ignoring 22 again) and 41, as our sample of ten. In sampling from a larger population, say from 3000 manors, we would simply take four digit groups of numbers and proceed as before.

Now that we have described the normal distribution and random sampling, we can proceed to show how they relate to the theory of sampling. Let us imagine that we repeatedly take random samples of N cases from a population; this population has a mean, which we will denote by μ, (pronounced mu) and a standard deviation which we will denote by σ (pronounced sigma). As we take each random sample, we calculate the mean of the sample; as we take more and more samples, these means will themselves form a frequency distribution, with its own mean and standard deviation. It can be shown that, provided N (the sample size) is large enough (in practice larger than 100), this frequency distribution of sample means (the sampling distribution) will be a normal distribution. Furthermore, the mean of the sampling distribution will be the same as the population mean μ and the standard deviation of the sampling distribution (known as the 'standard error') will be $\sigma/\sqrt{N}$ – that is, the standard deviation of the population, divided by the square root of N. This will be true whether or not the population itself is normally distributed, provided that the sample size is large enough.

These characteristics apply to the sampling distribution, not to the individual random samples themselves. However, since the sampling distribution is normal, we know that, for example, 68·26 per cent of cases in the distribution will fall between the mean of the distribution and one standard deviation either side of the mean. The cases making up the sampling distribution are the means of the individual random samples, and we can therefore say that 68·26 per cent of the random samples will have means within this range. We can turn this statement around, and say that in 68·26 samples out of 100, a random sample will have a mean within this range – or, equivalently, that there is a 68·26 per cent chance that any random sample will have a mean within this range. Similarly we can say that there is a 95·46 per cent chance that any random sample will have a mean within two standard deviations of the population mean.

It is these facts that provide the justification for the use of sampling methods. We know that, provided we take a reasonably large random sample (in practice over 100 cases), there is a very good, and precisely stated, chance that the mean of the random sample will be close to the mean of the population from which the sample is being drawn. Even if the sample is smaller the chances can also be stated with precision. The sample mean will thus be a good estimate of the population mean. Moreover, if we know the mean and standard deviation of the population, μ and σ, we know that there is a 68·26 per cent chance that the mean of a random sample of size N from that population will have a value in the range $\mu \pm \sigma/\sqrt{N}$. This knowledge can be extremely important in historical problems. Historians are increasingly using data collected by census enumerators in the nineteenth century, and are taking samples from the enumerators' books. Much of the material from these books was used in the published census reports, and such information as the mean and the standard deviations of the ages of people in particular census areas is available. The historian can therefore take a random sample from the enumerators' books, in the knowledge that, for example, in 95·46 samples out of 100, the mean should be in the range between the population mean plus two standard deviations and the population mean minus two standard deviations. If it is not, then he knows immediately either that he has made some mistake in taking his sample, or that he has been unlucky and his sample is one of the 4·54 samples in 100 in which the sample mean lies outside that range. If his sample mean is within that range, then he can be reasonably certain that nothing has gone wrong, and that he can use his sample to derive further information about the population from which he has sampled. (It is, of course, possible that he has made a mistake in drawing his sample, but that the sample mean has still fallen within the range; a sample mean within that range is therefore not necessarily a safeguard against a bad sampling method.)

In most historical studies, however, the mean and the standard deviation of the population are not known. Indeed, it is often the purpose of the sample to provide an estimate of them.

In these circumstances, we know that the sample mean should lie, in 95·46 samples out of 100, in the range $\mu \pm 2\sigma/\sqrt{N}$, but since we do not know the population standard deviation, σ, we do not know what that range is. The only information which we have comes from our random sample, and we therefore have to use that information to help us to estimate $\sigma/\sqrt{N}$. It can be shown that the best estimate of $\sigma/\sqrt{N}$ is $s/\sqrt{(N-1)}$ where s is the sample standard deviation, N is the number of cases in the sample and the sampling was random. When the population mean and standard deviation are unknown, therefore, we first take a random sample of size N from the population, and calculate the sample mean and sample standard deviation. Using the theorems that have just been presented, we can then say that in 95·46 per cent of all samples, the sample mean will lie within a range of $\pm 2[s/\sqrt{(N-1)}]$ – that is, two standard deviations (or standard errors) of the sampling distribution from the population mean. By this method, we use the sample to provide us with an estimate, which will be the best possible estimate, of the characteristics of the population in which we are interested.

We can illustrate the use of sampling to provide estimates of population characteristics by the use of a simple, hypothetical, example. Let us assume that we wish to estimate, by means of a sample, the mean age at first marriage of women in a particular town. We gather the information on marriage ages from the parish registers, and then take a random sample of 100 women. The mean age at first marriage, $\bar{X}$, is found to be 27, and the standard deviation, s, is found to be 2·2 years. We know from the theorems that have just been stated that the sample mean is the best estimate of the population mean, and that in 95·46 samples out of 100 the sample mean will lie in the range $\mu \pm 2\sigma/\sqrt{N}$. This is equivalent to saying that in 95·46 samples out of 100, the population mean will be somewhere in the range $\bar{X} \pm 2\sigma/\sqrt{N}$. Since we do not know σ, the population standard deviation, we use $s/\sqrt{(N-1)}$ as an estimate of $\sigma/\sqrt{N}$. We therefore know that, for our example, in 95·46 samples out of 100, the population mean will be in the range

$$\bar{X} \pm 2 \frac{s}{\sqrt{(N-1)}} = 27 \pm 2 \frac{(2\cdot2)}{(100-1)} = 27 \pm 0\cdot4444.$$

The population mean will therefore be between 26·5556 and 27·4444. The range around the mean, $\pm 0\cdot4444$, is known as the '95 per cent confidence interval', since we can say that we have approximately 95 per cent confidence that the population mean will lie in this range.

We have so far discussed the use of sampling theory in making estimates of characteristics of the population from which the sample has been drawn. We can, in addition, use sampling theory as an aid to the testing of hypotheses about sample results. A historian will often be interested to know whether a change in some characteristic of the subject he is studying has occurred between two dates. Using our hypothetical example, we may be interested in discovering whether the average age of marriage of women changed over the course of a century; since the number of children that may be born to a marriage is related to the age of the wife at marriage, it is important in under-standing population movements to know at what age most women married. Because of the very large number of marriages in the place we are studying, we need to use samples. Our first sample of 100 marriages at the beginning of the century shows a mean age at marriage of 27, with a standard deviation of 2·2 years, and our second sample of 100 marriages one hundred years later shows a mean age at marriage of 26·5 years, with a standard deviation of 1·6 years. At first sight, it would appear that the mean age of marriage fell by 0·5 years over the century. But we must remember that these are sample results, giving us only estimates of the population results; furthermore, since we are sampling, we must always remember the risk that the sample will not give us a very accurate estimate of the population result. We can imagine, for example, that the first sample overestimated the mean age at marriage, while the second sample underestimated it; it would only require an inaccuracy of 0·25 years towards each other in the estimates for the apparent change in age at marriage of 0·5 years to disappear. We therefore need to find some way of distinguishing between a difference in mean ages at marriage which might appear as the result of the process of sampling, and the real difference in the mean ages at marriage of the population. These two possibilities can be contrasted as follows:

1 No difference between population means, but difference between sample means as the result of the sampling process.
2 Difference between population means, reflected in difference between sample means.

In deciding between these possibilities, we make use of a test known as the difference of means test, which is dependent upon another theorem of sampling and the normal distribution. This theorem states that if we take a large number of independent samples of large size from two populations, and calculate the difference between the means of each pair of samples, the sampling distribution of these differences will itself be a normal distribution. It will have a mean equal to the difference between the population means, and its standard deviation (standard error) will be

$$\sqrt{\left(\frac{\sigma_1{}^2}{N_1} + \frac{\sigma_2{}^2}{N_2}\right)}.$$

We can make use therefore of the characteristics of the normal distribution, and can say, for example, that there is a 95·46 per cent chance that the difference between the means of two samples will lie in a range of

$$\pm 2\sqrt{\left(\frac{\sigma_1{}^2}{N_1} + \frac{\sigma_2{}^2}{N_2}\right)}$$

of the difference between the means of the population.

The first of the possibilities which we want to explore, in using the difference of means test, is that there is no difference between the population means. That is, if we subtract μ_2 (the mean of the first population) from μ_1 (the mean of the second population), the result will be zero. If this were so, then any difference between sample means that was non-zero would be the result of the chances of sampling; furthermore, in only

4·54 per cent (100 — 95·46) of samples would we be likely to have a difference of means greater than two population standard deviations from zero. The logic of the difference of means test is, therefore, as follows: calculate the difference between the two sample means, and divide by

$$\sqrt{\left(\frac{\sigma_1^2}{N_1} + \frac{\sigma_2^2}{N_2}\right)},$$

the standard error. If the result is greater than $+2$ or less than -2, there is only a 4·54 per cent chance that such a difference of sample means could have been the result of the chances of sampling had the population means really been equal. If the result is greater than $+2$ or less than -2, therefore, either we have been very unlucky in our sample, or the population means are not equal. If they are not equal, then they must be different, and we can therefore conclude that there was a difference in marriage age between the populations from which the samples were drawn.

In practice, we make use of a formula with which to calculate z, the difference of means divided by the number of pooled standard errors. Since we do not know the population standard deviations, we make use of the sample standard deviations as estimates. The formula for z, in the difference of means test, is

$$z = \frac{\bar{X}_1 - \bar{X}_2}{\sqrt{\left(\frac{s_1^2}{N_1 - 1} + \frac{s_2^2}{N_2 - 1}\right)}}.$$

For the hypothetical example which we have been using, $\bar{X}_1 = 27$, $s_1 = 2·2$, $\bar{X}_2 = 26·5$, $s_2 = 1·6$, $N_1 = N_2 = 100$, so

$$z = \frac{27 - 26·5}{\sqrt{\left(\frac{2·2^2}{99} + \frac{1·6^2}{99}\right)}} = 1·829.$$

Since z is 1·829, we know that there is a greater than 4·54 per cent chance that the difference between the sample means is a result of using samples, and that there is no difference between the population means. By the use of tables of the normal distribution, we can be more exact; there is a 6·73 per cent chance that the observed difference could have been the result of the chances of sampling, even though the population means were the same.

Now let us imagine that we had taken another sample of 100 marriages one hundred years later, and had found that the mean marriage age of this third sample was 24, with a standard deviation of 2·1 years. Applying the difference of means test to the second and third samples, we find that

$$z = \frac{26·5 - 24}{\sqrt{\left(\frac{1·6^2}{99} + \frac{2·1^2}{99}\right)}} = 9·42.$$

The result of this test, in which z is calculated to be much greater than $+2$, suggests that there is a very small chance that the difference of sample means was the result of the chances of sampling; the chance is considerably less than 1 in 100, or 1 per cent, and we can conclude that there was a real difference in mean marriage age between the two populations from which the samples were taken.

Similar tests can be carried out for other estimates from sample data, such as proportions or regression coefficients. For example, if the data on merchant ships in 1907, used in the last chapter, had been gathered by a sampling process, it would be sensible to check the results to see whether they might have occurred as the result of that sampling process rather than being representative of the underlying population from which the data were drawn. In Chapter 7, we concluded that the relationship between the two variables was

crew size $= 5·4481 + 0·0082$ tonnage

suggesting that the relationship was positive, and that crew size increased on average by 0·0082 crew members for every increase of 1 ton in the size of the ship. But can we be sure, with sample evidence, that this is so, and in particular can we be sure of our conclusion that crew size increased with tonnage; in other words, are we sure that, for the population of all ships, the coefficient of tonnage is different from zero?

As in the difference of means test, the test of the hypothesis that a particular regression coefficient is different from zero is based upon a comparison of the value of the regression coefficient with the standard error of the sampling distribution which would result from taking large numbers of samples from a population in which the true regression coefficient was zero. The standard error is estimated from the formula

$$\sqrt{\frac{\sum (Y - Y')^2/N - 2}{\sum (X - \bar{X})^2}}$$

where the Y' are the predicted values of Y from the regression equation. In the case of the shipping data, the standard error is found to be 0·00079; dividing 0·0082 (the regression coefficient) by 0·00079, we obtain the value 10·3797, which suggests immediately that the sample result of 0·0082 is unlikely to have been produced from a population in which the value of the regression coefficient was zero. A more exact test can be carried out by comparing the calculated value of 10·3797 with tables of the normal distribution (or in this case, since the sample size is small, of another probability distribution known as the t distribution) to ascertain what proportion of the values in the probability distribution lie further than 10·3797 standard deviations from the mean; the proportion is considerably less than 0·5 per cent, and we can safely conclude that the sample was not drawn from a population having a regression coefficient of zero.

The historian who wishes to assess the reliability of a regression coefficient (or other statistic) which has been calculated from sample data needs to know the value of the standard error, and it is therefore customary to state a regression result in the following form

$$Y = 5\cdot4481 + 0\cdot0082\,X$$
$$(0\cdot00079)$$

where the term in brackets is the standard error. Alternatively, it may be stated as

$$Y = 5\cdot4481 + 0\cdot0082\,X$$
$$(10\cdot3797)$$

where the term in brackets is the t statistic, calculated as in the last paragraph by dividing the regression coefficient by the standard error.

As this section has shown, different tests have to be undertaken with different sample results, and we have done no more than introduce some of the more important methods and concepts of sampling. Any historian who wishes to carry out sampling operations must, therefore, read more widely in the field of sampling theory before starting his study.

(c) The 'significance' of sample results

In discussing the use of sample methods in estimating population characteristics and in the difference of means test, we have described how it is possible to calculate the possibility that a sample result will be a good estimate of the population result. We have expressed this possibility in such terms as a 68·26 per cent chance, or a 95·46 per cent chance, or, in the last example, a 6·73 per cent chance that a difference in sample means could have arisen as a result of the chances of sampling. Once we have calculated these chances, we then need to use them to make historical judgements; we need, for example, to decide whether we will argue that there was, or was not, a change in the mean marriage age of the population. We know that there is a 6·73 per cent chance that the sample difference was produced by the sampling process, but is this a large or a small chance?

The decision as to whether we should take a chance (a 6·73 per cent chance), and state that there was a real difference in the mean marriage ages of the two populations, has to be a historical judgement. Statistical methods can tell us what the chances are (alternatively, what the probabilities are), but we have to make the decision as to what risk we are willing to take. Our decision will be dependent to some extent on the importance of the particular result to our inquiry; if we are only incidentally interested in mean marriage age, and nothing else depends on whether or not it changed, then we may be ready to accept a larger risk. If, on the other hand, our whole theory depends on knowing correctly what changes occurred in marriage age, then we will probably be willing to accept only a very small risk. The levels of risk which are customarily used in social research are 10, 5 and 1 per cent, often known as the 10 per cent, 5 per cent and 1 per cent 'significance levels'. This description gives rise to the naming of such tests as the difference of means test as 'significance tests', and to the appearance of such statements as 'the result was significant at the 5 per cent level'. This latter statement means simply that the risk that the result was produced by the sampling process was 5 per cent or less. Equivalent statements, both meaning the same thing, are that 'the result was significant ($p \leqslant 0.05$)', or that 'the null hypothesis could be rejected at the 5 per cent level'; the null hypothesis is normally the hypothesis that the result is produced by the chances of sampling so that in rejecting it one is accepting the hypothesis that the result is an accurate reflection of the characteristics of the population. In the difference of means test, for example, the null hypothesis is that there is no difference between the population means.

In these and similar statements, the term 'significant' refers only to whether the result confirms or rejects a hypothesis at a particular confidence level or level of significance. It has nothing to do with whether the result is historically significant, although the statistical 'significance' of a result may be a factor in determining the conclusions that the historian draws from it.

The use of significance tests is not confined to samples of interval data, although the tests we have discussed are appropriate only for such data. If only nominal or ordinal data are available, a number of other tests, often described as 'non-parametric' tests, may be used, of which the most used are the tests based on the chi-square statistic which we used in deriving the contingency coefficient. The logic of these tests is very similar to that of the tests we have described, but instead of the normal distribution they make use of other forms of probability distributions.

Tests of significance are invaluable when sample problems are being considered, and their use is essential when any estimates or inferences are to be made from sample data. However, they can easily be misused. They are, firstly, appropriate when, and only when, the data are gathered by the use of a method of probability sampling, such as the simple random sampling described earlier in this section. If the sample is not a probability sample, then to conduct tests of significance on it is theoretically meaningless, and may lead to misleading results. Secondly, many of the tests we have discussed may only be used when other restrictive assumptions are met: the difference of means test, for example, assumes interval data, normal populations or a large sample size, as well as independent random sampling. If these conditions are not fulfilled, then again the tests of significance are meaningless and misleading.

There can be no argument that the tests should not be applied to samples that are not probability samples, nor to data that violate any of the assumptions made by the tests. Statisticians and social scientists disagree, however, on the extent to which the tests can be sensibly applied to data that are not sample data at all. Let us assume, for example, that a historian is interested in studying the mean incomes attained, ten years after graduation, by Oxford and Cambridge students who studied between 1800 and 1900, in an effort to discover whether Oxford graduates were more successful in monetary terms than Cambridge graduates. Imagine that he managed to discover the incomes of all the graduates, so that there were no missing data, and that he discovered that Oxford graduates did in fact have higher incomes. In these circumstances, many social scientists would be tempted to carry out a difference of means test, and to quote the result of the test when giving their results, in some form such as 'the difference in mean incomes was significant at the 5 per cent level'. It would be perfectly feasible, arithmetically, to do this, but it is difficult to know what such a test, or its result, would mean. We do not have a sample of graduates, but all of them, so we cannot be testing to see whether the sample results differ from the population results; the two are by definition the same. In order to make some possible sense of tests of significance in these circumstances, in fact, we would have to hypothesize that there was some hypothetical, larger, population of Oxbridge graduates of whom all the actual Oxbridge graduates formed a simple random sample. However, it is difficult to believe either in the hypothetical population or in the random sampling, and therefore the significance test still has no meaning. There was a difference between the mean incomes, and that is an end of it.

This difficulty often arises when a historian wishes to generalize from a particular study, from one industrial town to all such towns, from one firm to an industry or from one man to a group of men. In such a case, it is arithmetically possible to carry out a significance test on, for example, the correlation coefficient between two characteristics of a town, such as size and expenditure on public services. Having discovered that the association is significant within that one town, the historian might feel happier about generalizing from it to other towns. But, in fact, carrying out a significance test has done nothing to help him to decide whether he can generalize from one town to all towns; it would have helped only if that one town had constituted a simple random sample of all towns. Only if the historian can establish that this is so, or if he is willing to assume that it is so, will the significance test have any meaning.

In spite of the difficulties of sampling theory, and of taking samples in practice, historians should not hesitate to use sampling methods rather than give up an analysis project because of the bulk of the records. The advantages of using samples are considerable in the amount of time and money that can be saved. This is particularly so since the accuracy of a sample is dependent on the size of the sample itself, not on the proportion that it forms of the total population. This can be seen from the fact that, if large random samples are taken, the accuracy of the estimate made from the sample is determined by the quantity $\sigma/\sqrt{N}$, where σ is the population standard deviation, and N the absolute size of the sample. The size of the population from which the sample is drawn does not appear in this quantity, and is therefore irrelevant for the purposes of determining the accuracy of the sample result. For this reason, no virtue attaches to a 10 per cent sample rather than to a sample of some other proportion of the population; what matters is the absolute size of the sample. A further important deduction that can be made from the quantity $\sigma/\sqrt{N}$ is that the accuracy of the sample depends on the square root of the sample size, rather than on the sample size directly. Doubling the sample size, for example, increases its accuracy only by $\sqrt{2} = 1\cdot4142$ times. Similarly, in order to double the precision of sample estimates we need to quadruple the size of the sample, since $\sqrt{4} = 2$. Both these facts – that the accuracy of the sample result is determined by the sample size, and that increasing the sample size does not increase its accuracy by the same amount – mean that it is often possible to derive very acceptable results from relatively small samples, with a relatively small amount of effort compared to the effort of studying the whole population.

(d) Too few data: the problems of missing data

By 'missing data problems' we mean all situations in which the data matrix that can be accumulated during the course of data collection does not fill the ideal data matrix that the historian has hoped to fill. The stereotypes (b), (c) and (d), which we distinguished at the beginning of this chapter (p. 165), are all examples of missing data situations. Such problems are both much more common in historical work than problems caused by having too many data, and much more difficult to solve. Typically, they arise through the destruction of records, or through the failure of the bureaucrats of the past to keep the type of records we would like to have. An example of the first would be, in English history, the parish records of baptisms, marriages and burials, which survive for some parishes but not for others. An example of the second would be the lack of adequate census data for most countries before the nineteenth century. It should be emphasized that there is very little statistical theory that helps with missing data problems, and the historian is therefore very dependent on his own ideas and resources in solving them.

(e) Data missing on one or more cases

Let us first take stereotype (b), in which data are missing on some complete cases. In this situation, we have a sample of the

cases, but not a probability sample (except in the extremely
unlikely case that the cases have survived after a process of
random sampling). Since we have sample data, we can use them
to make estimates of the characteristics of the total data set
which we would have had if it had survived. Since we do not
have a probability sample, however, we have little idea of how
accurate such estimates are. This does not of course make the
estimates valueless; they may be extremely interesting as
results in their own right. For example, it is a common feature
of business history that information has survived largely from
those firms that were prosperous and successful; firms that go
bankrupt rarely preserve their records. Thus a business historian is normally faced with a situation in which data are missing
on some cases (firms). Nevertheless, the information that he
has may tell him a great deal about the ways in which successful
firms operated, and, although this information cannot be used
statistically as estimates of the behaviour of other firms in the
industry, it may still be of interest.

In this example of business history it is clear that the sample
is deficient in two respects, judged against the standard of a
simple random sample. Firstly, the selection of cases has not
been done by random means, and secondly it is clear that the
sample is biased, since only the successful have survived. The
sample is, in other words, unrepresentative. This raises the
question of whether a sample that does not appear to be
biased in any way might, for the purpose of analysis, be treated
as if it were a random sample. This would enable statements
to be made about the likely accuracy of results derived from it,
and it would also provide a justification for using those results
as if they were derived from a data set without missing data.
Professor Lawrence Stone, for example, in his study of the
English aristocracy in the sixteenth century, suggests that a
sample composed of manors chosen because one of the parties
to their sale had a name beginning with the letter S can be
treated as if it were a random sample. 'Is there any reason',
he asks, 'to suppose that choosing the letter S in this case will
give results significantly different from taking a truly random
sample? . . . I deliberately avoided J, O and M as likely to

produce disproportionate numbers respectively of Welshmen, Irishmen and Scotsmen. But the letter S comprises over 10 per cent of all English names, and I fail to see what is likely to be peculiar about this particular group.'[1]

As Professor Stone knew, in strict statistical theory this procedure does not constitute drawing a random sample, and, again in theory, one is not justified in treating a non-random sample as if it were a random sample, even if there seems to be no reason why the sample one has is unrepresentative in any way. In practice, however, it seems justifiable for historians to proceed in the way that Professor Stone has done, provided firstly that they know what they are doing, and secondly that they make it clear to their readers what they are doing. One major difficulty raised by this advice is that of comparability between different historical findings; for example, let us assume that we sample English manors by one non-random method in 1535, as Stone did, and then by another non-random method using a later list. Are the differences between their ownership at each date due to real changes, or to differences between two non-random sampling methods? All that can be said is that one does not know, and one is adding that new possibility to all the other possible causes of changes in English landownership. But so long as both historian and reader are aware of the fact that this has been done, it is difficult to argue that the procedure is entirely wrong; something will be added to our knowledge, even if it has later to be modified when more studies have been carried out.

The importance of making it clear that a departure has been made from strict statistical procedure cannot be over-emphasized. Such departures are very common in historical work. Another example is that a number of attempts have been made to estimate the total value of cotton factories in the Industrial Revolution by multiplying the average value of a few factories, found from insurance records, by the total number of factories known to have existed. This procedure, considered strictly, involves the assumption that the factories whose values are known

[1] L. Stone, 'Lawrence Stone and the manors: rejoinder', *Economic History Review*, vol. XXIV (1971), p. 116.

constituted a random sample of all factories, which is unlikely to be true. Nevertheless, so long as this is made clear, and so long as not too much is built on the conclusion, the procedure is justifiable. What is unjustifiable, is to carry out such procedures without realizing, and making clear, what assumptions are being made.

The conclusion of our discussion of stereotype (*b*), in which data on cases are missing, must therefore be that although in strict terms the situation is nearly always hopeless, because of the lack of random sampling, in particular cases it may be possible to produce approximate answers by methods that violate statistical theory. The main need is for the historians to develop a greater awareness of what their methods entail.

(*f*) Data missing on one or more variables

The situation in which data are entirely missing for one or more variables is familiar to historians. Students of business history, for example, often know a great deal about manufacturing businesses, but not about the total value of the goods they made. Political historians often know little or nothing about the economic status of the politicians they study, although they may know such details as occupation and family background. In most cases, the total absence of data on a variable cannot be remedied. No information exists on which to form an estimate of the values of the variable, let alone to assess the accuracy of such an estimate. Faced with this situation, the historian can only search for more material, or limit his studies to those questions that can be answered without the aid of the missing variable.

The exception to this situation of hopelessness arises when the historian can be certain that there is some logical or statistical relationship between the variables such that he can estimate the values of the missing variable from the values of the variables on which he has information. In a trivial case, an economic historian who knows the cost of making a manufactured article, and the price at which it was sold, but has no direct knowledge of the profit made, can use his knowledge that profit equals price minus cost to estimate with precision the value of the missing variable. In this situation the relationship between the variables is straightforward, and there can be no objection to the procedure.

More difficulties arise when the relationship between the estimating and the estimated variables is derived not from a simple arithmetical relationship but from a theoretical model or from evidence from another historical period or place. The attempt to estimate the values of a missing variable by such means is particularly the hallmark of what has been called the 'new economic history' or 'econometric history' – econometrics being the branch of economics that tests economic theory against evidence by the use of statistical and mathematical techniques. The technique is, however, of wider use, and the 'new' economic historians are largely making explicit a technique that has often been employed, sometimes unconsciously, by other historians. For example, it is common for political historians to label with such descriptions as 'liberal', 'conservative' or 'fascist', even though no political parties existed with those names, and the people themselves would not have recognized such descriptions. Essentially, what a historian is doing, in using these descriptions, is to argue that he has information on several variables, such as attitudes to certain issues, behaviour in political debate, and so on. He feels that he can use this information to allow him to estimate the values of the missing variable, which we may call 'the political belief of the individual being studied', and, in calling a particular man a 'liberal', the historian is thus making an estimate of the value of a missing variable.

To illustrate the logic of the methods that have to be employed, and some of the possible dangers, we can look at two examples, one drawn from political and the other from economic history. The first example is that of Professor Aydelotte's efforts to establish spectra of political attitudes in the Parliaments of the 1840s. Professor Aydelotte argues that by studying votes on a large number of different issues, he can establish a scale of issues, and can rank M.P.s along this scale according to their attitudes to each issue. M.P.s who vote in favour on all issues on the scale will be ranked at one end, those who vote against at the other, and Aydelotte can then proceed to attempt to identify what pressures of party loyalty, background or ideology placed people at particular points along the scale. Essentially, he is trying to establish political attitudes – the missing variable – from political behaviour, made up of a set of variables on which the information exists. A number of criticisms may be made of this procedure; for example, it may be questioned whether Aydelotte has adequately eliminated the effects of party pressure or patronage, and whether contemporary politicians regarded the votes on particular issues as of great or no importance. In spite of these difficulties, Aydelotte's work has added a great deal to our knowledge of the 1840s, and he has been scrupulous in all his work in explaining the methods he has used, thus allowing critics to discuss his procedures.

Estimation procedures are used most explicitly in economic history. As an example, we can take Miss Deane and Professor Cole's work on British economic growth, and in particular their attempt to estimate the British production of grain in the eighteenth century. No figures for home grain production exist, although import and export figures are available. Deane and Cole's procedure is to take an estimate made in 1766 of the amount of grain eaten per head per year, and multiply this by the estimated population at the beginning of each decade. They then add exports, subtract imports, allow for the need to produce some corn for seed and arrive at a figure for estimated production of grain. Deane and Cole make it very clear that the possible errors in this procedure, and hence in the result, are very numerous. Their method involves the following assumptions:

(*a*) That the contemporary estimates for numbers in the population are correct.
(*b*) That the estimate of average consumption of grain in 1766 was correct.
(*c*) That the average consumption of grain did not change during the eighteenth century, in spite of changes in average income and grain prices.

(*d*) That the yield of grain – that is, the amount needed for seed corn – was accurately estimated in 1766, and was unchanged at that proportion during the whole century.

All these assumptions are defended by Deane and Cole, and are reasonable, at least when the object of the calculation is to produce an estimate of the missing variable, grain output, which is broadly rather than precisely accurate.[1]

Another example of a possible technique for filling in missing data is commonly used in econometric history, and consists in the use of regression estimates. For example, let us assume that we are studying merchant ships in 1907, and find that our data on one ship are incomplete; the crew size has not been recorded. If we had obtained our data on merchant ships, used in the last chapter (see p. 151), from a properly designed sample, and if we were confident of the regression estimates obtained, we could use the regression equation to help us to estimate the missing crew size. If we knew that the tonnage of the ship was 1600 tons, we could replace X in the regression equation, $Y = 5{\cdot}4481 + 0{\cdot}0082X$, by 1600, and calculate Y:

$$Y = 5{\cdot}4481 + 0{\cdot}0082\,(1600)$$
$$= 18{\cdot}5681.$$

Rounding off the digits after the decimal point, we can say that our best guess, on the basis of the available information, of the crew size of the ship is that it had nineteen seamen. The same information could, of course, be derived more quickly, if slightly less accurately, by inspection of the regression line plotted in Figure 7.1 (p. 149).

It can be seen from these examples that the possibility of making estimates of the values of missing variables depends on the theoretical basis linking other variables with the missing variable, and on the amount of trust that can be put on the information that is available. Furthermore, the historian must

[1] See P. Deane and W. A. Cole *British Economic Growth 1688–1959* (Cambridge, Cambridge University Press, 1964), pp. 62–68. For a discussion of these assumptions see N. F. R. Crafts, 'English Economic Growth in the Eighteenth Century', *Economic History Review*, vol. XXXIX (May 1976).

consider the importance of particular estimates of missing variables to the structure of his argument; if the estimates are crucial to his interpretation, then he will wish to be more certain of them than if they are only of peripheral interest. In any study, therefore, the historian must judge for himself whether he can undertake this type of estimation procedure, and his readers must judge whether he has been correct; for the latter purpose, the basis on which the estimates have been made must be made explicit.

(g) Data missing on one or more variables of one or more cases, but not on any complete case or variable

The methods that have been discussed in the last two sections can be applied to the third, and most common, of the stereo-types of missing data, in which odd pieces of data are found to be missing. That is, missing values can be estimated either by using the values of that variable or other cases to estimate the missing one, or by using the other variable values of that case to estimate the missing value. In terms of the data matrix, therefore, estimation can be made either vertically (by variable) or horizontally (by case), or by both methods as a check. A conflict between the estimates obtained by the two methods will suggest ways in which the estimating procedures can be refined and the estimates reconciled.

Although, with this last stereotype, the range of possible methods of overcoming the problem of missing data is wider than it was with the other stereotypes, the same objections apply. Taking firstly estimates from other cases, vertically on the matrix, it is still not possible to assume that the cases on which information exists form a random sample of all cases in the matrix, so that the danger that the estimates will be biased is still strong. Secondly, the possibility of estimating from other variables relating to the same case, horizontally on the matrix, is still dependent on the assumptions that can be made about the relationships between the variables. Once again, it is important that any use of estimation procedures should be stated as clearly as possible, so that the procedures can be adequately criticized and discussed.

9 Calculators, computers and historical data

All the statistical methods which have been explained in this book can be carried out by an electronic calculator. Moreover, the price of such calculators, and thus of the statistical power which they incorporate, is likely to continue to fall, as it has done rapidly in recent years. At the same time, much greater statistical power which can be employed to process and analyse historical data has become available through the widespread use of computers, which are now, or soon will be, available in schools, colleges and universities in many countries. So rapid has been the impact of what has been called the 'micro-processor' revolution, indeed, that the distinction between calculators and computers has become difficult to make, as programmable calculators compete in performance and price with micro- and mini-computers, which themselves can for many of the purposes of the historian match the performance of major university computers. Parallel to these developments in the 'hardware' of computing have come similar developments in 'software', the programs and sets of programs which enable calculators and computers to be used efficiently.

The historian, whether at school, university or even at home, as access to computers via television and telephone becomes possible, is therefore faced with a bewildering variety of possible aids to calculation and analysis of his materials. The purpose of this chapter is to explain some of the terminology of computing, to remove some of its mysteries, and to enable the historian to make an intelligent choice of the equipment and methods which will best aid the solution of his historical problem.

(a) The choice of equipment: electronic calculators

In broad terms, any of the statistical operations described in Chapters 1–5 of this book can be carried out either by hand, although this may be time-consuming and cumbersome, or with the simplest of pocket calculators. To carry out the analyses of Chapter 6, a simple calculator can be used in the way set out in the tables in that chapter, but many slightly more complex calculators, particularly those describing themselves as 'financial calculators', can calculate trend lines at the touch of a button. To calculate rates of growth directly requires that the calculator can evaluate the *n*th root of a number, for example

$$\sqrt[30]{\frac{X_n}{X_t}}$$

in the example on p. 94, although any simple calculator able to calculate logarithms, as most can, could be used in the way described on p. 95. Any calculator able to compute trend lines can also calculate *n*th roots, thus making it easy to calculate the log-linear trends described on p. 110. Simple linear regression and correlation analysis, the principal method described in Chapter 7, is available on many calculators marketed for scientific or statistical uses, and the methods of evaluation of sample data described in Chapter 8 can be calculated on such machines in association with tables of chi-square and the normal distribution. Only if one wishes to dispense even with such tables is it necessary to move to the upper end of the calculator market, to buy one able to carry out many statistical analyses too complex to be described in this book.

The historian therefore seems to need only to decide what he wishes to do to discover how complex a calculator he needs to buy. Yet this is not entirely true, for small electronic calculators have one disadvantage which is important in the analysis of historical data (although it may not matter very much if the historian wishes to use a calculator largely as an adjunct to reading, to check and calculate on the basis of data supplied in books and articles). The problem lies in the fact that many if not all historical problems can only be solved by the analysis of quite large sets of data, of many cases each with several variables. To take a very simple example, it might be necessary to calculate the mean and standard deviation of the data displayed in Table 3.1, concerned with swine in Essex in 1086 (see pp. 29–30). With many calculators, such a calculation can be done simply by entering the number, 1200 for the manor of Writtle, and then pressing a key marked $\sum X$, repeating these operations for each number in the list. Then keys marked $\bar{X}$ and S will give the result. This may seem simple, but it is worth noting that the set of operations which have just been described will involve 178 key depressions, one for each digit, 49 for $\sum X$, and once each for $\bar{X}$ and S. An error in any one of these must be noticed immediately so that it can be corrected; if it is not, the answer will be wrong, but the only way in which it can be checked will be to repeat all 178 key depressions. A more complex operation, such as correlating numbers of swine with some other characteristic of Essex manors, might well require 455 key depressions, although the exact number will depend on the design of the calculator.

The major defect of most calculators is, as this example shows, that entering data is cumbersome and that no permanent record of data entry exists which can be checked to see whether any mistakes have been made. This may not matter very much in many mathematical examples where the amount of data is small, but it is a serious problem in a subject such as history, which is 'data-bound' rather than being concerned with 'number-crunching', that is with complex calculations on small amounts of data. This problem can be overcome, but to do so is expensive; printers attached to calculators can be bought, but they are normally several times the cost of the calculator itself, use special and costly paper and reduce the advantages of portability and ease of use which small calculators possess. Other attempts have been made to overcome the problem, which is particularly troublesome when the same data are to be analysed several times; some expensive calculators allow data as well as 'programs' – sets of instructions for the manipulation of the data – to be recorded on magnetic strips for future use. But none of these methods is cheap, and none is convenient to use.

(b) *The choice of equipment: computers*

It is for these reasons that the historian with any amount of data to analyse should consider whether it would be sensible to use a computer. This depends upon ease of access to a computer, upon whether the data needs to be stored and upon whether it will be subjected to repetitive or complex calculations. It is impossible to generalize about access to computers, since the conditions and cost of using computers vary so much within and between different educational institutions, areas of countries and countries as a whole; all that can be said is that access is becoming easier and cheaper day by day.

To understand why storage of data and the nature of the calculations are important, it is necessary to know a little about the parts that make up an electronic computer. In essence, a computer consists of three parts: the central processing unit in which the arithmetical operations are performed; the memory in which data, results and sets of instructions – programs – are stored while the central processing unit is carrying out the instructions to process the data and produce the results; and the input–output devices through which data are transmitted to the memory and the results printed out. The historian need know very little more about the central processing unit than that it exists; the memory will affect him only if he intends to use a micro- or mini-computer or to process an enormous set of data with complex analysis programs. Anyone using a computer is, however, affected by the input–output devices and by the type of programs which can be used; the latter are discussed in Section (d) below.

The purpose of input devices is to transform data into a form in which it can be processed by the computer, which stores information as a series of electrical charges. Output devices do the reverse, allowing us to understand the results of the processing. The most common method of input to the computer is to transfer data and programs to 'machine-readable' form by typing them on to punch-cards, such as the card shown in Figure 9.1. Information is represented on cards of this type by small rectangular holes, or combinations of holes, which can be read by a card-reader attached to a computer and interpreted as numbers, letters or punctuation characters. In Figure 9.1, the information recorded is the details of the first ship shown in Table 4.1 (see p. 44). The first number recorded is 1697; the first digit of this number, 1, is represented by the hole punched through the first row of the first column. The second digit, 6, is punched in the second column in the sixth row, the third digit is punched in the third column in row 9, and the fourth digit in the fourth column in row 7. Each column of the card therefore represents one character, the characters being differentiated by the row in which the punch is made. Each ship is given an individual card, and each variable is punched in the same columns in each card. Since there are only ten rows printed on the card, it might seem that we could only represent ten characters on the card. To overcome this restriction, some characters are represented by two or more punches in the same column. For example, the name 'FLOUD 001' has been punched at the right-hand side of the card, as an identification. The letter F is represented by a punch in row 6, and by a punch in what is often known as the '+ punch' position, in a row at the top of the card. The letter L is represented by a punch in row 3 and a punch in the '− punch' position, a row between the '+ punch' row and the '0' row. By the use of these + and − punch rows, in conjunction with the other rows on the card, all letters of the alphabet, all numbers and many punctuation marks can be given unique combinations of punches. It is thus possible to punch alpha-betical and numerical characters on the card without any pos-sibility of confusion. The characters at the very top of the card are typed by the card punch machines, at the same time as the holes are punched, and thus allow the operator to check that he has punched the correct character.

Punched cards are convenient to use for many purposes, they can be corrected or duplicated easily, and the information con-tained on them is clearly visible. When they need to be used in large numbers, however, perhaps to record a very large amount of data, these advantages are outweighed by their weight and the ease with which they can be damaged. For this reason, it has long been common to use cards only for the first step in

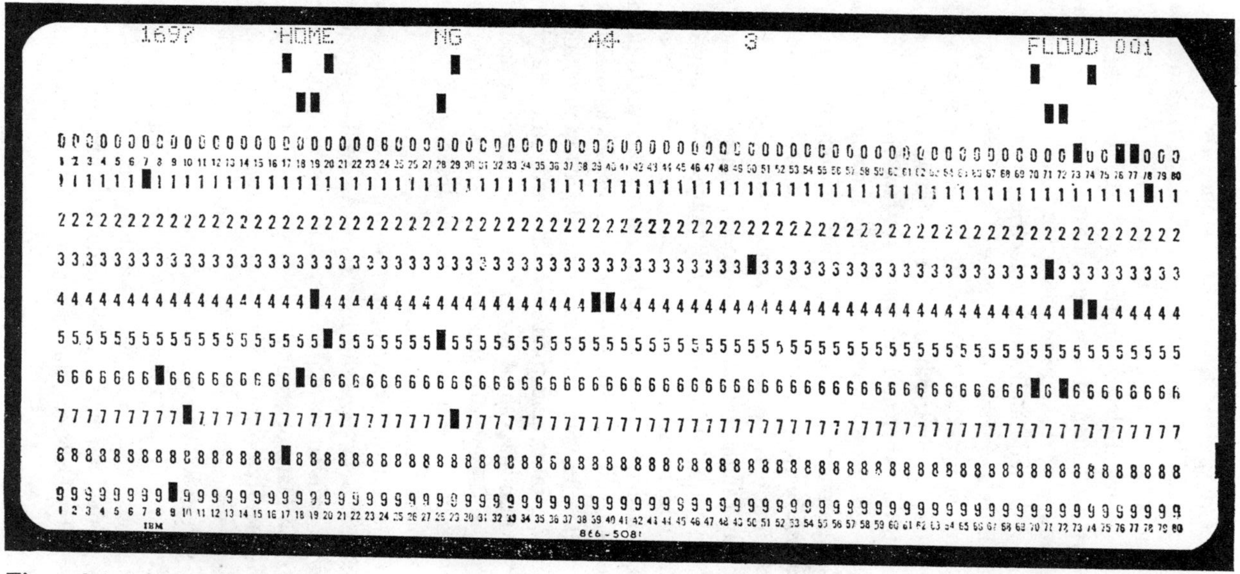

Figure 9.1 A punched card.

data processing; they are read only once by the computer, which then stores the information on another medium, usually a magnetic tape or magnetic disk, on which information is stored as electrical charges in the same way as on the tape in a tape recorder. A natural development is to transfer data immediately to tape or disk, and this can be done by typing on to a terminal, a device much like an electric typewriter attached to the computer. A further development is to record data on cassettes using terminals, which are about the same size and weight as an electric typewriter but which record whatever is typed on them both on paper and on magnetic tape in a cassette. Such terminals can be used anywhere that is convenient, and the cassette can be taken later to be read by the computer.

These developments in the hardware of computing are of immense importance to historians. This is because historical research and statistical methods applied to history are so heavily bound up with the collection and analysis of historical data; anything which makes such work easier and cheaper is important to historians. Until recently, the historian would need to go to a record office or other source of records, laboriously copy out the data he wished to use, take the copy to a punch-card machine operator, and then feed the cards into the computer. Now, the terminal can be taken to the record office and the data typed on to cassettes or small magnetic disks, to be taken later to the computer or even, if necessary, transferred to the computer along a telephone line.

In the same way, developments in the hardware of output devices can also help the historian. As well as receiving his results in printed form, the historian can now make the computer draw maps or graphs to display his results, or can preserve it permanently on microfilm or microfiche. He can display the data on a visual display unit (VDU), which is essentially a television screen with a keyboard attached, and can modify the data or give instructions to the computer by typing on the keyboard. He may also draw samples from his data and store them for future analysis on tape or disk, while the ability to make multiple copies safeguards his data against accidental damage or destruction.

Input–output devices are thus very varied, and new devices are constantly being developed. Their use is also becoming easier, because of a further development in the hardware of computing. Until recently, the computer and its input–output devices were physically located close together, normally in the computer centre of a university or college. Punched cards were brought to the computer centre, or prepared there; they were fed into the computer, and the results printed close by, to be collected by the research worker often after a substantial delay. Therefore, the computer user was, for almost all purposes, restricted to a computer physically close to him. He could not easily use computer programs which would suit his purpose but had not been designed for the particular computer system which he had to use, and transporting punched cards or even magnetic tapes to a distant computer was cumbersome.

Many of these difficulties have already disappeared, or will do so within the next few years, because of the development of what are called 'computer networks'. Within a particular institution, it is now common for input–output devices to be physically separated from the computer, close to the user and linked to the computer along telephone lines. Outside the university or college, many schools are now linked, again by telephone, to a central computer; they can send or receive data or results, and can store information on tape or disk at the central computer. Lastly, telephone lines also link the computers themselves, both within a particular country and between one country and another. This enables computing to be done wherever it is most efficient to do it, often a long way from the user. Specialized input–output devices, for example, to plot graphs or to produce microfiche, can be placed at the few specialized computers and used occasionally by scattered users. Because of the speed of electronic communication, the user sitting at his terminal has the illusion that he alone is using the computer, when in fact tens or hundreds of users may be doing so, each in his office, school, workshop or even home.

(c) Preparing historical data for the computer

Until very recently it was assumed by many people that the main benefits of computing related to the power to process numbers. This was not because computers could not store and process material which was in the form of words and letters, but because the most obvious early applications of computing were in the field of numerical processing; most effort, therefore, in the design of computers, of their input–output devices, and of the programming languages in which sets of instructions to the computer were given, went into increasing the speed and efficiency of numerical processing. While it was always possible to process material in alphabetical rather than numerical form, it was often awkward to do so and required greater expertise in computing than most historians would wish to acquire.

The potentialities of the computer for historical work were, however, as obvious as these disadvantages, and many historians and other social scientists therefore struggled to use computers. The most obvious way which could be used to make historical material in alphabetical form amenable to methods designed to process numbers was to transform the words into numbers by a process known as 'coding'. Let us imagine, for example, that the historian wished to study recruitment to the army in the eighteenth and nineteenth centuries and that he was particularly interested in the occupations and birthplaces of the recruits. In the original recruitment records the details were recorded in several ways, one British example of which is shown in Table 9.1. In order to transform such data into

Table 9.1 *A British Army recruitment record of the 1760s: Description Book of the 3rd Artillery Battalion, 1755–1831.* (Public Record Office volume W 054/272)

Date of recruitment	Name	Age		Stature		Occupation	Place of birth
		Yr	Mo.	Ft	In.		
17 November 1766	Brian Booth	26	3	5	7½	Sawyer	Chichester
19 November 1766	George Whiting	27	2	5	8½	Farrier	Northampton
26 November 1766	Ephraim Black	22	9	5	6¼	Baker	Tewkesbury

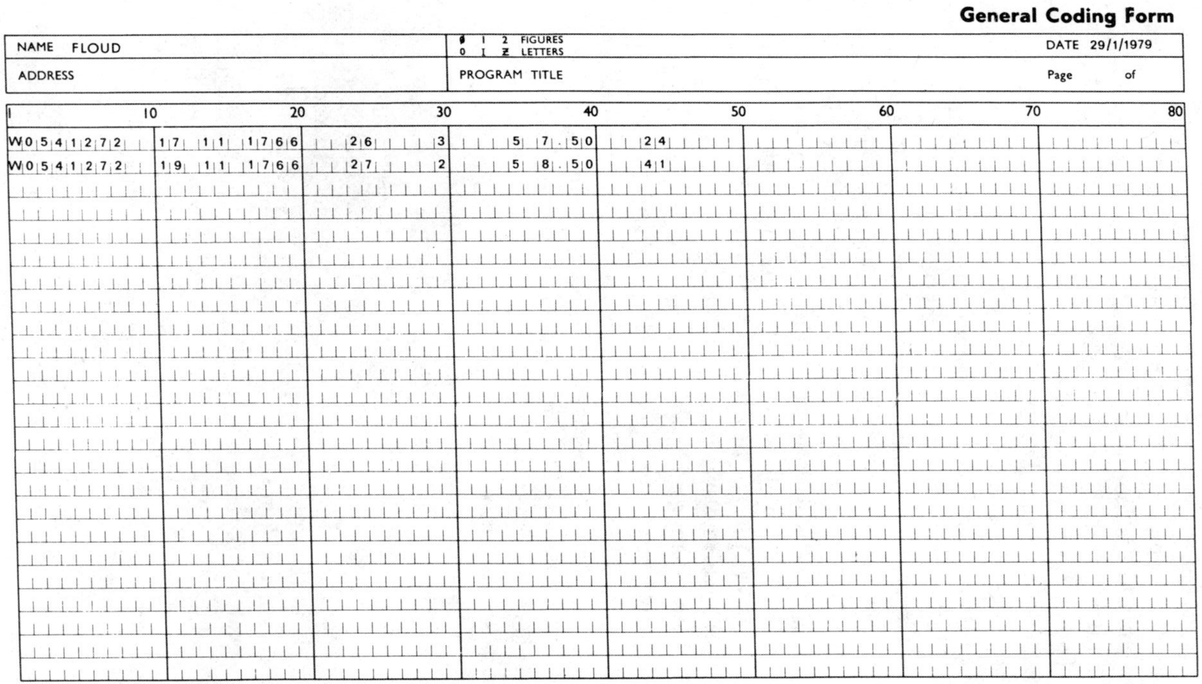

General Coding Form

NAME FLOUD | ∅ 1 2 FIGURES / 0 I Z LETTERS | DATE 29/1/1979

ADDRESS | PROGRAM TITLE | Page of

```
1        10        20        30        40        50        60        70        80
W0541272  17 11 1766   26    3    5 7.50   24
W0541272  19 11 1766   27    2    5 8.50   41
```

Figure 9.2 A coded version of part of Table 9.1, ready to be punched.

numerical form each occupation or birthplace must be assigned a number, which will be recorded on paper and punched card for entry to the computer; these successive stages are shown in Figures 9.2 and 9.3.

The problem which immediately arises, however, is how to assign the numbers. At one extreme, each occupation and birthplace might be given a unique number, which will recur only when that occupation or birthplace is encountered again. Thus all wheelwrights, for example, might be coded as 7, while Chipping Ongar, Essex would always appear as 215. The process of assigning numbers in this way is, however, extremely laborious, because there are so many possible occupations and birthplaces, each of which might appear in the records and therefore need to be assigned a number; there were over 900 occupations recorded even in the British census of 1841, while the number of possible birthplaces is much higher. Such a list of names and numbers is impossible to memorize, so that the process of recording the data as in Figure 9.2 is likely to be time-consuming and lead to inaccuracy. Moreover, the result will be a long list of numbers rather than a long list of occupations, and the historical analysis of the material will not have progressed.

It is to overcome these difficulties that many coding schemes intended to transform historical material into numerical form take a further step of embodying a logical classification of the material into the process of coding. This has the further benefit that the logic of the coding scheme can be used in analysis of the material. Table 9.2 shows some possible coding schemes. Scheme A is the result of assigning numbers to occupations simply in the order in which they are found in the data, while scheme B lists occupations alphabetically. The further step of a logical classification is taken in schemes C and D; the first, C, distinguishes between occupations dealing with different kinds of raw materials. Thus, all occupations working with wood are given numbers between 01 and 09, all occupations dealing with cloth are given numbers between 21 and 29, and so with other raw materials. A residual category, of numbers from 41 to 49, deals with occupations that are not concerned directly with the processing of raw materials. Scheme D, by contrast, classifies

Table 9.2 *Possible coding schemes for personal occupations*

A		B		C		D		E	
1	Iron moulder	1	Basket maker	01	Chairmaker	01	Coppersmith	1	Coppersmith
2	Coppersmith	2	Bookbinder	02	Sawyer	02	Iron moulder	1	Iron Moulder
3	Sawyer	3	Chair maker	03	Ship's carpenter	03	Whitesmith	1	Whitesmith
4	Ship's carpenter	4	Cloth dresser	04	Wheelwright	04	Ship's carpenter	1	Ship's carpenter
5	Painter	5	Coppersmith	11	Coppersmith	05	Rigger	1	Rigger
6	Gunmaker	6	Cordwainer	12	Gunmaker	21	Painter	2	Painter
7	Wheelwright	7	Farrier	13	Iron moulder	22	Plumber	2	Plumber
8	Cordwainer	8	Glove cutter	14	Whitesmith	23	Mason	2	Mason
9	Bookbinder	9	Gunmaker	21	Cloth dresser	24	Sawyer	2	Sawyer
10	Glove cutter	10	Hairdresser	22	Glove cutter	31	Chairmaker	3	Chairmaker
11	Basket maker	11	Iron moulder	31	Basket maker	32	Gunmaker	3	Gunmaker
12	Cloth dresser	12	Lighterman	32	Bookbinder	33	Cloth dresser	3	Cloth dresser
13	Lighterman	13	Mason	33	Cordwainer	34	Glove cutter	3	Glove cutter
14	Whitesmith	14	Painter	34	Painter	35	Basket maker	3	Basket maker
15	Plumber	15	Plumber	35	Plumber	36	Bookbinder	3	Bookbinder
16	Chairmaker	16	Rigger	36	Rigger	37	Cordwainer	3	Cordwainer
17	Farrier	17	Sawyer	37	Mason	38	Wheelwright	3	Wheelwright
18	Mason	18	Ship's carpenter	41	Farrier	41	Farrier	4	Farrier
19	Rigger	19	Wheelwright	42	Hairdresser	42	Hairdresser	4	Hairdresser
20	Hairdresser	20	Whitesmith	43	Lighterman	43	Lighterman	4	Lighterman

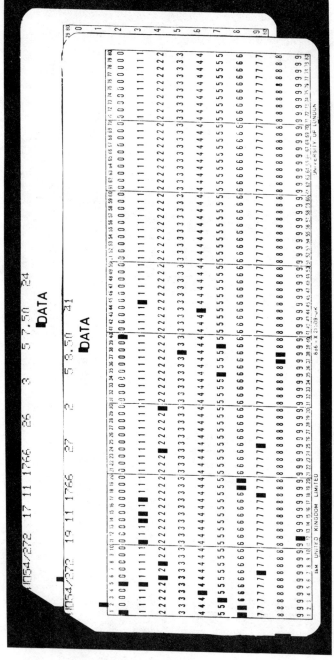

Figure 9.3 A coded version of part of Table 9.1, punched in fixed format.

occupations according to the industry of which they form a part. Thus the metal and shipbuilding trades receive numbers between 01 and 09, the building trades numbers between 21 and 29, and miscellaneous manufacturing industries are given numbers between 31 and 39. It would be possible to think of other logical schemes on the same pattern. Figures 9.2 and 9.3 show data coded according to scheme D.

A further step is to classify the occupations into groups, as in schemes C or D, but then to assign a single number to *all* the occupations falling within each group; all occupations in the building trades, for example, would be coded 2, all those in miscellaneous manufacturing 3, and so on. Such a grouped classification – shown as scheme E – is easier to remember, which facilitates coding and makes it less likely that errors of transcription will occur.

Considerable ingenuity has to be devoted, therefore, to the compilation of suitable coding schemes; properly devised, they are of considerable benefit to historians.[1] But coding can also be harmful if it is carried out too early in the process of the conversion of the data from historical record to machine-readable computer file, as we shall see below.

Coding can be done in one of two ways. First, it can be done by hand as the historian reads his original record and transcribes it as in Figure 9.2 on to sheets of paper, often called 'coding forms', from which a punch-card machine operator can work. One advantage of doing this is that, since the numerical code normally takes up less space than the original information, the amount of transcription and punching is less than if the record were transcribed in alphabetical form. This may make the process of transcription less expensive, and it is also convenient if all the information relating, for example, to one soldier, has to be recorded on one punched card.

There are, however, considerable difficulties and costs associated with this method of coding, often known as 'pre-coding', since it is done before the data are in a machine-readable form.

[1] See, for example, W. A. Armstrong's chapter 'The Use of Information about occupations' in E. A. Wrigley (ed.), *Nineteenth-Century Society* (Cambridge, Cambridge University Press, 1972).

The apparent savings in transcription costs may be outweighed by the difficulty of finding the appropriate numerical code in a list which may be very much longer than that shown in Table 9.2; the possibility of error is large. Most important, however, is that the coding scheme and the codes assigned during transcription are inflexible. Once the data have been coded according to a particular scheme it is very cumbersome to unscramble or to rearrange the data in an alternative logical basis to suit a new method of analysis. At the extreme, with a grouped coding scheme such as scheme E, to do so is impossible, since the fine detail of the original material has been irretrievably lost.

For these reasons historians are increasingly, and sensibly, making use of the second way of coding. Computing is now becoming attuned to the use of words as well as numbers, and it is as easy to input information in alphabetical as in numerical form. This makes it unnecessary for the historian to code his data before it is punched; instead, he can transcribe the data and have it punched as words, if necessary in exactly the same form as in the original historical document. This has been done in Figure 9.4, where the data have been punched with the addition only of a / between each piece of information, to enable a computer program to differentiate between information about, for example, height and information about occupation. Once the data is in machine-readable form, it is simple to write a computer program which will read the data and code it into whatever logical coding scheme is desired; moreover, because the original information is preserved, this coding by computer can be performed any number of times with little difficulty or cost. The information can also be understood easily if it is printed or displayed on a terminal, so that errors can be detected quickly; they can then be corrected using the editing commands which are available on most computing systems.

A further benefit of coding after the data are in machine-readable form is shown by a comparison of Figures 9.3 and 9.4. In Figure 9.3, a particular kind of information, for example that of occupation, is punched at the same place on each card, and the computer program is written to interpret all codes in that place as occupational codes; this is wasteful of space, since a

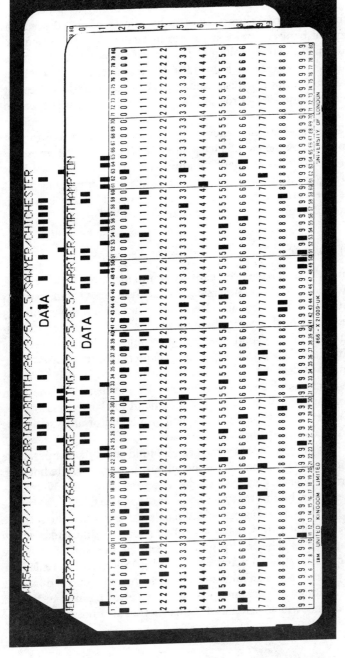

Figure 9.4 Uncoded version of Figure 9.2, punched in free format.

number of card columns have to be reserved for codes which may not be used, and it is easy to make errors and to place the code in the wrong column. This 'fixed-format' input, as it is called, is replaced in Figure 9.4 by 'free-format' input which does not have these disadvantages; if the data are later needed in a fixed format, a program can be written to convert them to this form.

The historian can, therefore, by careful use of free-format input and by the use of such symbols as / in Figure 9.4, preserve the character and shape of the original historical document throughout the input of material into the computer. Once input has been carried out, coding can be done and can be seen as an explicit step in the historical analysis.

(d) Analysing historical data with the computer

Once the data have been converted into machine-readable form and coded if that is necessary, the analysis may begin, starting with the rearrangement, classification and description which is described in the early chapters of this book, and progressing through and beyond the more complex analytical methods which are the subject of the later chapters. All these operations, simple or complex, have to be performed as the result of sets of instructions given to the computer by the historian: the term 'computer analysis' is merely shorthand for 'analysis using the computer', and the choice of which method of analysis to use still rests firmly with the historian.

Sets of instructions which can be followed by a computer are known as 'programs'. It is possible, but extremely tedious, to write programs which can be executed immediately by the computer, because they set out each step to be taken in immense detail. It is as if, instead of telling someone to cross the road we issued him with detailed instructions on each muscular action required to achieve that end. Since numerous such actions are required, repeated many times, it is clearly useful to be able to say 'Cross the road' and know that this will be followed by a set of actions. In the same way, it is useful to be able to write a program which contains the instruction to find the sum of a vector of numbers, without the need to specify exactly how this is to be carried out. To achieve this, programs are written in what are called 'high-level languages' which are then translated by a 'compiler' into the very detailed sets of instructions which can be followed, step by step, by the computer. The most widely known of such languages are FORTRAN and ALGOL, designed primarily for scientific and statistical uses, and COBOL, which is designed for business applications. There are, however, a host of such high-level languages, many of them specific to particular computers or even to particular computer centres; the historian must therefore seek advice as to the language which is both available and best adapted for his needs.

In most high-level languages it is possible to write a program which will carry out any of the descriptive or analytical techniques described in this book. It is, however, wasteful of effort for the historian to attempt to do so. To produce a contingency table or a set of regression results requires, even with a high-level language, a complex and quite lengthy program, but a program which (perhaps with slight modifications) could be applied time and again to different sets of data. It is for this reason that sets of programs known as 'packages' have been written to carry out all but the most specialized of analysis techniques; the historian using a package merely needs to specify the exact nature of the data which he wishes to analyse, and then to give an instruction such as 'CONTINGENCY TABLE' or 'RE-GRESS Y ON X'. These instructions will be translated by the package into sets of programs written in high-level languages, and by the compiler into sets of machine instructions to be followed by the computer.

As an example, the correlation and regression analysis of the shipping data of Table 4.1, which is described in Chapter 7 (see pp. 138–56), could be carried out by using the package known as SPSS (Statistical Package for the Social Sciences). This is the most widely used of statistical packages, and is therefore available for use on most university computers. There are many other such packages, some general and some, like TSP (Time Series Package) or COCOA (a concordance and text processing package) designed for specific types of analysis; once again, the computer centre where the analysis is to be carried out should be consulted about the most appropriate package to use.

A set of instructions for SPSS consists of four parts. The first, known as JCL (Job Control Language) is not part of SPSS, but tells the particular computer which is to be used that SPSS is to be used; the instructions vary from one computer to another. The remaining three parts are common to any SPSS 'job' (as a set of program and data submitted to a computer is called). The first is a set of instructions which controls the entry of data and describes the data, the second is a set of instructions which invokes particular types of statistical analysis, and the third is the set of data which is to be analysed. The complete set of instructions is set out in Figure 9.5, together with a commentary on each line of instructions, while the output from the job, including both the SPSS control cards and the results of the correlation and regression analysis are shown in the Appendix at the end of this chapter.

The existence of SPSS and similar packages makes it unnecessary for the historian to write his own programs for statistical analysis; not only would it be very time-consuming for him to do so, but the results of amateur programming in terms of efficiency and even accuracy are likely to be inferior to the results produced by the teams of expert programmers who have written packages. The historian has to learn how to give instructions to the packages, in the form of control cards and data, and of course has to have sufficient knowledge of statistics to choose the appropriate statistical routine from within the package. Neither of these tasks, however, requires the historian to have the ability to write computer programs.

There is, however, one reason why a historian may need to acquire such expertise. The example shown in Figure 9.5 and in the Appendix made use of a very straightforward set of data which required no manipulation before analysis could begin. When more complex data sets are to be used, and particularly when words are to be processed, coded and analysed in ways described in the last section, then it may be necessary for special purpose programs to be written to carry out these tasks before the rearranged data are submitted to analysis by packages such as SPSS. Many packages, including SPSS, will accept data far more complex than those used in Figure 9.5 and in the Appendix, but at the moment few will cope with the complexities which arise when historical documents such as parish registers, census returns or recruitment records are transferred direct into a machine-readable form. It may therefore be necessary for the historian to acquire sufficient ability in programming to do this for himself, or at least to know enough about the problems to give adequate instructions to a professional programmer. However, this need is now diminishing because of the development of new types of packages which are concerned not with analysis but with the storage and manipulation of data before analysis. 'Data-base management systems,' as these packages are called, are already in use in historical studies, as well as in many related fields such as indexing, cataloguing and bibliography; allied to statistical packages they provide powerful aids to historical research. Any historian who intends to record and analyse a large quantity of data should consider the use of such systems, and should seek professional advice about them.

The remarks in the last paragraph apply, however, only to a minority (although a growing minority) of uses of the computer by historians. In the majority of projects, the size and complexity of the data set is not sufficient to cause great difficulty, and the data management facilities within packages such as SPSS, aided by simple preparatory programs, will meet most needs. What is important, however, is that the historian should be aware of the potential problems, and should solve them before beginning to record his data. Otherwise, an enormous amount of time and effort may be needed to rearrange data for analysis, when a slightly different method of recording could have allowed the data to fit easily into the requirements of the analysis packages. All these packages are fully documented in published manuals which are available from any computer centre offering packages for use; they should be read at an early stage.

Computing offers immense opportunities to the historian, for its power allows him to organize, analyse and comprehend

```
JOB RCF2 2534 SPSS RUN, SAVE              —0001 ⎫
ROUTE UCL, TIME 10, LIMSTORE 200K         —0002 ⎪
PRINTER 3K                                —0003 ⎪
TR OVERNIGHT                              —0004 ⎬ Job control language
PHOENIX                                   —0005 ⎪
SPSS (SYSIN %H+)                          —0006 ⎭
RUN NAME        REGRESSION ANALYSIS OF    —0007  Title of the job
                CREWSIZE ON TONNAGE
VARIABLE LIST   TONNAGE, CREWSIZE         —0008  List of variables — two in this case
INPUT MEDIUM    CARD                      —0009  The input method — can be card, tape, disk
INPUT FORMAT    FIXED (F5.0,F3.0)         —0010  The format or place of the data on each card
N OF CASES      25                        —0011  No of cases
REGRESSION      VARIABLES = TONNAGE, CREWSIZE /   —0012 ⎫ Instruction to perform a regression
                REGRESSION = CREWSIZE WITH        —0013 ⎬
                TONNAGE (2) RESID = 0/            —0013 ⎭
STATISTICS      ALL                       —0014  Instruction to compute a number of optional statistics
READ INPUT DATA                           —0015  Instruction to read the following data
     44    3                              —0016 ⎫
    144    6                              —0017 ⎪
    150    5                              —0018 ⎪
    236    8                              —0019 ⎬ data
    739   16                              —0020 ⎪
    970   15                              —0021 ⎪
   2371   23                              —0022 ⎪
    309    5                              —0023 ⎭
```

```
—0024 ⎫
—0025 ⎪
—0026 ⎪
—0027 ⎪
—0028 ⎪
—0029 ⎪
—0030 ⎪
—0031 ⎬ data
—0032 ⎪
—0033 ⎪
—0034 ⎪
—0035 ⎪
—0036 ⎪
—0037 ⎪
—0038 ⎪
—0039 ⎪
—0040 ⎭
—0041  Instruction that job is to be concluded
—0042 ⎫ Job control language
—0043 ⎭
```

```
679   13
 26    4
1272  19
3246  33
1904  19
357   10
1080  16
1027  22
 45    2
 62    3
 68    2
2507  22
138    2
502   18
1501  21
2750  24
192    9
FINISH
+
//*
```

Figure 9.5 An SPSS job input. Data from Table 4.1.

historical data in ways that have never before been possible. There is, of course, no guarantee that the results of research will be interesting or valuable, but it is clearly desirable that a new range of sources should be open to historical investigation. How well historians use the new sources, and how well they use all the techniques described in this book, can be judged only when the work has been done.

Appendix to Chapter 9

Output from the SPSS job set out in Figure 9.5

```
STATISTICAL PACKAGE FOR THE SOCIAL SCIENCES                              01/31/79

SPSS FOR OS/360, VERSION H, RELEASE 7.2          DECEMBER 5, 1977

DEFAULT SPACE ALLOCATION        ALLOWS FOR      64 TRANSFORMATIONS
WORKSPACE    44800 BYTES                        256 RECODE VALUES = LAG VARIABLES
TRANSPACE     6400 BYTES                        1024 IF/COMPUTE OPERATIONS

         RUN NAME        REGRESSION ANALYSIS OF CREWSIZE ON TONNAGE
         VARIABLE LIST   TONNAGE, CREWSIZE
         INPUT MEDIUM    CARD
         INPUT FORMAT    FIXED (F5.0, F3.0)

         ACCORDING TO YOUR INPUT FORMAT, VARIABLES ARE TO BE READ AS FOLLOWS

         VARIABLE    FORMAT  RECORD  COLUMNS
         TONNAGE     F5. 0      1    1—    5
         CREWSIZE    F3. 0      1    6—    8

THE INPUT FORMAT PROVIDES FOR 2 VARIABLES. 2 WILL BE READ
IT PROVIDES FOR 1 RECORDS ('CARDS') PER CASE. A MAXIMUM OF 8 'COLUMNS' ARE USED ON A RECORD

         N OF CASES      25
         REGRESSION      VARIABLES = TONNAGE, CREWSIZE/
                         REGRESSION = CREWSIZE WITH TONNAGE (2) RESID=0/
         STATISTICS      ALL

····· REGRESSION PROBLEM REQUIRES 182 BYTES WORKSPACE, NOT INCLUDING RESIDUALS. ·····

         READ INPUT DATA


REGRESSION ANALYSIS OF CREWSIZE ON TONNAGE                               01/31/79

FILE  NONAME   (CREATION DATE = 01/31/79)

VARIABLE      MEAN      STANDARD DEV      CASES
TONNAGE     892.7600     965.8430          25
CREWSIZE     12.8000       8.7464          25


REGRESSION ANALYSIS OF CREWSIZE ON TONNAGE                               01/31/79

FILE  NONAME   (CREATION DATE = 01/31/79)

CORRELATION COEFFICIENTS

A VALUE OF 99.00000 IS PRINTED
IF A COEFFICIENT CANNOT BE COMPUTED.
```

```
                    TONNAGE      CREWSIZE
TONNAGE             1.00000      0.90936
CREWSIZE            0.90936      1.00000

REGRESSION ANALYSIS OF CREWSIZE ON TONNAGE                    01/31/79
FILE   NONAME   (CREATION DATE = 01/31/79)
 . . . . . . . . . . . . .  MULTIPLE REGRESSION  . . . . . . . .       VARIABLE LIST     1
                                                                      REGRESSION LIST    1

DEPENDENT VARIABLE         CREWSIZE
VARIABLE(S) ENTERED ON STEP NUMBER 1. .  TONNAGE
MULTIPLE R           0.90936      ANALYSIS OF VARIANCE       DF     SUM OF SQUARES      MEAN SQUARE         F
R SQUARE             0.82693      REGRESSION                 1.       1518.24230        1518.24230      109.98371
ADJUSTED R SQUARE    0.81940      RESIDUAL                   23.       317.75770          13.81555
STANDARD ERROR       3.71693
           VARIABLES IN THE EQUATION                  ------------VARIABLES NOT IN THE EQUATION------------
VARIABLE            B            BETA  STD ERROR B      F      VARIABLE      BETA IN    PARTIAL   TOLERANCE      F
TONNAGE       0.8234901D-02    0.90936   0.00079    109.894
(CONSTANT)    5.448210
MAXIMUM STEP REACHED
STATISTICS WHICH CANNOT BE COMPUTED ARE PRINTED AS ALL NINES.


REGRESSION ANALYSIS OF CREWSIZE ON TONNAGE                    01/31/79
FILE   NONAME   (CREATION DATE = 01/31/79)
 . . . . . . . . . . . . .  MULTIPLE REGRESSION  . . . . . . . .       VARIABLE LIST     1
                                                                      REGRESSION LIST    1
DEPENDENT VARIABLE CREWSIZE
                                    SUMMARY TABLE
VARIABLE       MULTIPLE R    R SQUARE    RSQ CHANGE    SIMPLE R           B              BETA
TONNAGE         0.0936       0.82693      0.82693       0.90936      0.8234901D-02      0.90936
(CONSTANT)                                                            5.448210

REGRESSION ANALYSIS OF CREWSIZE ON TONNAGE                    01/31/79
..... REGRESSION PROBLEM REQUIRES 2232 BYTES WORKSPACE INCLUDING RESIDUALS .....
```

REGRESSION ANALYSIS OF CREWSIZE ON TONNAGE   01/31/79
FILE   NONAME   (CREATION DATE = 01/31/79)
. . . . .   MULTIPLE REGRESSION   . . . . .

DEPENDENT VARIABLE: CREWSIZE   FROM   VARIABLE LIST 1
                                        REGRESSION LIST 1

SEQNUM	OBSERVED CREWSIZE	PREDICTED CREWSIZE	RESIDUAL	PLOT OF STANDARDIZED RESIDUAL
1	3.000000	5.810546	-2.810545	
2	6.000000	6.634035	-0.6340357	
3	5.000000	6.683445	-1.683445	
4	8.000000	7.391646	0.6083534	
5	16.00000	11.53380	4.466198	
6	15.00000	13.43606	1.563936	
7	23.00000	24.97314	-1.973159	
8	5.000000	7.992794	-2.992794	
9	13.00000	11.03971	1.960292	
10	4.000000	5.662317	-1.662317	
11	19.00000	15.92300	3.076996	
12	33.00000	32.17868	0.8213021	
13	19.00000	21.12746	-2.127460	
14	10.00000	8.388069	1.611930	
15	16.00000	14.34190	1.658096	
16	22.00000	13.90545	8.094546	
17	2.000000	5.818781	-3.818780	
18	3.000000	5.958774	-2.958774	
19	2.000000	6.008183	-4.008183	
20	22.00000	26.09309	-4.093105	
21	2.000000	6.584626	-4.584626	
22	18.00000	9.582130	8.417870	
23	21.00000	17.80879	3.191203	
24	24.00000	28.09418	-4.094187	
25	9.000000	7.029311	1.970689	

PLOT OF STANDARDIZED RESIDUAL
-2.0   -1.0   0.0   1.0   2.0

DURBIN-WATSON TEST OF RESIDUAL DIFFERENCES COMPARED BY CASE ORDER (SEQNUM).
VARIALBE LIST 1. REGRESSION LIST 1. DURBIN-WATSON TEST 1.91190

REGRESSION ANALYSIS OF CREWSIZE ON TONNAGE   01/31/79
FILE   NONAME   (CREATION DATE = 01/31/79)
. . . . .   PLOT: STANDARDIZED RESIDUAL (DOWN)   . . . .

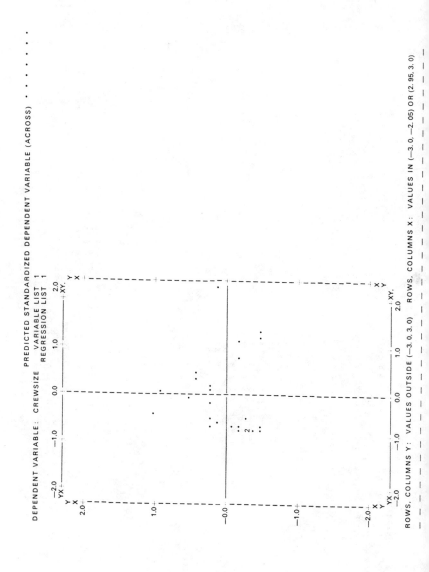

01/31/79

REGRESSION ANALYSIS OF CREWSIZE ON TONNAGE
CPU TIME REQUIRED..   0.38 SECONDS
           FINISH
     NORMAL END OF JOB.
        10 CONTROL CARDS WERE PROCESSED.
         0 ERRORS WERE DETECTED.
      0.1 TRACKS OF SCRATCH SPACE WERE NEEDED THIS RUN.

Bibliography

So many books and articles have been published which make use of the methods described in this book that it is impossible to list all, or even a large number, of them. Any bibliography must therefore be selective. In Section A are listed a number of books which cover topics that this book also covers, though with different emphasis and examples. Many of them devote more space than has been possible here to the theory of probability and sampling, and to more advanced statistical methods. Section B contains books which discuss the application of quantitative methods to historical problems, or which give examples of such work in a variety of historical fields and periods of time. Almost all contain extensive bibliographies, hence the reader of this book is recommended to search within the books in Section B for other books and articles relevant to his own interests.

A: Introductory books on statistics and quantitative methods

ALLEN, R. G. D., *Statistics for Economists* (London, Hutchinson University Library, 1966).

BLALOCK, H. M., *Social Statistics* (New York, McGraw-Hill, 1960).

CAULCOTT, E., *Significance Tests* (London, Routledge & Kegan Paul, 1973).

DOLLAR, C. M. and JENSEN, R. J., *Historian's Guide to Statistics: Quantitative Analysis and Historical Research* (New York, Holt, Rinehart and Winston, 1971).

DRAKE, M., *Historical Data and the Social Sciences:* Vol. I, *The Quantitative Analysis of Historical Data* (Milton Keynes, Open University Press, 1974).

GALTUNG, J., *Theory and Methods of Social Research* (London, George Allen and Unwin, 1967).

MORONEY, M. J., *Facts from Figures* (Harmondsworth, Penguin Books, 1960).

NIE, N. H. *et al.*, *Statistical Package for the Social Sciences* (New York, McGraw-Hill, 1975).

SIEGEL, S., *Nonparametric Statistics for the Behavioural Sciences* (New York, McGraw-Hill, 1956).

YEOMANS, K. A., *Statistics for the Social Scientist*: Vol. I, *Introductory Statistics*; Vol. II, *Applied Statistics* (Harmondsworth, Penguin Books, 1968).

B: Methodology and collections of quantitative historical studies

ANDREANO, R. L. (ed.), *The New Economic History: Recent Papers on Methodology* (New York, John Wiley, 1970).

AYDELOTTE, W. O., *Quantification in History* (Reading, Mass., Addison-Wesley, 1971).

AYDELOTTE, W. O., BOGUE, A. G. and FOGEL, R. W. (eds.), *The Dimensions of Quantitative Research in History* (London, Oxford University Press, 1972).

AYDELOTTE, W. O. (ed.), *A History of Parliamentary Behaviour* (Princeton, N.J., Princeton University Press, 1977).

BERKHOFER, R. F. jun., *A Behavioral Approach to Historical Analysis* (New York, Free Press, 1969).

BLALOCK, H. M. and A., *Methodology in Social Research* (New York, McGraw-Hill, 1968).

BOGUE, A. G. (ed.), *Emerging Theoretical Models in Social and Political History* (Beverley Hills and London, Sage Publications, 1973).

CLUBB, J. and SCHEUCH, E. K. (eds.), *Historical Social Research* (Stuttgart, Klett-Cotta, 1979).

CLUBB, J. and TRAUGOTT, M. W., *Using Computers* (Washington, D.C., American Political Science Association, 1978).

DAVIS, L. E. and NORTH, D., *Institutional Change and American Economic Growth* (Cambridge, Cambridge University Press, 1971).

DRAKE, M. (ed.), *Applied Historical Studies* (London, Methuen, 1973).

DRAKE, M., *Historical Data and the Social Sciences*: Vol. 2, *Historical Demography*; Vol. 3, *Introduction to Historical Psephology*; Vol. 4, *Exercises in Historical Sociology* (Milton Keynes, Open University Press, 1974).

ENGERMAN, S. L. and GENOVESE, E. D. (eds.), *Race and Slavery in the Western Hemisphere: Quantitative Studies* (Princeton, Princeton University Press. 1975).

FLOUD, R. C. (ed.), *Essays in Quantitative Economic History* (Oxford, Clarendon Press, 1974).

FOGEL, R. W. and ENGERMAN, S. L. (eds.), *The Re-interpretation of American Economic History* (New York, Harper and Row, 1971).

GLASS, D. V. and EVERSLEY, D. E. C. (eds.), *Population in History* (London, Edward Arnold, 1965).

GOULD, J. D., *Economic Growth in History* (London, Methuen, 1972).

HOLLINGSWORTH, T. H., *Historical Demography* (London, Hodder and Stoughton, 1969).

INTRILIGATOR, M. (ed.), *Frontiers of Quantitative Economics* (Amsterdam, North Holland, 1971).

IRSIGLER, F. (ed.), *Quantitative Methoden in der Wirtschafts- und Sozialgeschichte der Vorneuzeit* (Stuttgart, Klett-Cotta, 1978).

KURGAN, G. and MOUREAUX, P. (eds.), *La Quantification en Histoire* (Brussels, Brussels University Press, 1973).

LE ROY LADURIE, E., *Le Territoire de l'Historien* (Paris, Gallimard, 1973).

LANDES, D. S. and TILLY, C., *History as Social Science* (Englewood Cliffs, N.J., Prentice Hall, 1971).

LEE, C. H., *The Quantitative Approach to Economic History* (London, Martin Robertson, 1977).

LEE, R. D. (ed.), *Population Patterns in the Past* (New York, Academic Press, 1977).

LIPSET, S. M. (ed.), *Politics and the Social Sciences* (New York, Oxford University Press, 1969).

LIPSET, S. M. and HOFSTADIER, R. (eds.), *Sociology and History: Methods* (New York, Basic Books, 1968).

LORWIN, V. R. and PRICE, J. M., *The Dimensions of the Past. Materials, Problems, and Opportunities for Quantitative Work in History* (New Haven and London, Yale University Press, 1972).

MCCLELLAND, P. D., *Causal Explanation and Model Building in History, Economics and the New Economic History* (Ithaca, N.Y., Cornell University Press, 1975).

MCCLOSKEY, D. N. (ed.), *Essays on a Mature Economy: Britain after 1840* (London, Methuen, 1971).

MACFARLANE, A., *Reconstructing Historical Communities* (Cambridge, Cambridge University Press, 1978).

MERRITT, R. and ROKKAN, S., *Comparing Nations: The Use of Quantitative Data in Cross-National Research* (New Haven, Conn., Yale University Press, 1966).

O'BRIEN, P., *The New Economic History of the Railways* (London, Croom Helm, 1977).

ROWNEY, D. K. and GRAHAM, J. Q. jun. (eds.), *Quantitative History: Selected Readings in the Quantitative Analysis of Historical Data* (Homewood, Ill., Dorsey Press, 1969).

SCHNORE, L. F. (ed.), *The New Urban History. Quantitative Explorations by American Historians* (Princeton, N.J., Princeton University Press, 1975).

SILBEY, J. H., BOGUE, A. G. and FLANIGAN, W. H., *The History of American Electoral Behavior* (Princeton, N.J., Princeton University Press, 1978).

Studies in Quantitative History and the Logic of the Social Sciences (Middletown, Connecticut, Wesleyan University Press. *History and Theory*, supplement 9, 1969).

SWIERENGA, R. P. (ed.), *Quantification in American History* (New York, Atheneum, 1970).

TEMIN, P. (ed.), *The New Economic History* (Harmondsworth, Penguin Books, 1973).

TILLY, C. (ed.), *Historical Studies of Changing Fertility* (Princeton, N.J., Princeton University Press, 1978).

WACHTER, K. A. with E. A. HAMMEL and P. LASLETT, *Statistical Studies of Historical Social Structure* (New York and London, Academic Press, 1978).

WILLIAMSON, J. G., *Late Nineteenth Century American Development. A General Equilibrium History* (Cambridge, Cambridge University Press, 1974).

WRIGLEY, E. A. (ed.), *An Introduction to English Historical Demography* (London, Weidenfeld and Nicolson, 1966).

WRIGLEY, E. A. (ed.), *Nineteenth Century Society. Essays in the Use of Quantitative Methods for the Study of Social Data* (Cambridge, Cambridge University Press, 1972).

WRIGLEY, E. A. (ed.), *Identifying People in the Past* (London, Edward Arnold, 1973).

Four Figure Logarithms

	0	1	2	3	4	5	6	7	8	9	1	2	3	4	5	6	7	8	9
											Mean Differences.								
10	0000	0043	0086	0128	0170	0212	0253	0294	0334	0374	4	8	12	17	21	25	29	33	37
11	0414	0453	0492	0531	0569	0607	0645	0682	0719	0755	4	8	11	15	19	23	26	30	34
12	0792	0828	0864	0899	0934	0969	1004	1038	1072	1106	3	7	10	14	17	21	24	28	31
13	1139	1173	1206	1239	1271	1303	1335	1367	1399	1430	3	6	10	13	16	19	23	26	29
14	1461	1492	1523	1553	1584	1614	1644	1673	1703	1732	3	6	9	12	15	18	21	24	27
15	1761	1790	1818	1847	1875	1903	1931	1959	1987	2014	3	6	8	11	14	17	20	22	25
16	2041	2068	2095	2122	2148	2175	2201	2227	2253	2279	3	5	8	11	13	16	18	21	24
17	2304	2330	2355	2380	2405	2430	2455	2480	2504	2529	2	5	7	10	12	15	17	20	22
18	2553	2577	2601	2625	2648	2672	2695	2718	2742	2765	2	5	7	9	12	14	16	19	21
19	2788	2810	2833	2856	2878	2900	2923	2945	2967	2989	2	4	7	9	11	13	16	18	20
20	3010	3032	3054	3075	3096	3118	3139	3160	3181	3201	2	4	6	8	11	13	15	17	19
21	3222	3243	3263	3284	3304	3324	3345	3365	3385	3404	2	4	6	8	10	12	14	16	18
22	3424	3444	3464	3483	3502	3522	3541	3560	3579	3598	2	4	6	8	10	12	14	15	17
23	3617	3636	3655	3674	3692	3711	3729	3747	3766	3784	2	4	6	7	9	11	13	15	17
24	3802	3820	3838	3856	3874	3892	3909	3927	3945	3962	2	4	5	7	9	11	12	14	16
25	3979	3997	4014	4031	4048	4065	4082	4099	4116	4133	2	3	5	7	9	10	12	14	15
26	4150	4166	4183	4200	4216	4232	4249	4265	4281	4298	2	3	5	7	8	10	11	13	15
27	4314	4330	4346	4362	4378	4393	4409	4425	4440	4456	2	3	5	6	8	9	11	13	14
28	4472	4487	4502	4518	4533	4548	4564	4579	4594	4609	2	3	5	6	8	9	11	12	14
29	4624	4639	4654	4669	4683	4698	4713	4728	4742	4757	1	3	4	6	7	9	10	12	13
30	4771	4786	4800	4814	4829	4843	4857	4871	4886	4900	1	3	4	6	7	9	10	11	13
31	4914	4928	4942	4955	4969	4983	4997	5011	5024	5038	1	3	4	6	7	8	10	11	12
32	5051	5065	5079	5092	5105	5119	5132	5145	5159	5172	1	3	4	5	7	8	9	11	12
33	5185	5198	5211	5224	5237	5250	5263	5276	5289	5302	1	3	4	5	6	8	9	10	12
34	5315	5328	5340	5353	5366	5378	5391	5403	5416	5428	1	3	4	5	6	8	9	10	11
35	5441	5453	5465	5478	5490	5502	5514	5527	5539	5551	1	2	4	5	6	7	9	10	11
36	5563	5575	5587	5599	5611	5623	5635	5647	5658	5670	1	2	4	5	6	7	8	10	11
37	5682	5694	5705	5717	5729	5740	5752	5763	5775	5786	1	2	3	5	6	7	8	9	10
38	5798	5809	5821	5832	5843	5855	5866	5877	5888	5899	1	2	3	5	6	7	8	9	10
39	5911	5922	5933	5944	5955	5966	5977	5988	5999	6010	1	2	3	4	5	7	8	9	10
40	6021	6031	6042	6053	6064	6075	6085	6096	6107	6117	1	2	3	4	5	6	8	9	10
41	6128	6138	6149	6160	6170	6180	6191	6201	6212	6222	1	2	3	4	5	6	7	8	9
42	6232	6243	6253	6263	6274	6284	6294	6304	6314	6325	1	2	3	4	5	6	7	8	9
43	6335	6345	6355	6365	6375	6385	6395	6405	6415	6425	1	2	3	4	5	6	7	8	9
44	6435	6444	6454	6464	6474	6484	6493	6503	6513	6522	1	2	3	4	5	6	7	8	9
45	6532	6542	6551	6561	6571	6580	6590	6599	6609	6618	1	2	3	4	5	6	7	7	8
46	6628	6637	6646	6656	6665	6675	6684	6693	6702	6712	1	2	3	4	5	5	6	7	8
47	6721	6730	6739	6749	6758	6767	6776	6785	6794	6803	1	2	3	4	5	5	6	7	8
48	6812	6821	6830	6839	6848	6857	6866	6875	6884	6893	1	2	3	4	4	5	6	7	8
49	6902	6911	6920	6928	6937	6946	6955	6964	6972	6981	1	2	3	4	4	5	6	7	8
50	6990	6998	7007	7016	7024	7033	7042	7050	7059	7067	1	2	3	3	4	5	6	7	8
51	7076	7084	7093	7101	7110	7118	7126	7135	7143	7152	1	2	3	3	4	5	6	7	8
52	7160	7168	7177	7185	7193	7202	7210	7218	7226	7235	1	2	2	3	4	5	6	6	7
53	7243	7251	7259	7267	7275	7284	7292	7300	7308	7316	1	2	2	3	4	5	5	6	7
54	7324	7332	7340	7343	7356	7364	7372	7380	7388	7396	1	2	2	3	4	5	5	6	7

Four Figure Logarithms

	0	1	2	3	4	5	6	7	8	9	Mean Differences.								
											1	2	3	4	5	6	7	8	9
55	7404	7412	7419	7427	7435	7443	7451	7459	7466	7474	1	2	2	3	4	5	5	6	7
56	7482	7490	7497	7505	7513	7520	7528	7536	7543	7551	1	2	2	3	4	5	5	6	7
57	7559	7566	7574	7582	7589	7597	7604	7612	7619	7627	1	2	2	3	4	5	5	6	7
58	7634	7642	7649	7657	7664	7672	7679	7686	7694	7701	1	2	3	4	4	5	6	7	
59	7709	7716	7723	7731	7738	7745	7752	7760	7767	7774	1	1	2	3	4	4	5	6	7
60	7782	7789	7796	7803	7810	7818	7825	7832	7839	7846	1	1	2	3	4	4	5	6	6
61	7853	7860	7868	7875	7882	7889	7896	7903	7910	7917	1	1	2	3	4	4	5	6	6
62	7924	7931	7938	7945	7952	7959	7966	7973	7980	7987	1	1	2	3	4	4	5	6	6
63	7993	8000	8007	8014	8021	8028	8035	8041	8048	8055	1	1	2	3	3	4	5	6	6
64	8062	8069	8075	8082	8089	8096	8102	8109	8116	8122	1	1	2	3	3	4	5	5	6
65	8129	8136	8142	8149	8156	8162	8169	8176	8182	8189	1	1	2	3	3	4	5	5	6
66	8195	8202	8209	8215	8222	8228	8235	8241	8248	8254	1	1	2	3	3	4	5	5	6
67	8261	8267	8274	8280	8287	8293	8299	8306	8312	8319	1	1	2	3	3	4	5	5	6
68	8325	8331	8338	8344	8351	8357	8363	8370	8376	8382	1	1	2	3	3	4	4	5	6
69	8388	8395	8401	8407	8414	8420	8426	8432	8439	8445	1	1	2	3	3	4	4	5	6
70	8451	8457	8463	8470	8476	8482	8488	8494	8500	8506	1	1	2	2	3	4	4	5	6
71	8513	8519	8525	8531	8537	8543	8549	8555	8561	8567	1	1	2	2	3	4	4	5	5
72	8573	8579	8585	8591	8597	8603	8609	8615	8621	8627	1	1	2	2	3	4	4	5	5
73	8633	8639	8645	8651	8657	8663	8669	8675	8681	8686	1	1	2	2	3	4	4	5	5
74	8692	8698	8704	8710	8716	8722	8727	8733	8739	8745	1	1	2	2	3	4	4	5	5
75	8751	8756	8762	8768	8774	8779	8785	8791	8797	8802	1	1	2	2	3	3	4	5	5
76	8808	8814	8820	8825	8831	8837	8842	8848	8854	8859	1	1	2	2	3	3	4	5	5
77	8865	8871	8876	8882	8887	8893	8899	8904	8910	8915	1	1	2	2	3	3	4	4	5
78	8921	8927	8932	8938	8943	8949	8954	8960	8965	8971	1	1	2	2	3	3	4	4	5
79	8976	8982	8987	8993	8998	9004	9009	9015	9020	9025	1	1	2	2	3	3	4	4	5
80	9031	9036	9042	9047	9053	9058	9063	9069	9074	9079	1	1	2	2	3	3	4	4	5
81	9085	9090	9096	9101	9106	9112	9117	9122	9128	9133	1	1	2	2	3	3	4	4	5
82	9138	9143	9149	9154	9159	9165	9170	9175	9180	9186	1	1	2	2	3	3	4	4	5
83	9191	9196	9201	9206	9212	9217	9222	9227	9232	9238	1	1	2	2	3	3	4	4	5
84	9243	9248	9253	9258	9263	9269	9274	9279	9284	9289	1	1	2	2	3	3	4	4	5
85	9294	9299	9304	9309	9315	9320	9325	9330	9335	9340	1	1	2	2	3	3	4	4	5
86	9345	9350	9355	9360	9365	9370	9375	9380	9385	9390	1	1	2	2	3	3	4	4	5
87	9395	9400	9405	9410	9415	9420	9425	9430	9435	9440	0	1	1	2	2	3	3	4	4
88	9445	9450	9455	9460	9465	9469	9474	9479	9484	9489	0	1	1	2	2	3	3	4	4
89	9494	9499	9504	9509	9513	9518	9523	9528	9533	9538	0	1	1	2	2	3	3	4	4
90	9542	9547	9552	9557	9562	9566	9571	9576	9581	9586	0	1	1	2	2	3	3	4	4
91	9590	9595	9600	9605	9609	9614	9619	9624	9628	9633	0	1	1	2	2	3	3	4	4
92	9638	9643	9647	9652	9657	9661	9666	9671	9675	9680	0	1	1	2	2	3	3	4	4
93	9685	9689	9694	9699	9703	9708	9713	9717	9722	9727	0	1	1	2	2	3	3	4	4
94	9731	9736	9741	9745	9750	9754	9759	9763	9768	9773	0	1	1	2	2	3	3	4	4
95	9777	9782	9786	9791	9795	9800	9805	9809	9814	9818	0	1	1	2	2	3	3	4	4
96	9823	9827	9832	9836	9841	9845	9850	9854	9859	9863	0	1	1	2	2	3	3	4	4
97	9868	9872	9877	9881	9886	9890	9894	9899	9903	9908	0	1	1	2	2	3	3	4	4
98	9912	9917	9921	9926	9930	9934	9939	9943	9948	9952	0	1	1	2	2	3	3	4	4
99	9956	9961	9965	9969	9974	9978	9983	9987	9991	9996	0	1	1	2	2	3	3	3	4

Four Figure Antilogarithms

	0	1	2	3	4	5	6	7	8	9	Mean Differences.								
											1	2	3	4	5	6	7	8	9
·00	1000	1002	1005	1007	1009	1012	1014	1016	1019	1021	0	0	1	1	1	1	2	2	2
·01	1023	1026	1028	1030	1033	1035	1038	1040	1042	1045	0	0	1	1	1	1	2	2	2
·02	1047	1050	1052	1054	1057	1059	1062	1064	1067	1069	0	0	1	1	1	1	2	2	2
·03	1072	1074	1076	1079	1081	1084	1086	1089	1091	1094	0	0	1	1	1	1	2	2	2
·04	1096	1099	1102	1104	1107	1109	1112	1114	1117	1119	1	1	1	1	2	2	2	2	2
·05	1122	1125	1127	1130	1132	1135	1138	1140	1143	1146	0	1	1	1	1	2	2	2	2
·06	1148	1151	1153	1156	1159	1161	1164	1167	1169	1172	0	1	1	1	1	2	2	2	2
·07	1175	1178	1180	1183	1186	1189	1191	1194	1197	1199	0	1	1	1	1	2	2	2	2
·08	1202	1205	1208	1211	1213	1216	1219	1222	1225	1227	0	1	1	1	1	2	2	2	3
·09	1230	1233	1236	1239	1242	1245	1247	1250	1253	1256	0	1	1	1	1	2	2	2	3
·10	1259	1262	1265	1268	1271	1274	1276	1279	1282	1285	0	1	1	1	1	2	2	2	3
·11	1288	1291	1294	1297	1300	1303	1306	1309	1312	1315	0	1	1	1	2	2	2	2	3
·12	1318	1321	1324	1327	1330	1334	1337	1340	1343	1346	0	1	1	1	2	2	2	3	3
·13	1349	1352	1355	1358	1361	1365	1368	1371	1374	1377	0	1	1	1	2	2	2	3	3
·14	1380	1384	1387	1390	1393	1396	1400	1403	1406	1409	0	1	1	1	2	2	2	3	3
·15	1413	1416	1419	1422	1426	1429	1432	1435	1439	1442	0	1	1	1	2	2	2	3	3
·16	1445	1449	1452	1455	1459	1462	1466	1469	1472	1476	0	1	1	1	2	2	2	3	3
·17	1479	1483	1486	1489	1493	1496	1500	1503	1507	1510	0	1	1	1	2	2	2	3	3
·18	1514	1517	1521	1524	1528	1531	1535	1538	1542	1545	0	1	1	1	2	2	2	3	3
·19	1549	1552	1556	1560	1563	1567	1570	1574	1578	1581	0	1	1	1	2	2	3	3	3
·20	1585	1589	1592	1596	1600	1603	1607	1611	1614	1618	0	1	1	1	2	2	3	3	3
·21	1622	1626	1629	1633	1637	1641	1644	1648	1652	1656	0	1	1	2	2	2	3	3	3
·22	1660	1663	1667	1671	1675	1679	1683	1687	1690	1694	0	1	1	2	2	2	3	3	3
·23	1698	1702	1706	1710	1714	1718	1722	1726	1730	1734	0	1	1	2	2	2	3	3	4
·24	1738	1742	1746	1750	1754	1758	1762	1766	1770	1774	0	1	1	2	2	2	3	3	4
·25	1778	1782	1786	1791	1795	1799	1803	1807	1811	1816	0	1	1	2	2	2	3	3	4
·26	1820	1824	1828	1832	1837	1841	1845	1849	1854	1858	0	1	1	2	2	3	3	3	4
·27	1862	1866	1871	1875	1879	1884	1888	1892	1897	1901	0	1	1	2	2	3	3	4	4
·28	1905	1910	1914	1919	1923	1928	1932	1936	1941	1945	0	1	1	2	2	3	3	4	4
·29	1950	1954	1959	1963	1968	1972	1977	1982	1986	1991	0	1	1	2	2	3	3	4	4
·30	1995	2000	2004	2009	2014	2018	2023	2028	2032	2037	0	1	1	2	2	3	3	4	4
·31	2042	2046	2051	2056	2061	2065	2070	2075	2080	2084	0	1	1	2	2	3	3	4	4
·32	2089	2094	2099	2104	2109	2113	2118	2123	2128	2133	0	1	1	2	2	3	3	4	4
·33	2138	2143	2148	2153	2158	2163	2168	2173	2178	2183	0	1	1	2	2	3	3	4	4
·34	2188	2193	2198	2203	2208	2213	2218	2223	2228	2234	1	1	2	2	3	3	4	4	5
·35	2239	2244	2249	2254	2259	2265	2270	2275	2280	2286	1	2	2	3	3	4	4	5	5
·36	2291	2296	2301	2307	2312	2317	2323	2328	2333	2339	1	2	2	3	3	4	4	5	5
·37	2344	2350	2355	2360	2366	2371	2377	2382	2388	2393	1	2	2	3	3	4	4	5	5
·38	2399	2404	2410	2415	2421	2427	2432	2438	2443	2449	1	2	2	3	3	4	4	5	5
·39	2455	2460	2466	2472	2477	2483	2489	2495	2500	2506	1	2	2	3	3	4	5	5	5
·40	2512	2518	2523	2529	2535	2541	2547	2553	2559	2564	1	2	2	3	4	4	5	5	5
·41	2570	2576	2582	2588	2594	2600	2606	2612	2618	2624	1	2	2	3	4	4	5	5	5
·42	2630	2636	2642	2649	2655	2661	2667	2673	2679	2685	1	2	2	3	4	4	5	5	6
·43	2692	2698	2704	2710	2716	2723	2729	2735	2742	2748	1	2	3	3	4	4	5	5	6
·44	2754	2761	2767	2773	2780	2786	2793	2799	2805	2812	1	2	3	3	4	4	5	5	6
·45	2818	2825	2831	2838	2844	2851	2858	2864	2871	2877	1	2	3	3	4	5	5	5	6
·46	2884	2891	2897	2904	2911	2917	2924	2931	2938	2944	1	2	3	3	4	5	5	5	6
·47	2951	2958	2965	2972	2979	2985	2992	2999	3006	3013	1	2	3	3	4	5	5	5	6
·48	3020	3027	3034	3041	3048	3055	3062	3069	3076	3083	1	2	3	4	4	5	6	6	6
·49	3090	3097	3105	3112	3119	3126	3133	3141	3148	3155	1	2	3	4	4	5	6	6	6

Four Figure Antilogarithms

	0	1	2	3	4	5	6	7	8	9	1	2	3	4	5	6	7	8	9
·50	3162	3170	3177	3184	3192	3199	3206	3214	3221	3228	1	1	2	3	4	4	5	6	7
·51	3236	3243	3251	3258	3266	3273	3281	3289	3296	3304	1	2	2	3	4	5	5	6	7
·52	3311	3319	3327	3334	3342	3350	3357	3365	3373	3381	1	2	2	3	4	5	5	6	7
·53	3388	3396	3404	3412	3420	3428	3436	3443	3451	3459	1	2	2	3	4	5	6	6	7
·54	3467	3475	3483	3491	3499	3508	3516	3524	3532	3540	1	2	2	3	4	5	6	6	7
·55	3548	3556	3565	3573	3581	3589	3597	3606	3614	3622	1	2	2	3	4	5	6	7	7
·56	3631	3639	3648	3656	3664	3673	3681	3690	3698	3707	1	2	3	3	4	5	6	7	8
·57	3715	3724	3733	3741	3750	3758	3767	3776	3784	3793	1	2	3	3	4	5	6	7	8
·58	3802	3811	3819	3828	3837	3846	3855	3864	3873	3882	1	2	3	4	4	5	6	7	8
·59	3890	3899	3908	3917	3926	3936	3945	3954	3963	3972	1	2	3	4	5	5	6	7	8
·60	3981	3990	3999	4009	4018	4027	4036	4046	4055	4064	1	2	3	4	5	6	6	7	8
·61	4074	4083	4093	4102	4111	4121	4130	4140	4150	4159	1	2	3	4	5	6	7	8	9
·62	4169	4178	4188	4198	4207	4217	4227	4236	4246	4256	1	2	3	4	5	6	7	8	9
·63	4266	4276	4285	4295	4305	4315	4325	4335	4345	4355	1	2	3	4	5	6	7	8	9
·64	4365	4375	4385	4395	4406	4416	4426	4436	4446	4457	1	2	3	4	5	6	7	8	9
·65	4467	4477	4487	4498	4508	4519	4529	4539	4550	4560	1	2	3	4	5	6	7	8	9
·66	4571	4581	4592	4603	4613	4624	4634	4645	4656	4667	1	2	3	4	5	6	7	9	10
·67	4677	4688	4699	4710	4721	4732	4742	4753	4764	4775	1	2	3	4	5	7	8	9	10
·68	4786	4797	4808	4819	4831	4842	4853	4864	4875	4887	1	2	3	4	6	7	8	9	10
·69	4898	4909	4920	4932	4943	4955	4966	4977	4989	5000	1	2	3	5	6	7	8	9	10
·70	5012	5023	5035	5047	5058	5070	5082	5093	5105	5117	1	2	4	5	6	7	8	9	11
·71	5129	5140	5152	5164	5176	5188	5200	5212	5224	5236	1	2	4	5	6	7	8	10	11
·72	5248	5260	5272	5284	5297	5309	5321	5333	5346	5358	1	2	4	5	6	7	9	10	11
·73	5370	5383	5395	5408	5420	5433	5445	5458	5470	5483	1	3	4	5	6	8	9	10	11
·74	5495	5508	5521	5534	5546	5559	5572	5585	5598	5610	1	3	4	5	6	8	9	10	12
·75	5623	5636	5649	5662	5675	5689	5702	5715	5728	5741	1	3	4	5	7	8	9	10	12
·76	5754	5768	5781	5794	5808	5821	5834	5848	5861	5875	1	3	4	5	7	8	9	11	12
·77	5888	5902	5916	5929	5943	5957	5970	5984	5998	6012	1	3	4	5	7	8	10	11	12
·78	6026	6039	6053	6067	6081	6095	6109	6124	6138	6152	1	3	4	6	7	8	10	11	13
·79	6166	6180	6194	6209	6223	6237	6252	6266	6281	6295	1	3	4	6	7	9	10	11	13
·80	6310	6324	6339	6353	6368	6383	6397	6412	6427	6442	1	3	4	6	7	9	10	12	13
·81	6457	6471	6486	6501	6516	6531	6546	6561	6577	6592	2	3	5	6	8	9	11	12	14
·82	6607	6622	6637	6653	6668	6683	6699	6714	6730	6745	2	3	5	6	8	9	11	12	14
·83	6761	6776	6792	6808	6823	6839	6855	6871	6887	6902	2	3	5	6	8	9	11	13	14
·84	6918	6934	6950	6966	6982	6998	7015	7031	7047	7063	2	3	5	6	8	10	11	13	15
·85	7079	7096	7112	7129	7145	7161	7178	7194	7211	7228	2	3	5	7	8	10	12	13	15
·86	7244	7261	7278	7295	7311	7328	7345	7362	7379	7396	2	3	5	7	8	10	12	13	15
·87	7413	7430	7447	7464	7482	7499	7516	7534	7551	7568	2	3	5	7	9	10	12	14	16
·88	7586	7603	7621	7638	7656	7674	7691	7709	7727	7745	2	4	5	7	9	11	12	14	16
·89	7762	7780	7798	7816	7834	7852	7870	7889	7907	7925	2	4	5	7	9	11	13	14	16
·90	7943	7962	7980	7998	8017	8035	8054	8072	8091	8110	2	4	6	7	9	11	13	15	17
·91	8128	8147	8166	8185	8204	8222	8241	8260	8279	8299	2	4	6	8	9	11	13	15	17
·92	8318	8337	8356	8375	8395	8414	8433	8453	8472	8492	2	4	6	8	10	12	14	15	17
·93	8511	8531	8551	8570	8590	8610	8630	8650	8670	8690	2	4	6	8	10	12	14	16	18
·94	8710	8730	8750	8770	8790	8810	8831	8851	8872	8892	2	4	6	8	10	12	14	16	18
·95	8913	8933	8954	8974	8995	9016	9036	9057	9078	9099	2	4	6	8	10	12	15	17	19
·96	9120	9141	9162	9183	9204	9226	9247	9268	9290	9311	2	4	6	8	11	13	15	17	19
·97	9333	9354	9376	9397	9419	9441	9462	9484	9506	9528	2	4	7	9	11	13	15	17	20
·98	9550	9572	9594	9616	9638	9661	9683	9705	9727	9750	2	4	7	9	11	13	16	18	20
·99	9772	9795	9817	9840	9863	9886	9908	9931	9954	9977	2	5	7	9	11	14	16	18	20

Index

Index